The New Naturalist

LOCH LOMONDSIDE
GATEWAY TO THE WESTERN HIGHLANDS
OF SCOTLAND

John Mitchell

With 8 colour plates and over 120 black
and white photographs and line drawings

HarperCollins*Publishers*

HarperCollins*Publishers*
77–85 Fulham Palace Road
Hammersmith
London W6 8JB

The HarperCollins website address is:
www.**fire**and**water**.com

Collins is a registered trademark of HarperCollins*Publishers* Ltd.

First published 2001

The author asserts his moral right to be identified as
the author of this work
ISBN 000 220145 3 (Hardback)
ISBN 000 220146 1 (Paperback)

Printed and bound in Great Britain by The Bath Press
Colour reproduction by Saxon Photolitho Ltd.

Contents

List of Plates

Plate 1 The diversity of the lochside aquatic flora in the Balmaha Marshes is a reflection of the site's sheltered position.

Plate 2 The magnificent royal fern was brought to the brink of local extinction through over-collecting.

Plate 3 Floristically rich fens such as the Aber Bogs are found in few parts of Scotland.

Plate 4 The River Endrick below Balfron bridge has a well-developed river bank flora.

Plate 5 An eye-catching plant, the Loch Lomond dock is found nowhere else in Britain.

Plate 6 Tussocks of elongated sedge in periodically flooded woodland.

Plate 7 Undisturbed by the plough, the grassland fringing Dumbrock Loch is particularly rich in orchid species.

Plate 8 The tufted loosestrife is a characteristic member of the Endrick flood meadow community.

Plate 9 Short-eared owls are attracted by the high number of voles found in young conifer plantations (John Knowler).

Plate 10 A male capercaillie at his courtship display area in spring (John Knowler).

Plate 11 A hen capercaillie incubates her eggs at the foot of an aspen tree in deciduous woodland.

Plate 12 Cloudberry is abundant on the slopes of Hart Hill in the Campsies.

Plate 13 Red campion and mossy saxifrage grow in profusion on a basalt cliff in the Campsie Fells.

Plate 14 A red carpet of nationally scarce waterworts on the exposed bed of Kilmannan reservoir.

Plate 15 A red-throated diver nests beside a lonely high-level lochan (John Knowler).

Plate 16 The mountain ringlet is Britain's only alpine butterfly (Norman Tait).

Editors' Preface

Scotland is the only country in Europe which does not have a National Park. Almost half a century after their establishment in England and Wales, the Scottish Secretary, Donald Dewar, announced in September 1997 that Scotland will have National Parks, with the Loch Lomond and Trossachs area as the first. Yet, despite the fame of the district for its natural and cultural heritage, there has been no single comprehensive treatment to make knowledge of this available to the visitor. The addition of this latest regional volume on the celebrated Loch Lomonside to the New Naturalist Series is thus highly appropriate and well timed.

The district is one of the most diverse and beautiful in the Highlands, ranging from the lowland woods, farms and rivers of the gently contoured southern section, to the Loch itself with its numerous and mostly wooded islands, and the high alpine peaks of the mountains forming the northern watershed. Its natural history is rich and complex in similar measure, and no one is better qualified than the author of this book to do it justice. John Mitchell was, between 1966 and 1994, the Senior Warden of the Loch Lomond and Ben Lui National Nature Reserves established by the Nature Conservancy (now devolved in Scotland as Scottish Natural Heritage). In this role he was responsible for the care and management of the Reserves, including welcoming and informing the visiting public, which he did with great dedication. With the southern end of Loch Lomond lying within 16 km of Glasgow and its two million or so human inhabitants, the loch and its surrounds are extremely popular as a recreational area. There is a great love of the district and a demand for knowledge about it, but also a relentless pressure of people that increases the problems of nature conservation.

Besides his intimate acquaintance with the Reserves themselves, John Mitchell has gained a comprehensive knowledge of the wildlife of the whole district, together with its human history and the interactions between the two. His enthusiasm for animals and plants led him to explore the hidden corners of Loch Lomondside in his spare time, and to write extensively on his findings in the journals of both local and national societies. A natural warmth won him many friendly and helpful contacts among farmers, shepherds, foresters, gamekeepers, fishermen and other countryfolk, to whom he was the Nature Conservancy's ambassador in this district. He continues in retirement to live within it, and to add to his 35 years' knowledge of the area and its wildlife. This natural history, ecological insight and historical research he has admirably distilled into the writing of this book, which the Editors are pleased to welcome to the series, as in the best traditions of the New Naturalists.

Author's Foreword and Acknowledgements

'While I gazed on this Alpine region, I felt
a longing to explore its recesses …'

Frank Osbaldistone in *Rob Roy*
Sir Walter Scott (1817)

Ever since tales of the adventures of Rob Roy MacGregor first drew Loch Lomondside to the nation's attention, generations of travellers have followed in Sir Walter Scott's literary footsteps. They too may have shared Frank Osbaldistone's desire to know more of the region on first seeing it stretched out before him on the southern approach, a prospect that has since become known as the Queen's View (see Figure below). In the foreground the open moorland with its mosaic of subdued colours gradually falls away to an orderly patchwork of plantations and enclosed green fields. Beyond that and studded with wooded islands is the wide expanse of the loch itself, almost completely encircled by a backdrop of rugged mountains which were once the remote fastness of the Highland clans. Such is its scenic reputation, the area attracts more than two million visitors every year, many from overseas. Landscape entirely un-defaced by man may have long since vanished, yet to most eyes Loch Lomondside still reflects the wild country so vividly portrayed by Scott. And once away from the beaten track and the confines of man-made boundaries, a feeling of open space and solitude may still be experienced, belying the fact that the largest concentration of people living in Scotland is encompassed within a one hour car journey.

Every book has a point of conception, and in this case it occurred some years ago when I was invited to prepare a course of lectures on Loch Lomondside's

Loch Lomondside from near the Queen's View.

natural history and nature conservation for the University of Glasgow's Department of Further Education. It was the students' need for a readily available and modestly priced work on the history and wildlife of Loch Lomond and surrounds that brought together a group of tutors to produce *A Natural History of Loch Lomond* (1974), a booklet which is still in print and available from the Loch Lomond Park Authority's visitor centres. The intention of this greatly expanded account is to examine in turn each of Loch Lomondside's component physical, historical and economic features, before describing the principal wildlife habitats and their dependent species, concluding with a summary of the gradual awakening to the national importance of the region's wealth of wild places, plants and animals. Particular attention is drawn to the influence of man on the natural environment, especially those changes brought about by agriculture, forestry, urban and industrial water demands, together with recreation in all its forms. If, as intended, the present work not only answers many of the enquiring reader's questions as to what, where and when, but stimulates a wider awareness of the significance of Loch Lomondside's diverse wildlife heritage, then the book's aim as a New Naturalist will have been achieved.

In the gathering of material for the book, help has been forthcoming from many directions. First I would like to acknowledge a considerable debt to all those historians, geographers and biologists – past and present – who have published or permanently recorded in some way the results of their investigations in the Loch Lomond area. Without such a rich legacy of the written word to draw upon, the project could not even have begun. Considerable assistance with obtaining these publications and reports was given by Scottish Natural Heritage, Stirling and Dumbarton library services. Thanks are also due to fellow members of the Loch Lomond & Trossachs Research Group (based at the University Field Station near Rowardennan) for helpful discussions on various subjects outwith my own experience. Similarly, I would like to extend my thanks to a number of former colleagues in the Nature Conservancy Council and associates at the Universities of Glasgow, Paisley and Stirling, the Royal Botanic Garden, Edinburgh, the Natural History Society of Glasgow and the Scottish Entomologists' Group, who generously made available their expertise on specialist groups from bryophytes to beetles, freshwater life to fungi. Members and staff of the Scottish Ornithologists' Club, the British Trust for Ornithology, the Royal Society for the Protection of Birds, the Botanical Society of the British Isles, the British Bryological Society, the British Lichen Society, the Scottish Wildlife Trust, the National Trust for Scotland, the Forestry Commission and the Loch Lomond Angling Improvement Association have between them furnished many additional biological records. The Scottish Climate Office in Glasgow kindly provided much of the recent meteorological data. A large proportion of the accompanying photographic plates and figures have been drawn from my own collection; those from other sources are individually acknowledged. Preparation of these photographs for publication was undertaken by Norman Tait.

To Allan Stirling – my field companion on Loch Lomondside on many an occasion – I am especially grateful for giving his time and unfailing patience to read through and comment on the entire draft manuscript. Finally, I would like to take this opportunity to pay a personal tribute to Dr Derek Ratcliffe of the New Naturalist Editorial Board; not only for overseeing the manuscript through its early stages, but for his encouragement and guidance over many years.

John Mitchell, Drymen, July 2000

Part I

The Physical Environment

1

An Introductory Overview of the Region

'Nothing can well be more striking than the first view of Loch
Lomond: its spacious expanse of silvery water, its lovely islands, the
rich meadows and trees by which it is bounded, and the distant scene
of fading hills, among which Ben Lomond rears its broad and gigantic
bulk, like an Atlas to the sky.'

The Highlands and Western Islands of Scotland
John MacCulloch (1824)

The main route from Glasgow to the western Highlands and Islands follows the
glacially carved Loch Lomond Valley. As the city with its suburban sprawl is left
behind and a view north to the Grampian Highlands gradually unfolds, first
time visitors to Loch Lomondside are left in little doubt that this is the
Scotland of their expectations – a country aptly described as a land of mountain and flood (Fig. 1.1). Over the centuries the loch itself has been known by
several names, two of the earliest reflecting its well-wooded shores. Loch

Fig. 1.1 Admiring the beauties of Loch Lomondside by passenger boat has been popular with
visitors for nearly 200 years.

Lomond's catchment is approximately 780 km², but with the addition of the loch's outlet to the Clyde Estuary, plus several other adjoining small areas that are essential to the story or add in some way to the historical and scientific interest of Loch Lomondside, the total coverage of the present regional study is nearer 800 km².

For general locations and the many individual place names mentioned in this account, the recommended Ordnance Survey Sheet is the 1:25000 Outdoor Leisure 39 *Loch Lomond*, supplemented by Pathfinder Series sheets NS 47/57, 48/58, 68/78 and NN 22/33 covering southeast and north of the central area.

The loch and its catchment

By any yardstick Loch Lomond is very impressive. Shaped roughly like an elongated triangle, the narrow and deep northern half is typical of most Highland lochs, but its wide and relatively shallow southern end bears more than a passing resemblance to the island-strewn loughs of Ireland. Between the contrasting upper and lower portions of the loch lies a transitional zone, the Luss–Strathcashell basin. This central basin is bounded to the north by the Inverbeg bar and to the south by a close assemblage of islands between Bandry and Arrochymore Points, barriers that partially restrict the free circulation of water throughout the loch as a whole.

At 71 km², Loch Lomond has the largest surface area of any water body in Britain. Most of the northern half of Loch Lomond is under 1.5 km in breadth, but it broadens out to a maximum of 6.8 km at its widest point in the south. Lomond's 36.4 km length is outdistanced only by Lochs Ness and Awe. The greatest depth of water at 190 m in the loch's over-steepened northern trench is exceeded only by Lochs Ness and Morar. Ness again is the only loch to outmatch Loch Lomond's massive volume of water, the latter estimated in 1903 at 92,805 million cubic feet (2,628 million m³) during Murray and Pullars' historic survey of Scottish freshwater lochs. From north to south, the main unimpeded rivers discharging into Loch Lomond are the Falloch, Douglas, Luss, Endrick and Fruin. The others – Inveruglas, Arklet and Finlas Waters – are impounded at some point by reservoir dams and, except following periods of heavy rain, are now mere shadows of their former selves. The River Leven is the loch's only outlet. Despite the massive storage capacity of the Lomond basin lessening the effect of sudden surges of incoming water, at peak flow from the loch the Leven is understandably one of the fastest rivers in Scotland and provides a significant discharge of fresh water into the Inner Clyde Estuary.

With the extremely high annual rainfall experienced in the mountainous region of Loch Lomondside, the inflow from the northern catchment is twice that of the much larger southern catchment. Overall, it has been calculated (using pre-1970 rainfall figures) that in an average year, the total inflow is equivalent to an 18 m rise in loch level. With only the one outlet to the sea, autumn and winter peaks in precipitation inevitably lead to a severe imbalance between inflow and outflow, producing the occasional exceptional rise in the level of the loch and extensive flooding of adjoining low-lying land. Between 1770 and 1841, no fewer than four different schemes were promoted to lower the surface level by dredging the loch's outlet, thereby alleviating winter flooding and improving the often waterlogged peripheral agricultural land. Nothing came of them because, in each case, not all the riparian owners were

Fig. 1.2 The bed of the shallow southeast corner of the loch exposed during the drought of 1984.

willing to bear their share of the cost. In the twentieth century an engineering project did go ahead; not to lower the water surface, but to impound the loch and raise its level as a major water supply for central Scotland. Prior to completion of the work in 1971, the modal loch level stood at 7.6 m Ordnance Datum, but this has since risen to about 7.9 m OD.

The highest loch level on record of 10.05 m OD occurred in March 1990, following persistent rainfall over two and a half months, equal to almost three times the rainfall normally expected for mid to late winter. The lowest known loch level of 6.75 m OD was recorded in August 1984 (Fig. 1.2), after a period of below average rainfall that had lasted five months. These two extremes in surface level can be seen to differ by 3.3 m (almost 11 ft), possibly the greatest fluctuation of any lake in Britain, confirming once again that everything about Loch Lomond is on the grand scale.

On reading through a selection of descriptive accounts of Loch Lomond it becomes apparent that there is a lack of agreement over the number of islands or 'inches'. Those with an eye to their financial value list only the larger habitable and cultivable islands, whereas others have inflated the figure by the inclusion of rocky islets, some of which are only exposed during low water. Taking a middle course by including only those islands with some permanent tree cover, regardless of economic worth or loch level, then the total stands at 39. Not that the number is static for all times; Inchmoan and Inchcruin were evidently the one island before a narrow isthmus eroded away. Wave erosion continues to play its part; the main body of Clairinsh is well on its way towards separating from its 'fish-tail'-shaped southwestern end. Since the surface level was raised by the construction of a barrage across the loch's only outlet, a small islet at the Endrick Mouth has been completely washed away. In contrast, Wallace's Isle has been lost as an island by becoming firmly joined to the main-

Fig. 1.3 A much enlarged Loch Arklet is incorporated into Glasgow's water supply.

land shore through silting at the mouth of Inveruglas Water. Of Loch Lomond's 39 islands with at least some tree cover, Inchmurrin at 116 ha is by far the largest, followed by Inchlonaig at 75 ha, Inchtavannach at 63 ha and Inchcailloch at 56 ha. Only two islands – Inchmurrin and Inchtavannach – are permanently occupied and farmed, although several other islands are seasonally occupied by residents and/or grazed by farm stock.

It would be remiss not to include in a description of the loch at least a brief mention of its famous three 'marvels' where fact and fiction merge:

Waves without Wind
Fish without Fins
and a Floating Island

Historians have puzzled over the marvels' authenticity for centuries, yet there are plausible explanations for all three. 'Waves without Wind' are undoubtedly seiches. These can occur when a particularly strong wind suddenly drops, allowing the piled-up water on the windward side of the loch to move back in the other direction. To the casual observer, the waves now breaking on the opposite sheltered shore would appear to have no obvious cause. The duration of such water movement is usually short, but one exceptional seiche was timed oscillating back and forth for well over 12 hours. 'Fish without Fins' can be accounted for by the unusual presence in the loch of the river lamprey (*Lampetra fluviatilis*) which, in the Highlands of Scotland, was once regarded as a creature of ill omen. A mat of loch shore vegetation breaking loose as the result of floods or a storm is not that rare an event; it is the size of these 'Floating Islands' that has been subject to gross exaggeration in travellers' tales.

Because of its dominant presence in the landscape, Loch Lomond tends to overshadow the presence of other bodies of standing water in its catchment. In the early days of harnessing water power, a number of small lochans were enlarged to keep each district's corn mill working when the rivers ran low. As the local demand for water increased, more substantial, entirely man-made reservoirs were constructed in the southern foothills to serve the developing industries and an expanding urban fringe. Later still, Loch Arklet (Fig. 1.3) and Loch Sloy in the high rainfall Highlands had their natural storage capacities massively enlarged for water supply and hydro-electric power respectively for consumers much further afield.

The native woodlands

Even before the appearance of early man with his grazing animals, axe and fire, the extent and composition of the native forest cover would have been ever-changing in response to the prevailing climatic conditions. Loch Lomondside is fortunate compared to most areas in the Scottish Highlands in retaining large stands of semi-natural broad-leaved woodland clothing the islands and the lower mountain slopes. This is no accident, but the result of several hundred years of sustainable coppice management designed to meet the raw material needs of industrial Clydeside, the oak woods in particular retaining some of their commercial value until the early twentieth century. Since then, these descendants of the 'wildwood' have faced an uncertain future, as most former coppice woodlands have been left open to grazing and browsing by farm stock, feral goats and deer. Replacement of broad-leaved trees by quick growing conifers and the invasion of many woodland stands by the widely planted non-native rhododendron (*Rhododendron ponticum*) have also taken their toll. A recent revival of interest in native woodlands on Loch Lomondside, more especially for their wildlife and landscape value, may yet tip the balance in their favour.

The uplands

The land surrounding Loch Lomond ranges in height from near sea level to the 1,130 m (3,708 ft) peak of Ben Lui (Fig. 1.4), although because it is set

Fig. 1.4 Ben Lui in the distance is the highest of the Loch Lomondside mountains.

apart, Ben Lomond at 974 m (3,194 ft) is the summit that first draws the eye.
On the windswept and winter-frozen summit ridges of all the mountains
approaching this height, only the hardiest life forms can survive all the year
round. The Luss Hills on Loch Lomond's southwestern flank are, by comparison, more gently rolling in character. Despite lacking the height and sculptur-
ing of the northern peaks, these hills can still offer the keen walker over a
dozen named tops above 2,000 ft (610 m). To the south of the Highland Line
(a geographical boundary that marks out the Lowland/Highland divide in
Scotland) Earl's Seat at 578 m is the highest point of the Kilpatrick, Campsie
and Fintry–Gargunnock Hills, which once formed a continuous plateau before
being divided into three distinct blocks by glacial breaching.

For the most part, the uplands are covered in acidophilous vegetation, the
region's high rainfall having washed much of the natural fertility out of the
soil. They have also been subject to intensive sheep grazing for over 250 years,
which, together with an equally long history of regular burning, gradually
transformed much of the former heathy cover to a sward of nutritionally poor
grasses, with bracken (*Pteridium aquilinum*) covering large areas of the lower
slopes. Now that the carrying capacity for high numbers of sheep on the
Lomondside uplands is lost, large tracts of this degraded pasture have been
planted with massive blocks of closely packed conifers, almost invariably foreign species.

Agriculture, industry and settlements

From the arrival of the early agriculturists to the advent of the Industrial
Revolution, most of the inhabitants of Loch Lomondside were dependent on
farming for their livelihoods. Once cleared of the forest cover, the soils of the
low-lying land proved both fertile and workable for mixed farming, but on the
less productive hill ground the accent was placed on the grazing of stock.
Although land use continued to be dictated by the rhythm of the seasons, the
early communal system evolved into individual farms, particularly during the
period of agricultural improvement which began in the mid-1700s. One result
of this change, which included the introduction of mechanised farm implements, was a lessening of the need for manpower, emigration of the people
from the land further encouraged by the development of an industrial economy requiring a new workforce along the area's southern fringe.

The rapid transformation of an inwardly-looking rural area to manufacturing and exporting on a world scale reflected the entrepreneurial spirit of the
age. Away from the one-time sea port of Dumbarton at the mouth of the River
Leven, whose initial industrial growth was based on glass making and ship-
building, most of the centres of population in the low-lying agricultural belt of
southern Loch Lomondside can trace their development as eighteenth to
nineteenth-century textile villages taking advantage of the abundant supply of
clean, fast flowing water in the manufacture and colouring of yarn and cloth.
For Strathendrick and district, the employment opportunities brought about
by the textile industry were short-lived, the switch to coal-fired steam power by
competitors having rendered the more outlying water powered mills uncom-
petitive. Better placed, with more diversification of manufactories and closer
links with centres of commerce on the River Clyde, the small industrial townships in the Vale of Leven continued to expand, so that today there is virtually
no break in urban settlement between Dumbarton and Balloch on Loch

Lomond's southern shore. Over the last 50 years, the small settlements in the southeast of the region have all grown as dormitory villages to the centres of employment in the Glasgow conurbation.

By road, rail and water

As a tourist attraction, Loch Lomondside is unchallenged as the most popular countryside recreational destination in Scotland, in addition to its importance as the main through-route to the northwest of the country.

Up to the early 1930s, for a predominantly rural area, the southernmost part of Loch Lomondside enjoyed a comprehensive public transport system. Although bypassed by the main West Highland line, three other railway lines linked the centres of population; and despite having just lost its tramway connection between Balloch and Glasgow, faster and more flexible bus services were reaching even the most outlying villages. Paddle steamers based at Balloch still operated on the loch all the year round. Yet even as the expanding bus services led to the closure of two of the railway lines, the bus services themselves were facing increasing competition from the motor car. Initially, the west of Scotland was slow in taking up car ownership, but today the private motor reigns supreme.

Faced with nose-to-tail traffic on roads not designed for such a heavy volume of cars and commercial vehicles, considerable improvements have been carried out to the main A82 up the west side of Loch Lomond and again further north through Glen Falloch, necessitating the removal of earth and rock on a massive scale. Large swathes of deciduous woodland were cut down in the process. In other places the natural shoreline was embanked where the re-aligned road runs alongside the loch. Comparatively little road reconstruction work has been carried out on the east side of the loch, where the B837 goes no further than Rowardennan. On particularly fine summer weekends, the traffic congestion created by recreation seekers on this access route to the east shore

Fig. 1.5 In summer the shores of Loch Lomond can draw large numbers of recreation seekers.

of the loch (Fig. 1.5) can be such that it is not unknown for the road to be temporarily closed to all but local residents.

The era of a few large pleasure steamers and work boats on Loch Lomond has given way to the age of small, high-powered craft; some permanently based, the rest trailer-borne day-to-day. Survey figures show that with increased leisure time the number of recreational powerboat owners taking advantage of the public right of navigation on the loch has been steadily rising year by year, with no upper limit set at the present time. The majority concentrate their activities in the southern half of the loch, in particular the shallow offshore waters which up to now have supported the greatest variety and abundance of lochside-edge and aquatic wildlife.

Loch Lomondside for the naturalist

The diversity of wildlife habitats to be found on Loch Lomondside, where the low country and the uplands meet, is unrivalled anywhere in central Scotland. Much of Loch Lomondside's biological distinctiveness is owed to its close proximity to Scotland's western seaboard, but with the region's generally mild oceanic climate locally modified by high ground. This includes more than a dozen mountain summits over 3,000 ft (914 m). Such is the rapid fall in temperature and change in vegetation with increasing altitude, that with a little imagination the last part to the ascent of any of these high tops can become a journey back in time to an immediate postglacial age. Conversely, around the lochside edge and on the islands, the presence of the most expansive body of water in the country can ameliorate the effect of all but the severest winter cold. With such contrasting physical and climatic variations side by side, opportunities exist for a wide range of plants and animals within a relatively small area. In those parts subject to high rainfall the western elements of the British flora and fauna are well represented, but both northern and southern species commonly occur – a number of them reaching the limits of their geographical distribution in the British Isles. Not unexpectedly, the region holds the largest concentration of *Red Data Book* rare plants and animals of any district in Strathclyde. Add to this ready accessibility, and it becomes clear why Loch Lomondside has attracted the attention of both amateur naturalists and professional biologists over a long period.

In this work, for the purposes of describing such a varied flora and fauna, Loch Lomondside has been arbitrarily divided into four broad biogeographical zones: the loch and surrounds, the Lowland fringe, deciduous and coniferous woodlands, muirs and mountains (Chapters 9–12). At species level, however, there can be considerable overlap between all four zones. No better example of adaptation to a wide range of ecological niches need be given than the wren (*Troglodytes troglodytes*), just about the smallest bird in Britain. On Lomondside, the wren not only finds a habitable spot in the reed beds alongside the lower River Leven's intertidal waters, but in town gardens, parks, farmland, broad-leaved woodlands and conifer plantations, this tiny creature even managing to eke out a living amongst the jumble of fallen rocks around the summits of the highest mountains.

2

The Rocks Beneath

'Mica schist hills ... as we approach their grey rocks of silky lustre, we find that they are curved, wrinkled, contorted, so as to remind us of pieces of ill-laid-by satin, that bear on their crushed surfaces the creases and crumplings of a thousand careless foldings.'

Sketch-book of Popular Geology
Hugh Miller (1859)

Loch Lomondside has long held a fascination for the geologist. Although the region's exposed rocks are representative of only a small part of Scotland's incredibly long geological history, they still present an extremely varied cross section, not least because of massive overfolding that dominates the geological sequence in the southern Highlands. Throughout most if not all of the rocks' formation, what is now central Scotland lay beneath or surrounded by warm seas in tropical latitudes of the world's surface. As the result of movements of the earth's crust and varying degrees of metamorphism, the geological structure of Loch Lomondside as seen today is very complex, with opinions as to the origins and age of the rocks under continual review.

   Most of the region is covered by the British Geological Survey 1:50000 sheets 30 and 38(W). Sheet 46(W), which takes in the Glen Falloch area, has been out of print for many years, but may be consulted in major libraries.

The Cambrian period

The Dalradian rocks of the Cambrian period, which are named after the ancient Scots kingdom of Dalriada, make up the greater part of the Highland portion of Loch Lomondside. Dating back at least 570 million years, the Dalradians were formed from the top 15 km of 24 km of marine sands and muds deposited in a major subsidence in the earth's crust known as the Highland Trough. Evidence that the lower Dalradian rocks in the most northerly part of Loch Lomondside are made up of sediments which were moved around by cross currents suggests that they were laid down on a shallow sea shelf. In contrast, the well-preserved graded bedding of the upper Dalradian rocks found elsewhere in the region's Highland area is more typical of deep water sedimentation. The lower and upper parts of the sequence are separated by a thin, very fragmented band of crystalline limestone – the Loch Tay Limestone.

   After many millions of years of deposition these sedimentary beds were com-pressed, heated and re-crystallised to different degrees during the Caledonian orogeny or mountain-building era, when new land was thrust up by massive folding of the earth's surface. Three broad zones representing the degree of metamorphism to which the original sediments were subjected are charac-

Fig. 2.1 One of many new road cuttings with fresh exposures of mica schist.

terised by their respective index mineral. The rocks of the southern zone, where the least amount of metamorphism took place, contain the green mineral chlorite, which imparts a pearly lustre to the surface. In the central zone, where the metamorphism was more intense, the rocks contain biotite, a dark coloured mica. Maximum metamorphism, restricted to the extreme northwest corner of the region, can be identified by red crystals of garnet. Occasional garnets occur further south, but only where the country rock has come into contact with the intense heat of an igneous intrusion.

The Dalradian succession in the southernmost part of the Loch Lomond Highlands – the chloritic zone – is represented by the Luss–Aberfoyle Slates and Leny Grits. A blue-black limestone that outcrops in Glen Fruin also appears to be Dalradian in age. Slate, which is derived from fine-particled muds and still clearly showing their well-marked bedding, was subjected to immense pressure but relatively little re-crystallisation. Grits contain abundant angular grains of quartz and felspar that have been carried in suspension by water currents. Both slates and grits become progressively more deformed northwards with increased metamorphism. A bright surface sheen resulting from its increased mica content indicates a change from slate to phyllite, which feels greasy to the touch. The accompanying grits become steadily more schistose. With many new rock cuttings freshly exposed with the road re-alignment and widening programme on the west side of Loch Lomond (Fig. 2.1), the traveller along the A82 has a unique opportunity to see the effects of increasing metamorphism and repeated folding of the mica schists within a relatively short distance.

Only the roots or stumps of the once great Dalradian range remain today, the consequence of millions of years of erosion that followed the mountains' creation. These remnant layers of rock run approximately NE–SW, with the narrowest banding occurring in the southern zone. Examination on the ground shows progressive dipping of the rock layers from more or less horizontal in the central zone to almost vertical along the Highlands' southern edge. This resulted from massive southeasterly overfolding hinged around Ben Lui in the northwest. Known as the Tay Nappe, evidence of this folding in the northern zone is the inversion of the Dalradian sequence, older rocks overlying those much younger. Although largely worn away in the southernmost part of the Highlands, the nose of the recumbent fold turns down sharply, with the steeply inclined slates at the nose's core flanked on either side by grits.

Almost immediately to the south of the nose of the Nappe lies a major structural displacement – the Highland Boundary Fault. The Fault's initial establishment is obscure, but substantial movements along the fracture line were to occur right up to the late Devonian period (see below). Even today, the southern edge of the Highland Boundary Fault zone is a prominent feature in the landscape, the glacially breached Ben Bowie–Conic Hill ridge running right through Loch Lomondside, physically dividing the gently undulating Scottish Lowlands in the south from the mountainous Highlands to the north.

The Ordovician period

Between the turned-down nose of the Tay Nappe and the Ben Bowie–Conic Hill ridge is a narrow zone of discontinuous wedges of former marine sediments, laid down initially in deep sea conditions followed by an uplift into shallow water at the beginning of the Ordovician period some 500 million years ago. Younger than their Highland neighbours, these sedimentary rocks were not subjected to the main peak of Dalradian metamorphism. Best represented are the black shales of Glen Fruin and the Highland Border Grit at Arrochymore. Closely associated with these exposures of shales and grits is a much altered band of an ultra basic igneous rock – serpentinite. At first considered to be a dyke intruded along the line of the Highland Boundary Fault, recent recognition of the serpentinite's fragmentary nature suggests a second sedimentary phase with a history of uplift alongside the fault. As a group, these Ordovician rocks are referred to as the Highland Boundary Series or Complex.

The lack of Dalradian debris in the make-up of the Highland Boundary Complex testifies to the fact that these remnants of the floor of a long-dead ocean were far removed from the Scottish Highlands at the time of their formation. Evidence of microfossil marine creatures obtained from Aberfoyle's Dounans limestone quarry, an exposure of the Highland Border Complex just a short distance east of Loch Lomondside, points to the limestone being similar in composition to one found in eastern North America.

The Silurian period

Further uplift, folding and metamorphism of the Dalradian rocks occurred during the Silurian period, 440–410 million years ago. Although no sedimentary deposits of this period are known to survive locally, it was from late Silurian times that intrusive masses of molten magma were emplaced below ground northwest of Arrochar, around Garabal Hill and elsewhere in Loch Lomondside's Highland region. Of these slowly cooled, coarsely crystalline plutonic rocks, diorite at the northeast end of the Arrochar Complex is the one most readily seen in an abandoned quarry in Coiregrogan Glen near Loch Sloy. Less accessible is a huge boss of granitic rock centred on Maol Breac further north. Contemporaneous with the plutonic rocks is the Inverbeg–Roward-

Fig. 2.2 Lower Old Red Sandstone conglomerates along the fault line on Conic Hill.

ennan Lamprophyre Dyke, an igneous intrusion that can be traced both sides of the loch.

The Devonian period

Beginning about 410 million years ago, the Devonian period saw the waning stages of mountain building, followed by erosion of the elevated land on a considerable scale. With little vegetation to protect the land surface from the weather elements, the eroded material was washed away by fast-flowing rivers and seasonal torrents, to be deposited elsewhere in the form of cobbles, pebbles and sand. The Devonian period is represented for the most part by a broad band of red sandstone of great thickness sandwiched between the Highland Boundary Fault to the north and an overlying lava plateau to the south. The red coloration of the sandstone is due to oxidation of iron, indicative of the regular drying-out of a semi-arid plain. Scotland's Stone of Destiny, for hundreds of years an integral part of the pomp and ceremony associated with the crowning of kings and queens, was hewn from Lower Old Red Sandstone at Scone near Perth.

The basal layers of reddish-brown and purplish Lower Old Red Sandstones contain thick beds of water-rounded cobbles and pebbles set in a matrix of coarse-grained sandstone (Fig. 2.2). These are known as conglomerates and consist mainly of ubiquitous hard quartz and quartzite; but, as in the Highland Boundary Complex, there is a significant absence of soft and easily worn-away pebbles of schist or other Dalradian rocks. This, together with the abrupt northern limit of the Lower Old Red Sandstone, clearly proves that these particular conglomerates are not made up of material of local origin, but were moved into their present position by a sideways shift along the line of the fault from a great distance away, in the process displacing the original sediments washed down from the southern Highlands. Examination of the quartz and quartzite cobbles show that many were sheared during the displacement process.

Deposits of Middle Old Red Sandstone, well developed in the extreme northeast of Scotland, are unrepresented in the central belt. Renewed earth movements at this time, however, led to further uplift of the Dalradian Highland rocks, but subsidence of Lowland rocks south of the fault. The steeply inclined beds of Lower Old Red Sandstone conglomerates exposed on Conic Hill alongside the Highland Boundary Fault are directly related to this downthrow to the south.

By 390 million years ago, the southern crustal block was sliding along the fault line into its final position. Erosion of the mountains to the north continued as before, with vast quantities of sands and gravels deposited in the present day Midland Valley, a 65 km wide rift valley that was gradually sinking under the weight of the accumulating material. Some outwash was also laid down just north of the Highland Line, to rest unconformably on the near vertical Dalradian and Ordovician strata. This second deposition of sandstone – the Upper Old Red Sandstone, which is distinguished from its Lower counterpart by a brighter red coloration – can be seen to advantage in the water-worn ravine of Finnich Glen (Fig. 2.3) that passes beneath the Glasgow–Drymen road. Compared to the con-

Fig. 2.3 Finnich Glen; a water-worn ravine in the Upper Old Red Sandstone.

Fig. 2.4 Alternating beds of cementstones and mudstones in Ballagan Glen.

glomerates of Lower Old Red Sandstone, the Upper Old Red Sandstone conglomerates are composed of more angular (less travel worn) fragments. The
presence of pebbles of soft Highland schist confirm its local origin.

With the exception of an area around Killearn, where a shallow dome of
Lower Old Red Sandstone rises through the overlying Upper Old Red Sandstone, the boundary between the two occurs only along the lines of faults. The
Devonian rocks on Loch Lomondside are singularly unfossiliferous, the exceptions being a few plant remains from Lower Old Red Sandstone quarries at
Buchanan Castle and near Balloch. Rarer still are the fossil fish scales obtained
from an Upper Old Red Sandstone quarry on Carman Muir.

Further movement along the Highland Boundary Fault followed. This time
the downthrow was to the north, which was later to protect the Upper Old Red
Sandstone on the Highland side of the fault from total erosion. Immediately to
the south of the Highland Line the Upper Old Red Sandstone has been completely worn away, but reappears within a few kilometres where it has again been
protected by a downthrow, this time on the south side of the Gartness Fault.

The close of the Devonian sandstone period beginning about 360 million
years ago is characterised by the presence of cornstones – terrestrial concre-
tionary limestones – formed by rapid evaporation of mineral-rich ground water
precipitating calcium carbonate in the surface soils. As the semi-arid desert was
gradually replaced by conditions where the land never completely dried out,
the red sandstones gave way to green, grey and white deposits, initially alternating with the red oxide layers before replacing them entirely. Exposures of
these Calciferous Sandstones skirt the northern and western lava scarps of the
Campsie Hills, but are cut out on the southern side of these foothills by the
Campsie Fault. The sequence can be considered as a transition zone between
the late Devonian and early Carboniferous periods.

The Carboniferous and early Permian periods

A transgression of a warm shallow sea over the sunken Midland Valley of Scotland marked the beginning of the Carboniferous period in Scotland around 350 million years ago. The basement group of sedimentary deposits laid down during the early Carboniferous – the Ballagan Beds – comprises some 180 m of alternating beds of cementstones and thin-bedded silty mudstones. Whereas the mudstones are derived from material washed down from the high ground during rainy seasons, the cementstones are impure limestones precipitated during extended periods of drought. Occasional complete drying out of the shallow lagoons is indicated by the presence of gypsum and the cavities left by dissolved crystals of salt. Few fossils have been found in these sediments, as animal life was sparse in this highly saline environment. At the type locality in Ballagan Glen (Fig. 2.4), at least 100 distinct bands of cementstone of varying thickness are exposed. The Ballagan Beds are overlain by a thick band of hard Spout of Ballagan Sandstone, usually overhanging as the much softer mudstones and cementstones beneath erode at a more rapid rate.

Carboniferous sedimentation in the partially submerged Midland Valley was interrupted after the first 10 million years by widespread volcanic activity. From a large number of vents penetrating the marshy ground, voluminous quantities of volcanic ash were discharged, in which is preserved one of the richest assemblages of fossilised plants known for this age. The ash in turn was followed by layer after layer of molten magma – the Clyde Plateau Basaltic Lavas. At the centre of this volcanic activity it is probable that the lava flows accumulated to a depth in excess of 600 m, although thinning away towards the edge of the plateau. Well over 70 volcanic vents, plugged either by basalt or an agglomeration of debris, have been identified in the Kilpatricks and Campsies, but none in the Fintry–Gargunnock Hills. They range from relatively small multiple plugs to eye-catching landscape features such as Dumgoyne (Fig. 2.5) above

Fig. 2.5 Dumgoyne; a striking volcanic plug in the Clyde Lava Plateau.

Strathblane and Dumbarton Rock. Millions of years of denudation have greatly reduced the extent and thickness of the Clyde Plateau Lavas, the only remaining evidence of their former presence north of the Highland Line is to be found capping the summit of Ben Bowie on the west side of the loch. Just south of the Highland Line is the isolated volcanic plug of Duncryne near Gartocharn; so low lying that it is the only one in the district that can be seen to penetrate the Lower Old Red Sandstone. Not all of the formation can be examined at any one spot, but at least 30 lava flows amounting to a thickness of over 300 m have been identified along the steep scarps of the Kilpatrick, Campsie and Fintry–Gargunnock Hills. The well-defined terracing of these scarps is due to structural and weathering differences between individual layers of lava, with the tiers picked out here and there by a waterfall descending in a series of cascades. Although the intense volcanic activity had extinguished life over a wide area, the mineral richness of the lava bequeathed a new fertility to the land, which in turn was fully exploited by the recolonising plants and animals.

With the gradual subsidence and irregular submergence of the Midland Valley, sedimentation become possible once more. Below the southern face of the Campsie Hills, on the downthrow side of the Campsie Fault, lies Muirhouse Muir with its Craigmaddie White Sandstones and associated quartz conglomerates. The lower Craigmaddie Sandstones comprise mainly rounded quartz pebbles. These are overlain by beds of finer sand containing some remains of fossilised plants. The bedding of the Craigmaddie Sandstones suggests the earlier material was carried down from the north by braided streams, followed in turn by flood plain deposition. The Craigmaddie Sandstones are not quite the youngest rocks to be found in southern Loch Lomondside, for cutting through them and the nearby Clyde Plateau Lavas is an intrusive igneous dyke, which can be seen to the south of Loch Ardinning. Of similar composition and presumed age to the great quartz–dolerite sill on which Stirling Castle sits, this would place the intrusion in the late Carboniferous–early Permian period, between 290 and 280 million years ago. Other quartz–dolerite dykes are present in the Highland Region.

The laying-down of sedimentary beds in the southern part of Loch Lomondside continued throughout all subsequent geological periods, but these overlying younger rocks have long since eroded away into the sands of time.

Earthquakes and tremors

It is fortunate indeed that the Highland Boundary Fault – one of the great fractures in the earth's crust – seems to have remained dormant within historical time. Periodic earthquake swarms near to the line of this massive fault have been recorded in the Comrie area of Perthshire, but apparently attributable to a neighbouring fault.

Most of the earth tremors that have occurred in the region since records were kept would seem to have originated from the still settling down Campsie and Gartness Faults, the former running west along the south face of the Campsie Hills and the northern edge of the Kilpatrick Hills, the latter through Balfron, Croftamie and Balloch. The two faults almost converge in the vicinity of Dumbarton. From several documented accounts of earth tremors in Dumbarton, one of the strongest took place during the hours of darkness on 8 November 1608, the townsfolk scurrying from their homes to the kirk, where with their minister they prayed for deliverance from imminent destruction.

Situated almost directly on the Campsie Fault, Strathblane too is no stranger to seismic activity, the most recent incident severe enough to attract newspaper coverage in January 1990. What must be one of the strongest tremors recorded in Strathblane occurred mid-morning on 6 January 1787, the terrified inhabitants running for safety to the open fields as their houses shook and locked doors flew open. The sounds accompanying these sudden movements in the earth's crust have been variously described as a loud rumbling or rushing noise to a deep-seated cavernous growl.

A famous incident involving Loch Lomond itself began suddenly at 9.30 a.m. on 1 November 1775, at the same time as the great Lisbon earthquake. Without warning, the surface of the loch rose rapidly about 2.3 ft (0.7 m) in height, then dropped to a level only seen during the driest summers. The sudden rise in water level was almost immediately repeated, the oscillations continuing at five minute intervals for an hour and a half before gradually subsiding, leaving behind a 'tide-line' of debris and small boats up to 40 yards (37 m) from the shore.

Rocks in the service of man

Man's ingenuity in utilising the most readily available materials is well reflected in the region's rocks. Serving both local and distant needs, almost every type of rock found on Loch Lomondside has been put to practical use at some time. As timber dwellings gave way to something more permanent, the earliest buildings and defensive walls were simple constructions made from gathered loose stones. Only with the development of rock-cutting implements came the use of quarried stone hewn to the desired shape and size. First choice was the easily extracted and dressed red sandstones, as many of the older houses show. Not all was used locally; for many years, flags of Old Red Sandstone used for flooring and pavements were transported by boat from the Port of Aber on the loch's southern shore. For more durable roofing, the early turf and thatch coverings were replaced by readily split slate, from quarries opened up on workable seams both sides of the loch (Fig. 2.6). Like the sandstone flags, slate was also exported by boat. The coming of the railway and the increasing use of building stone from further afield was to lead to the closure of the Loch Lomondside sandstone and slate quarries one by one. Gone too are the clay pits, which had been opened up to meet the need for field drainage tiles at the height of nineteenth-century agricultural improvement. Still continuing in demand by the building industry, glacial gravels and sands have been worked in a number of localities around the southern end of the loch. Crushed, washed and screened, the Craigmaddie Sandstone, until recently quarried on Muirhouse Muir, produced an aggregate of the highest grade. In the more northern part of Loch Lomondside, well over 300,000 tonnes of coarse-grained diorite was used as a crushed hard-rock aggregate in the construction of the hydro-electric reservoir dam at Loch Sloy.

Like the earliest stone houses, the hundreds of kilometres of dry-stone dykes (unmortared field and boundary walls) were invariably built from the nearest source to hand. In contrast, the choice of suitable road stones in pre-Tarmacadam days was far more selective. Lowland igneous rocks (whinstone) and Highland grits were frequently used as road 'metal', the softer sandstones and schists proving totally unresilient to wheeled traffic.

Agricultural mineral fertilizers were at one time obtained from burning ser-

Fig. 2.6 Camstradden slate quarry when actively worked in the nineteenth century (G.W. Wilson/Author's collection).

pentinite (some of the Lomondside outcrops having high concentrations of calcium), cornstones and cementstones in specially built kilns. In the absence of any coal deposits in the immediate vicinity, large amounts of peat were used as fuel in the firing process. At the other end of the cereal production cycle, millstones were quarried in several places, but the local material was not of a high enough quality for the industry to be sustained.

Not all past quarrying or mining operations in the region have surviving records. There appears, for example, to be no documentation on graphite extraction from the blue-black limestone in Glen Fruin, or on the barytes mine beside Kilmannan Reservoir. A reputed venture to extract gold from Lomondside quartz ca.1880 and a worked-out vein of silver near Dungoil in the Campsies must equally have tales to tell. The only deposit of precious metals to be worked in recent years is just outside the Loch Lomond area at the abandoned Cononish lead mine, immediately northeast of Ben Lui. Test results show that the Cononish mine can produce on average 11.3 grams of gold and 60.1 grams of silver for each tonne of processed rock.

Finally there is the influence of the underlying rocks on the locally produced 'water of life'. According to whisky connoisseurs, it is the water draining from the mineral-rich lavas and sandstones of the Campsie Hills to a well-known distillery at the foot of Dumgoyne that helps impart to the finished product its distinctive flavour.

Mineralogy

The collections of local minerals and semi-precious stones housed in the museums of Glasgow and Edinburgh bear witness to the dedicated work of the amateur collector. In Scotland, agates are always the first to come to mind, but Loch Lomondside's Carboniferous Lavas cannot compare in either numbers or variety of these 'scotch pebbles' which occur in the earlier Devonian Lavas of the Ochils east of Stirling or the Carrick Hills and coastal cliffs to the south of Ayr. But what the Lomondside foothills lack in agates is more than made up for by a richness in zeolites and associated minerals, with the Kilpatrick Hills a hunting ground of world renown. Zeolite crystals are found where mineral-laden water has permeated into fissures and cavities within the cooling lava. Amongst the best known types are:

• stilbite: sheaf-like aggregations of crystals coloured orange-red due to the presence of iron oxide, the finest specimens up to 38 mm long;
• heulandite: locally taken specimens are also orange, but with 'coffin-lid'-shaped (wider in the middle) crystals;
• thomsonite: white, occasionally flushed or lined with orange; and
• prehnite: very similar in composition to a zeolite; crystals usually pale green.

In the mid-nineteenth century, a mini-bonanza of zeolites was made available to the keen-eyed opportunist from rock spoil heaps as tunnelling work for the Loch Katrine aqueduct progressed through the Strathblane–Mugdock area en route to the Glasgow water supply reservoirs at Milngavie.

Amongst other minerals described for Loch Lomondside, gypsum and garnet have already been mentioned. Gypsum as a sedimentary evaporite is well known from the Ballagan Beds, and both red and yellow varieties are easily collected. Garnets are common in the highly metamorphosed schists in the northwest, but the stones are generally small and lack gem quality. Elsewhere in the Highland region, crystals of tourmaline have been obtained from schists on An Caisteal and titanite in the plutonic rocks of Garabal Hill. Not to be forgotten are the local veins of both banded and interwoven red and yellow jasper, an opaque form of quartz which occurs in the Clyde Plateau Lavas. Jasper takes a fine polish, and in the past was made into seals and buttons. In modern times, a specially chosen specimen from the Campsie Hills was used to decorate the ceremonial baton carrying the Queen's message to the 1986 Commonwealth Games.

The overlying soils

The wide variety of rock types found in the region has given rise to a complex pattern of derived soils. At one extreme are the Highland sub-alpine soils, characteristically shallow and containing parent material that is little altered. In complete contrast to these immature soils at high levels are the Lowland forest brown earths and river flood plain silts that have both been extensively utilised for arable farming. Such soils have long since lost their natural profiles through centuries of ploughing; their chemical composition changed with repeated applications of mineral fertilizers.

Loch Lomondside is covered by 1:250000 sheets 4 and 6 from the Macaulay Institute's soil survey of Scotland.

3

Shaping of the Landscape

'Loch Lomond ...it is as excellent a specimen of an excavated basin as
the heart of a glacialist could desire.'

The Great Ice Age
James Geike (1876)

The chronology of events leading to the present day topography of Loch
Lomondside is still not completely understood, which is not surprising considering the number of times the face of the land has been altered by the play
of natural forces. In addition to millions of years of sedimentary deposition
and mountain building, followed by erosion and re-deposition of the region's
geological fabric, the landscape as it appears today has been further shaped by
successive ice sheets and valley glaciers.

The pre-glacial drainage pattern of the region

Long before the north–south glacial trench now occupied by Loch Lomond
was gouged out by ice, most of the area's rivers flowed through a high-level
plateau in a generally easterly direction (Fig. 3.1). Some river valleys on the
west side of the loch have their counterparts in the east, the perfect match of
the Inveruglas and Arklet glens a good example. At the head of the loch, the
alignment of Strath Dubh-uisage points to its waters once flowing northeast-
wards towards Glen Dochart, being joined en route by the other northern
watercourses including the River Falloch. To the south, the Douglas and Luss
Waters combined to flow southeasterly via what is now Strathendrick. The
Finlas Water and River Fruin converged in a more southerly course, the original channel (now buried under glacial meltwater deposits) running past the
east side of Dumbarton Rock rather than the River Leven's present course to
the west. There is also the evidence of high-level 'wind-gaps' – water-eroded
channels through which no major watercourse now flows. One of these can be
seen above the Corrie of Balglass on the north face of the Campsies, a former
wide river valley that once headed southeastwards across the Clyde Lava
Plateau, which in the immediate post-Carboniferous period extended considerably further north.

The age of ice

Two million years ago, a period of global cooling began as the Oceanic Polar
Front moved southwards, and the warming influence of the North Atlantic
Drift or Gulf Stream was deflected in a more easterly direction well away from
Britain. An accumulation of countless snowfalls, which compacted when they
failed to melt, led to icecaps forming over much of northern Europe. Just how
many ice sheets waxed and waned over the northern hemisphere is uncertain,

but the evidence gained from sediment cores taken from the bed of the North Atlantic suggests repeated major glacial episodes, although only a few of these have been positively identified on land in the British Isles. As each fresh ice sheet altered the appearance of the preceding glacial and interglacial environments, relatively little is known of the effects on the land surface of any of these glacial episodes except the last – the Devensian. Therefore it can only be a guess as to when Loch Lomond's north–south trench first began to be excavated by accumulating ice overriding the northeast to southwest strike or grain of the Dalradian Highland rocks, in the process breaching several watersheds to link their separate drainage systems.

The calibrated radiocarbon dates used throughout the rest of this chapter should be treated as approximations, as techniques in determining the ages of past events are continually being refined.

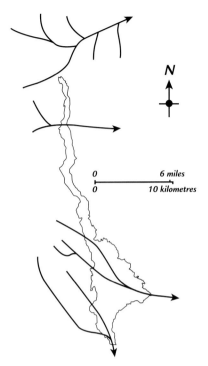

N

0   6 miles
0   10 kilometres

Fig. 3.1 Reconstruction of the pre-glacial river system of the Loch Lomond area.

Right from the very beginning of the Devensian period, the Scottish Highlands experienced alternating valley glaciers and peri-glacial conditions. With intensification of the arctic cold between 30,000 and 25,000 years ago, a massive build-up of ice in the western Highlands signalled the start of the Dimlington Stadial, with an ice sheet eventually moving over the entire Scottish land mass. By the time this last great ice sheet had reached its full extent, covering two-thirds of Britain, even the highest Lomondside mountains had been completely covered, obliterating all plant and animal life in the region. Large mammals such as the mammoth (*Mammuthus primigenius*) and the woolly rhinoceros (*Coelodonta antiquitatis*) had roamed over Scotland for the last time.

A return northwards of the Oceanic Polar Front marked the start of the warmer Windermere Interstadial, causing the ages-old ice sheet covering Scotland to decay. In the southern part of Loch Lomondside the melting ice left behind a covering of reddish-brown sandy clay containing locally derived boulders of Highland rocks, red sandstone and Carboniferous lavas – the Wilderness Till. Proglacial lakes of meltwater together with drainage water from the southern foothills formed in the Endrick and Blane Valleys, temporarily dammed by stagnant ice before this retreated sufficiently northwards to allow the impounded water to escape into the Clyde Estuary through the Vale of Leven. It is probable that Loch Lomondside was entirely clear of residual ice by 14,500 years ago.

With the land surface that had been compressed by the great burden of ice only just beginning to rebound, the disappearance of the ice was followed by a marine incursion through the Vale of Leven and into the Loch Lomond basin. Evidence that the area became an arm of the Firth of Clyde can be traced on ground since elevated to 33 m OD. As the land surface continued to rise, the sea level correspondingly fell, eventually stabilising at what now stands at 12 m OD to leave a well-marked shoreline around the southern end of Loch Lomond. During the submergence by the sea, large amounts of silts and clays were laid down. These marine sediments, which contained a rich arctic–boreal mollusc fauna, are known as the Clyde Beds.

This amelioration of the climate proved to be a false start, and a return to much colder conditions about 12,900 years ago heralded the appearance once more of glacial ice. With winter deposition of snow again exceeding the rate of summer melting, substantial accumulations of ice began to build up to the north. Formed from the coalescence of a number of tributary glaciers, the southwards-moving Lomond glacier did not develop into a full-scale ice sheet covering the entire land. Nevertheless, some indication of its immense thickness can be gained from signs of its passing through the northern end of the Lomond Valley detected at over 600 m on the flanks of Beinn Dubhchraig. Initially confined within the narrow but deep Highland 'fjord', the valley glacier spread out into a broad lobe when it reached the softer and easily eroded sedimentary rocks of the southern basin. This last resurgence of ice has been alternatively described as the Loch Lomond Advance or Readvance, depending on whether or not it is believed that small remnants of the last great ice sheet had lingered on in Scotland's highest mountain corries during the brief period of climatic warming. To date there is no conclusive proof for either the presence or absence of relic ice at this time, so the return of ice is referred to here as the Loch Lomond Stadial glaciation. The slowly moving ice finally came to a halt about 11,900 years ago along the lower northern slopes of the Kilpatrick Hills, the extent of the glacier clearly demarcated by terminal and lateral moraines, together with a widespread covering of glacial till. Described as the Gartocharn Till, it is characterised by marine shell fragments scraped up from the Clyde Beds. Here and there occur boulders of Highland rock carried some distance by the ice. A few of these erratic boulders are so large and immovable (Fig. 3.2) that generations of farmers have been obliged to work their fields around them.

Undisturbed marine deposits in the Vale of Leven just outwith the reach of the Loch Lomond glacier contain well-preserved remains of cold water molluscs, most notably the bivalve *Portlandica arctica*, its optimal habitat the muddy environment near a melting glacier snout. Although the ground in the vicinity of the glacier would have been subject to extreme periglacial processes such as frost heaving, further away the physical evidence of the earlier Dimlington Stadial and Windermere Interglacial remained relatively intact, making southern Loch Lomondside one of the classic areas for the study of the waning stages of 'the age of ice' in Britain, including several type examples of glacial landforms.

With the onset of the present Flandrian Interstadial ca. 11,500 years ago, rising temperatures led to rapid ice melt. Proglacial lakes again formed in the

Fig. 3.2 A massive erratic boulder left behind by the retreating Loch Lomond glacier.

Endrick and Blane Valleys, their free drainage impounded by a mass of decaying ice. Sediments carried into the lakes by meltwater led to an accumulation of bottom deposits many metres thick. A similar ice-dammed lake with substantial bottom deposits formed in Glen Fruin. Outwash from the retreating glacier led to massive accumulations of fluvio-glacial sands and gravels around the southern end of Loch Lomond.

As the climate continued to warm, the southern Lomond basin was almost certainly clear of ice by 11,300 years ago. With the Vale of Leven choked with glacial debris to a height of at least 15 m OD, the Lomond Valley held a freshwater lake for about 3,000 years. However, with ocean levels rising at a faster rate than the depressed land, as water was unlocked from melting ice sheets throughout the northern hemisphere, the Lomond Valley once more became an arm of the sea. At the southern end of the valley the late glacial 12 m OD shoreline was exhumed and re-cut, with raised deltas and estuarine flats forming around the mouths of the inflowing Rivers Endrick and Fruin. The marine layer of black, silty clay in the loch sediments is distinguished by the disappearance of spores of the freshwater common quillwort (*Isoetes lacustris*) and the appearance of marine plankton in the form of dinoflagellate cysts, the species composition within the assemblage responding to changes in the salinity of the water. Deposits of marine molluscs have been reported from Ross Arden Bay and elsewhere, amongst them the common mussel (*Mytilus edulis*), common cockle (*Cardium edule*) and the Baltic tellin (*Macoma balthica*), all still present in the Clyde Estuary today.

A brief disappearance of dinoflagellates in the loch sediments indicates that a very short-lived freshwater interval took place just over 7,000 years ago, possibly as the result of a temporary blockage reoccurring in the Vale of Leven. A final marine incursion lasted until about 6,300 years ago, by which time the continuing rebound of the ice-compacted land had uplifted the Lomond Valley beyond the reach of the sea. Loch Lomondside's remoulded topography as it appears now was complete.

A glaciated landscape

Just how recent all these events are in terms of geological time is more readily pictured if Scotland's hundreds of millions of years of evolution are condensed to the scale of a 24-hour clock. When considered on such a reduced timescale, it can be calculated that the Loch Lomond Stadial glaciation occurred little more than a second ago. Scotland is, in fact, still rising at rates between 0.5 and 2 mm per year, as the land continues to recover from the great weight of its former covering of ice. With such fresh evidence available, there can be few regions in Britain better placed than Loch Lomondside to see erosional and depositional features of a late-glacial landscape, in the following cases without having to leave the public road.

The erosional features are particularly striking. Beginning in the north, where the Loch Lomond glacier was confined to a narrow valley, the ice gouged out the bed of the loch to a depth greater than the North Sea separating Britain from the rest of northern Europe. The lower parts of the side glens were cut away to be left as alternating truncated spurs and hanging valleys, the latter well illustrated at Inverarnan by the Beinglas Falls. During the Loch Lomond Stadial the main thrust of ice was joined by small local glaciers. Glen Mallochan, above Luss, with its over-steepened U-shaped valley is one such site of a former corrie glacier. A smaller, but still eye-catching landmark at Gartocharn showing the direction taken by the ice is the crag-and-tail of Duncryne. Other signs of ice movement can be found on the east side of the loch, with both grooved and smoothed-over lochside rocks beside Rowardennan pier. Often overlooked on account of its large size, Strathblane is one of Scotland's best examples of glacial breaching on a massive scale as the ice ground its way right through the Clyde Lava Plateau.

Glacial debris can also be seen easily from the car, a drive from north to south offering hummocky moraine along the valley floor of Glen Falloch and the remains of eskers in the form of sinuous ridges beside the main A83 at Auchentullich between Luss and Arden. Approximately 1.6 km west from the Crosskeys, the lower Glen Fruin road crosses a morainic ridge. The ridge is mainly composed of material pushed up in front of the glacier, rather than meltwater debris. The noticeably flat floor to Glen Fruin itself was formed from the accumulated bottom deposits of an ice-dammed lake. Another short drive, this time from Gartocharn along the backroad to Croftamie, takes the observer through an undulating 'swarm' of drumlins, each huge mound with its long axis running WNW to ESE, the direction of movement taken by the ice.

From tundra to high forest

As already described, the disappearance of the last great ice sheet from the area ca. 14,500 years ago was followed by an incursion of the sea into the Lomond Valley. A similar marine incursion occurred in the neighbouring Forth Valley to the east. With the depressed land still to recover from the weight of the ice, the converging waters of the two estuaries covered ground that now stands at over 33 m OD, leaving an isthmus less than 12 km wide joining the northern half of Scotland with the rest of Britain. Such a narrow link, before the land surface began to rebound, must have influenced the rate of plant and animal recolonisation north of this point. The Muirpark ridge (Fig. 3.3) at the centre of this land bridge stood just high enough to separate the Lomond and Menteith (Forth) glaciers when they returned to both valleys during the Loch Lomond Stadial. Because the Muirpark remained free of permanent ice, it has become one of central Scotland's most thoroughly investigated sites for interpreting postglacial plant colonisation, the history of which has lain preserved in the form of partially decayed, but still identifiable plant

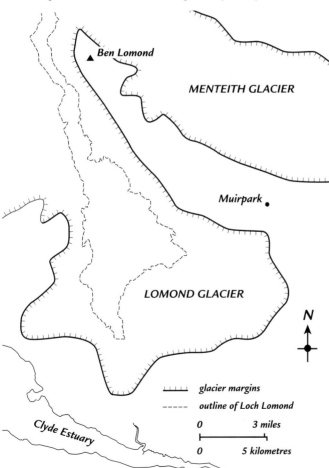

Fig. 3.3 The Muirpark ridge stood above the twin valley glaciers of the Loch Lomond Stadial.

remains within the sediments and overlying peat at the edge of a small lochan. Studies of these layered deposits undertaken by palaeoecologists has led to tremendous advances in our understanding of the vegetation succession and comparative abundance of species through several climatic periods. By microscopic analysis of the number of pollen grains present for each species represented, it has proved possible to reconstruct a chronological sequence of Loch Lomondside's woodland history from the first dwarf shrubs appearing on the tundra, to climax forest dominated by birch, oak or pine.

All of the land that had been overridden by ice was left covered in unsorted glacial till. Although rich in minerals, these skeletal soils initially lacked the organic material essential for the growth of higher plants. After the pioneering phase of mosses, lichens, grasses and sedges, which were the first to be able to colonise the bare rock and immature soils in response to the rising temperatures of each summer thaw, the Muirpark pollen profile shows the establishment of the first exposure-resistant low-growing shrubs: dwarf birch (*Betula nana*) and dwarf willow (*Salix herbacea*) (Fig. 3.4), together with an expansion of heathland plants such as crowberry (*Empetrum nigrum*) and a dwarf form of juniper (*Juniperus communis* ssp. *nana*). Reindeer (*Rangifer tarandus*), a migratory species that feeds mainly on lichens, was almost certainly amongst the first animals to push north. The blue or mountain hare (*Lepus timidus*) would not have been far behind. With the onset of the Loch Lomond Stadial, lowering temperatures and the subsequent reappearance of ice, the Muirpark just above the Lomond and Menteith glaciers became subject to repeated freeze-thaw processes, resulting in lower concentrations and poorer preservation of pollen in the frost disturbed ground. In the ice-filled Lomond and upper Forth Valleys below, however, all trace of the early plant cover was entirely destroyed.

The re-greening of the Lomondside landscape from the end of the Loch Lomond Stadial glaciation to the maximum development of forest cover in

Fig. 3.4 The dwarf willow is a relict species from the immediate postglacial period (Allan McG. Stirling).

central Scotland has been studied at a number of sites in the region, from the Campsie Hills in the south to Glen Falloch in the north. This research into vegetation succession has shown that the colonisation phase of mosses and lichens was again followed by grasses, sedges, ericaceous species, small willows and dwarf birch. Into this tundra-type vegetation cover came an immigration of tree-sized downy birch (*Betula pubescens*), encouraged by the steadily improving climatic conditions. As the birch forest expanded during the dry Boreal period, the ericaceous heath and low-growing shrubs declined, unable to compete on the lower ground with the increasing shade cast by canopy trees. Dwarf birch has apparently been lost to Loch Lomondside, but some of the small willows still persist on the higher ground north of the Highland Line. Hard on the heels of the birch forest came a rapid colonisation by hazel (*Corylus avellana*) beginning about 10,300 years ago, a clear indication of continuing climatic warming and developing organic woodland soils. Aspen (*Populus tremula*), rowan (*Sorbus aucuparia*), bird cherry (*Prunus padus*) and tree-sized willows (*Salix* spp.) all established themselves as constituent members of the birch–hazel forest. The early presence of holly (*Ilex aquifolium*) and ivy (*Hedera helix*) at this time is considered noteworthy for the Highland region.

Between 9,000 and 10,000 years ago, towards the end of the Boreal period of warm and dry summers, came the arrival and expansion of sessile oak (*Quercus petraea*). Apart from in the extreme north of the area, oak gradually replaced birch as the dominant canopy tree on all but the higher forest ground. At the Dubh Lochan near Rowardennan, pollen values obtained for oak are amongst the highest recorded for Scotland; and many of these oaks would have grown to a great age and size. In the eighteenth and nineteenth centuries, when the carseland in the adjoining Forth Valley was undergoing agricultural improvement, huge 'bog oaks' reputedly over 300 years old were dug out of the enveloping peat. Wych elm (*Ulmus glabra*) appeared on the scene about the same time as oak. Its virtual disappearance from Loch Lomondside some 3,500 years later parallels the elm decline recorded in other parts of Scotland. Modern-day outbreaks of Dutch elm disease suggest that the cause of the elm's virtual disappearance is most likely to have been pathological, the tree's potential for a full recovery limited by a change to wetter conditions and leaching of minerals from the soils. With the beginning of the Atlantic or wet climatic period came the establishment and spread of the moisture loving alder (*Alnus glutinosa*), which has been dated from about 7,400 years ago. Ash (*Fraxinus excelsior*) was detected for the first time in the pollen profiles after the rise in alder, but the species never became a dominant tree on Loch Lomondside except where there were localised pockets of lime-rich soils.

The time of arrival and extent of Scots pine (*Pinus sylvestris*) woodland throughout the country has been a subject of lively debate. Pine is prolific in the production of pollen; and with air sacs attached, the pollen grains can be carried in the wind for great distances from their source. So, although small amounts of pine pollen have been shown to be present at Muirpark from early postglacial times, without the corroborative evidence of macro-remains of the tree as well, it does not necessarily follow that pine was actually growing on site between the retreat of the last ice sheet and the return of the Lomond and Menteith glaciers. Towards the end of the Boreal period, however, it can be deduced from a steep rise in the representation of pine pollen that the species had not only established itself, but was spreading in the more open and well-drained birch forest then covering the lava foothills and the Muirpark. This colonisation phase of pine in southern Loch Lomondside was to be cut short. With the onset of the Atlantic period came the development of bog moss (*Sphagnum*) peat over much of the pine forest floor as dead vegetation failed to decompose completely in the cold and wet conditions.

A change once again to a warmer and drier climate during the Sub-boreal period, about 5,750–2,250 years ago, brought a second migration of Scots pine into the area, but this time spreading in from the west Highland pine forests to the north. Able to regenerate freely on the drying-out peat surface, a condition probably accelerated by fire, caused by lightning strike or just possibly the activities of earliest man, pine pushed south down Glen Falloch, and from there into Gleann nan Caorann, Lairig Arnan, Strath Dubh-uisage and Glen Sloy. Remains of pine have been found up to 500 m in the now treeless landscape of the Caorann Plateau. In the main Lomond Valley, it would appear that the well-established and dense oak–hazel forest proved an effective barrier to a major expansion of pine further south. With the climatic deterioration of the cool and wet Sub-Atlantic period from 2,600 years ago, peat accumulation in the highest rainfall areas once again began to overwhelm the pine forest floor

Fig. 3.5 An ancient pine stump exposed by eroding peat.

and stifle future generations of young trees. Where this covering of peat has subsequently eroded, the preserved roots of long-buried pines are occasionally exposed (Fig. 3.5).

To summarise the results of the pollen analysis studies carried out on Loch Lomondside, the climax forest on the lower ground over much of the region comprised mainly oak and hazel, with smaller amounts of elm, alder, birch and other mainly deciduous species. The proportions of the forest mix altered with increasing altitude, the early colonist birch remaining the dominant tree on the higher ground. Only in the northernmost parts were there extensive stands of Scots pine, representing a southern outlier of the ancient Caledonian pine forest. Loch Lomondside at peak forest development can thus be regarded as a transition zone between the oak–hazel forest of central Scotland and the pine–birch forest of the northwest, with only the mountain summits unclothed by trees. The changes that were about to be made on this forest cover with the arrival of man between 6,000 and 5,000 years ago are discussed in Chapter 5.

One of the consequences of a more equable climate and the spread of dense forest into postglacial Loch Lomondside was the retreat northwards and upwards of the tundra vegetation. The arctic–alpine element of the region's flora and fauna became confined to the highest ground – in effect biological 'islands' above the tree line – none more so than on Ben Lomond in its isolated position in relation to the rest of Loch Lomondside's mountain terrain.

4

A Wealth of Weather

'Loch Lomondside ... this country is justly styled the Arcadia of
Scotland; and I don't doubt that it may vie with Arcadia in everything
except climate.'

Matt Bramble in *The Expedition of Humphrey Clinker*
Tobias Smollett (1771)

Others have been far more outspoken than the Welsh squire Matt Bramble
when expressing their views on the vicissitudes of the climate in the west of
Scotland. One, a disgruntled eighteenth-century Hanoverian army officer stationed in the Highlands, bemoaned: 'It is a rarity to see the sun, but constant-
ly black skies and rusty looking mountains, attended with wintry rains and cutting winds'. Because of its changeability, it is a not infrequent assertion that
Loch Lomondside does not have a climate at all, merely a hotchpotch of
weather; a place where all four seasons can be experienced during the course
of a single day. An exaggeration maybe, but it is certainly true to say that any
region close to Scotland's western seaboard rarely enjoys long periods of settled conditions, as the mobile influences of the Atlantic Ocean continually do
battle with the more stable conditions of the Eurasian land mass to the east.
Needless to say, any mention of just how frequently weather fronts move across
the country to bring rain to Loch Lomondside is discreetly omitted from the
tourist brochures. Yet for those with an eye for wild beauty, a spell of wet weather can have its compensations. Writing from the west Highlands in July 1841,
the novelist Charles Dickens enthused: 'This is a wondrous region. The way the
mists were stalking about today, and the clouds lying down upon the hills; the
deep glens, the high rocks, the rushing waterfalls and the roaring rivers down
in deep gulfs below; were all stupendous.' (Fig. 4.1).

Rainfall, humidity, cloud cover and mist

Of all the elements that combine to make up Loch Lomondside's weather, the
most comprehensive meteorological figures available are for mean annual
rainfall. The rainfall map closely matches the contoured relief map of the
region, with roughly a 2450 mm difference between sea level in the south and
the mountain tops in the north, where moisture-laden air currents cool and
condense as they are forced to rise over the high ground. In a little more
detail, average annual rainfall figures for the period 1941–1970 put
Dumbarton on the Clyde Estuary at 1150 mm and the summits of Ben Lui,
Beinn Dubhchraig and Beinn Ime at almost 3600 mm. Between 1971 and
1990, however, rainfall statistics from various sources have all shown that the
northern Clyde catchment area has experienced an overall rise in mean annual rainfall of up to 30 per cent, the increase largely concentrated in the winter

Fig. 4.1 The foaming waters of the Falls of Falloch attract many sightseers.

months. A corresponding increase in annual mean flow in the region's rivers, together with accelerated erosion of their fragile banks, has also been observed.

The heaviest downpour over a 24-hour period ever recorded in Scotland fell on Loch Lomondside on 17 January 1974, with 238.4 mm (9.39 in) measured at Loch Sloy in the Arrochar Hills – 'a land swept by savage rains' according to the poet Robert Burns when he toured the area in 1787. Climatic events as experienced at Loch Sloy are fortunately rare, as the damage caused by exceptionally heavy rain can be severe. Two such incidents in Strathblane followed cloudbursts over the Campsie Hills on 13 August 1795 and 12 August 1884, when the greatly swollen River Blane carried crops, bridges and roads before it. Yet another flash flood, this time in the neighbouring Endrick Valley, resulted in 400 sheep being swept away from their riverside pastures in September 1836. A more recent incident affecting almost the entire region occurred in the summer of 1985, when several weeks of wet weather culminated in a torrential downpour on 25 July. Scores of cars were abandoned as floods, spate debris and a collapsed bridge rendered the main A82 on the west side of the loch impassable for two days. The Inversnaid road was also blocked for a while. Still in evidence from that particular deluge are the landslip swathes cut through the forestry plantation just south of Cailness. Flooding due to lengthy periods of unbroken rain rather than sudden cloudbursts is much more common, the two most vulnerable areas being the lower reaches of the River Endrick and Dumbarton at the mouth of the River Leven. Flowing across countryside with a gentle gradient, the lower Endrick is usually slow to respond to persistent rain, but once its banks are overtopped, the flood water can spread over a wide area (Fig. 4.2). At Dumbarton, problems with flooding arise when a swollen River Leven meets up with a high tide in the Clyde Estuary being forced upstream by a strong southwesterly wind. In an extreme case of a storm-

Fig. 4.2 The River Endrick can overtop its banks at any time of the year.

driven tidal surge up the estuary recorded on 6 February 1856, the water rose some 1.5 m (5 ft) above the edge of the riverside quay, inundating all but the highest parts of the town. Measures taken to protect Dumbarton from flood damage, including the construction of wooden bulwarks, stone and earthen levees, are known to date back several hundred years.

With Loch Lomondside's barely inland position, the average number of thunderstorms experienced in a year is probably no more than seven. Thunder and lightening are usually triggered by intensive convective activity, most occurring during the warmer weather of summer. Occasional stories of close encounters with potentially fatal lightening strikes, which have been reported since the earliest days of mountain exploration in the area, all point to the exposed high tops not being places to linger at the onset of such a storm. One freak incident involved a 'ball' of lightening brushing past two startled hill walkers as they stood beside Ben Lomond's metal-topped summit cairn.

Historically, it has been clusters of wet summers when grain crops failed to ripen in the sunless conditions before the onset of early frosts that have proved the most injurious to Loch Lomondside's farming-dependent inhabitants. During what became known as 'King William's ill years', a succession of poor harvests towards the end of the seventeenth century led to a retreat downwards from the highest intakes of land where cereal growing had just been possible, leaving behind overgrown furrows well up the hillside for today's passer-by to chance upon and perhaps puzzle over the cause of their abandonment. A hundred years later a period of climatic deterioration set in again. In the *Statistical Account* for Buchanan, the minister tells us that in 1782 particularly heavy autumn rains were followed by extensive flooding of the low-lying agricultural land around the Endrick Mouth, after which 'there came snow and intense frost, so that in some places people walked on ice above the standing corn'.

As impressive as some of the records of heavy rainfall appear, it is the distribution in time of the annual precipitation that has most effect on the abundance and luxuriance of the region's western types of vegetation, especially the ferns, mosses and liverworts (Fig. 4.3). The greater the number of 'rain days' – days over the course of a year on which 0.2 mm or more of rain is recorded in each 24-hour period – the higher and more constant the humidity. On Loch Lomondside, pre-1970 figures showed that the mean number of rain days ranged from just under 200 in the southeast to 250 (classed as extremely humid) in the northwest. Since the post-1970 increase in mean annual rainfall, a gauge monitored at Inversnaid has shown that it is now not unusual for a figure of 300 rain days to be attained in a year. In these same cloudy and cool upland areas, loss of water back into the atmosphere through evaporation is usually very low, the surface runoff factor in excess of 80 per cent.

With the frequency of frontal depressions moving in from the Atlantic Ocean, cloud and mist shroud the upper parts of the region's northwestern mountains for over half the year. The reduced visibility can be a hazard to those who take to the hills for work or pleasure, but relatively few stretches of Loch Lomondside's public roads are affected by low cloud base; the exceptions are the upper Glen Fruin road and the summits of the routes that cross the southern foothills. The Crow Road through the Campsies, for instance, ascends to over 337 m at its highest point near the Muir Toll. Water droplets from low-lying cloud cling tenaciously to one's clothes and hair, something met with by the nineteenth-century American writer, Nathaniel Hawthorne. After staying at Inverarnan on Loch Lomondside in July 1857, Hawthorne entered in his journal: 'the clouds came down and enveloped us in a drizzle, or rather a shower, of such minute drops that they had not weight enough to fall. This,

Fig. 4.3 Boulders completely draped in mosses and liverworts testify to the high atmospheric humidity.

Fig. 4.4 Dense mist trapped in the Blane Valley by a temperature inversion.

I suppose, was a genuine Scotch Mist; and as such it is well enough to have experienced it, though I would willingly never see it again.' During still, anti-cyclonic conditions, all routes in the uplands are subject to cold air gravitating down the hill slopes, occasionally leading to a thick mist forming at the valley bottoms (Fig. 4.4).

Drought conditions in the Loch Lomond area are infrequent and there are few historical records. Dumbarton was put on an alert footing during the 'Grit Drouth' of 1628, for with most of the older houses built from wood and thatched with straw, lack of water meant that the town was at serious risk of destruction by accidental fire. Memories of the last sustained drought in the summer of 1984 are already beginning to fade. Starting in late April that year, almost continuous dry weather lasted throughout May, with only two-thirds of the average rainfall in June and even less in July. Apart from the occasional wet day here and there, the normal rainfall pattern did not return until the end of August. Its unprecedented effect on the level of Loch Lomond has already been described.

It has often been observed that when a long dry spell does eventually come to an end, the rain appears unstoppable. A nineteenth-century minister at Bonhill was in the act of fervently praying for rain on behalf of his drought-stricken parish, when a sudden thunder clap and a deafening downpour of rain on the roof of the church interrupted the service. Such was the deluge, it is said that he ended his remarkably successful petition with the words 'in mod-eration Lord'.

No description of Loch Lomondside's rainfall and cloud cover would be complete without reference to 'acid rain', although to be absolutely correct the phenomenon includes all precipitation including hail and snow. It was a Scot, Robert Angus Smith, who first coined the term acid rain in the mid-nine-teenth century, having observed its damaging effects on stonework and trees in Glasgow and several other large manufacturing towns. Loch Lomondside is sufficiently close to urban and industrialised Clydeside to be affected by its pollutant gases, which combine with water in the upper atmosphere to produce dilute sulphuric and nitric acids. Although the level of pollutants carried towards the region by southerly air currents may be generally small, they can still achieve significant concentrations in the upland areas as a consequence of higher rainfall and often persistent hill mist. The general scarcity of the more susceptible lichens and the occasional abundance of the pollutant-tolerant species *Lecanora conizaeoides* growing on exposed trees around the loch is an indication that the area is indeed subject to acid rain. Where this mildly acidic precipitation falls on peaty soils covering impermeable Highland rocks, especially those planted with monocultures of conifers, its effects can cause localised problems. A stream draining one such afforested area near Rowardennan was found to have a seasonal pH of 3.9, which is far to low to sustain those aquatic life forms sensitive to acidification, including the eggs and small young of Atlantic salmon (*Salmo salar*) and brown/sea trout (*Salmo trutta*). Some freshwater feeding birds can also be affected; the disappearance of the dipper (*Cinclus cinclus*) from its traditional haunts is often the first sign that the stream's invertebrates have succumbed to acidification. The lack of any buffering effect to acid rain where the bedrock is particularly hard or mineral deficient was clearly demonstrated on the hills above Loch Sloy. During a country-wide study carried out in the mid-1980s, two lochans sited on the Maol Breac granite were shown to be fishless, whereas two neighbouring lochans on the softer schists with a more readily dissolved mineral content had normal populations of brown trout. To raise the pH of an acidified lochan in another Loch Lomondside upland area, the proprietors of the fishings resorted to treating the water with lime.

Snow and hail

Loch Lomondside is situated at a similar latitude to Edmonton in Canada and Moscow in Russia, yet the amount of snowfall experienced in winter only infrequently disrupts peoples' day-to-day lives. Inevitably there are some exceptions, as every hill sheep farmer would be quick to point out; and the recently opened upper road in Glen Fruin is fitted with snow gates should this high-level route become impassable and have to be closed. The 1894 summer opening of the West Highland Railway, which threads its way through the northern half of the area en route to Fort William, was followed by a winter with the most severe snow storms experienced within living memory. In January and February 1895 one blizzard came after another, with several trains held fast by snowslides coming off the Loch Lomond hills. Heavy snowfall in January–February 1940 and March 1947 also closed down the line. Fortunately, loss of life through snowfall is rare. One tragic case occurred in February 1821, when several travellers perished after being overtaken by a blizzard while attempting to cross Campsie Muir. Snow storms at times other than winter are not entirely unknown. A highly unusual case was reported on 29–30 May 1809, when almost 1 ft (30 cm) of snow fell on the Lowland parish of Kilmaronock, breaking down the branches of fully-leaved deciduous trees under its immense weight.

Snowfall on the lower ground can be expected on less than 15 days per year, and the occasional winter passes by with virtually no snow at all. On the higher ground the number of snowfall days goes up with increasing altitude.

Although systematic weather recording on Loch Lomondside's highest summits has never been carried out, enquiry made to hill shepherds and deer stalkers suggests that the mountains in the northern half of the region experience
snow from just a flurry to a heavy fall between 75 and 100 days per year. Despite
the limited extent of high-level snow gathering ground in the dissected southwestern Highlands, substantial amounts of drifting snow can accumulate on
mountain slopes facing directly into the northerly winds. In the high corries
and gullies facing away from the sun, snow melt in spring is often delayed,
some patches lingering on well into June and occasionally early July. In the
upper northern corrie of Ben Lui – Corrie an Lochain – winter can be very
reluctant to leave, with lying snow known to persist into August. In the late
snow lie year of 1903, Ben Lui's upper ground was found to be still locked in
ice just below the surface in July, while in contrast, the foot of the mountain
basked in the warm sunshine of mid-summer. Within only weeks of the last
high-level snow patches disappearing, the first of the autumn snow gently pow-
ders the mountain summits. This can be as early as September, creating the
offchance of finding snow, however briefly, somewhere on Loch Lomondside's
highest ground in just about every month of the year.

As the experienced winter hill walker is very much aware, the build-up and
eventual collapse of overhanging snow cornices along the edge of a windswept
summit ridge can trigger an avalanche. But the underlying cause of most
avalanches in the region is a layer of unstable wet snow sitting directly on a
hard frozen snow base, resulting from the alternating freeze-thaw temperatures commonly experienced on high ground near the west coast of Scotland.
Ben Lui is very prone to avalanche conditions, especially where snow gathers
in its steep northeastern corrie (Fig. 4.5). One well-documented incident,
when a snow slide swept down a party of climbers, occurred as late in the
avalanche season as mid-May.

There is less information available on the number of days that precipitation
takes the form of hail. It is no more than a few days per year on the low ground,
but anecdotal reports – again largely gleaned from shepherds and stalkers –
point to hail showers being a more frequent occurrence over the hills.

Sunshine

'By yon bonnie banks and by yon bonnie braes,
Where the sun shines bright on Loch Lomond.'

Regrettably, not as often as the above world-famous song would have us
believe. Loch Lomondside is by no means the least sunny place in Scotland
during the winter months, but the short days of December produce on average only about one hour of daily sunshine. With the mountains crowding-in on
some of the Highland glens, mid-winter sunshine can barely reach the valley
bottoms if at all. Restricted sunshine at that time of the year is not confined to
the northernmost parts of the area; the main street of Fintry – wedged in
between the River Endrick and the shade-casting north face of the Campsie
Hills – sees nothing of the mid-winter sun for about six weeks.

Although the region's latitudinal position results in long day length in summer, frequent cloud cover ensures that even June averages only 5.5 hours of
daily sunshine. A mean figure of 9.4 hours (maximum, 16.3 hours) of sunshine

Fig. 4.5 An accumulation of snow in the northeast corrie of Ben Lui (Donald Bennet).

recorded in June 1995 was quite exceptional. Twilight at these latitudes is considerably extended in mid-summer. This too caught the attention of the ever observant Nathaniel Hawthorne, noting in his Loch Lomondside journal that 'there was almost no night, for at twelve o'clock there was still a golden daylight, and yesterday, before it died, must have met the morrow.'

Temperature

With its moist oceanic climate, the region normally experiences a relatively small range of average temperatures. Corrected to sea level, the mean daily temperature in July is 14.5°C, falling to 4.5°C in December. Superimposed on these figures however, is the effect of increasing altitude, air temperature dropping at a rate of about 0.7°C for every 100 m of height. This well-marked temperature lapse rate is reputed to be amongst the most rapid anywhere in the world, explaining why on Loch Lomondside, temperate and sub-arctic habitats can be found in relatively close proximity. The fall in temperature from the Rowardennan car park to the top of Ben Lomond (974 m) can be as much as 7.0°C. Add to this the effect of wind chill, which accelerates the loss of body temperature, and it becomes clear why many of the summer visitors who make their way up the popular Ben Lomond path find themselves inadequately clothed for the bleak conditions often encountered on the exposed summit ridge.

Overnight ground frosts, especially where cold air settles in the more sheltered glens, can occur in just about any month of the year, although the severest are to be expected between December and March. The most penetrating frost in recent years produced air temperatures as low as -20.0°C (ground temperatures down to -24.5°C) during the last week of December 1995, killing off

Fig. 4.6 Delivering the Royal Mail on foot to Loch Lomond's ice-locked islands, February 1963 (A.J. Macfarlane collection).

large areas of native common gorse (*Ulex europaeus*) and many garden plants and shrubs. Spring frosts can prove a real headache to the horticulturist attempting to get the growing season off to an early start; the unseasonable ground temperatures recorded in early May 1997 – down to -7.4°C – proved very destructive to tender seedlings.

To those who have known the loch for a very long time, really sustained frost equates with the magnificent spectacle of southern Loch Lomond's wide expanse of water frozen over with bearable ice. As one admirer observed: 'the sight of such an immense sheet of frozen water with an amphitheatre of beautiful mountain slopes around, leaves an impression not readily effaced.' The list of documented occurrences is far from complete, but the southern half of Loch Lomond is known to have been completely frozen over on at least eight occasions during the nineteenth century. In the twentieth century, the loch's southern waters were totally locked with thick ice in only three winters – 1947, 1959 and 1963 (Fig. 4.6), although there have been other times when the southern loch was at least partially frozen. In early March 1929, for example, the Balloch-based steamer that was to carry the mails to the head of the loch was unable to break free. For the real grip of winter ice within historical times, however, one must look back to the few surviving records of the swift-flowing River Leven freezing over, at a time when the more scientifically-minded travellers noted 'permanent' snow fields on Scotland's highest hills during the so-called 'Little Ice Age'. Details of local events are sketchy, but safe passage on foot across the frozen Leven is known to have been achieved in 1434–5, 1607, 1795 and 1802. There are also several probable occasions, such as the early 1700s – a succession of severe winters on Loch Lomondside having been detected in the annual ring pattern of an old yew tree (*Taxus baccata*); in 1740, when the mechanism of all but one of the water-driven meal mills in the district froze solid; and again in 1784–85, the severity of that particular winter allowing a 'frost fair' to be held at Glasgow on the frozen River Clyde. Ice did cover the River Leven from bank to bank during the particularly cold weather of February 1895, when the Endrick was hard frozen and Loch Lomond attracted skaters and sightseers in their thousands, but not of sufficient thickness on the Leven to tempt even the foolhardy.

Wind

Scotland ranks not only amongst the wettest, but the windiest countries in Europe, the number of totally still days in a year near the west coast just about countable on the fingers of one's hands. Loch Lomondside was amongst the potential areas considered for harnessing wind power, with at least one feasibility study carried out into the siting of wind turbines on the Fintry Hills. Given the region's geographical position and the regularity with which low pressure areas develop over the north Atlantic, the most common airflow direction is not unexpectedly from the southwest. Even where meteorological data is lacking, the persistence of the Atlantic winds can be inferred from the asymmetrical shapes of trees growing in exposed situations.

All winds, from whatever direction, when funnelling through the glens will increase in speed as they become constricted by the high ground either side. Little wonder that the more mountainous parts of Loch Lomondside have a reputation for 'horizontal' rain; and the loch itself for sudden squalls (Fig. 4.7), which have on occasions proved fatal to those who ignored the warning signs. The music world came close to being deprived of the Hebrides Concert Overture and other fine compositions during the young composer Felix Mendelssohn's tour of Scotland in 1829, when his small boat almost cap-

Fig. 4.7 Loch Lomond has a deserved reputation for sudden squalls (Author's collection).

sized in the face of a violent squall as he attempted to cross the loch. On 18 December 1873 Sir James Colquhoun and four of his gamekeepers were not as fortunate, for all lost their lives when their laden boat was engulfed by a sudden storm while returning from a hunting expedition to the deer park on Inchlonaig.

The prevailing wind may be southwesterly, but the region does have its season for continental winds from the east. Most frequent from late March to the end of May, these cold and usually drying winds generally follow the establishment of a high pressure area over Scandinavia. This is an anxious time for the forester, with the tinder-dry plantations at risk from fire. Moor gamekeepers fret too, for harsh winds can lead to heather browning, reducing the nutritional value of the young heather shoots to red grouse (*Lagopus lagopus*). Similarly, the hill farmer engaged in lambing knows from experience that prolonged east winds will hold back the new growth of grass at this most critical of times in the shepherd's calendar.

A number of gale force winds can be guaranteed every year. Because of the structural damage to buildings, woodlands laid waste and even loss of life that has occurred, there are records of the most catastrophic storms dating back at least 250 years. Looking through the documented occurrences, January tops the list as the month for greatest frequency of exceptionally strong winds. Any conversation on the subject almost invariably turns to the great gale that swept through the area during the early hours of 15 January 1968. Local information on the strength of the wind at the height of the storm is lacking, but an hourly mean wind speed of 98 km/h with hurricane force gusts of up to 166 km/h, was recorded at the nearest full-time meteorological station at Abbotsinch, a near sea level site beside the River Clyde. The speed of these winds as they squeezed through Loch Lomondside's glens and over its mountain summits would have been far in excess of the above figures. Damage sustained by native woodlands and conifer plantations in the area during the storm was unprecedented. The problems for woodland managers did not end at clearing away uprooted and snapped trees, for the gaps opened up in the canopy left the stands vulnerable to subsequent storms. One in particular hit the region on 13 February 1989, when Abbotsinch meteorological station recorded gusts up to hurricane force of 119 km/h. As just one example of the damage sustained on that occasion, an oak wood traditionally used by good numbers of nesting grey herons (*Ardea cinerea*) suffered so badly from secondary wind-throw, that it led to the break-up of the colony. A legacy of these recent severe storms has been a reluctance amongst foresters to continue the practice of periodically thinning the commercial conifer plantations, which would increase the risk of wind-throw, particularly on the poor soil structures and exposed situations of the upland sites. The result is the new generation of tightly packed trees ensures that the maturing plantations are even gloomier and less attractive to wildlife than before.

Climatic change and Loch Lomondside's wildlife

Apart from major shifts in climate experienced over millennia, Scotland's weather patterns have always been subject to short-term variability. A mere quarter of a century ago it was considered by many that Western Europe was undergoing a period of temperature cooling. Birds with their superior mobility are the most responsive of all the land vertebrates to climatic change, and ornithologists in this country were delighted with the boreal species colonising the Scottish Highlands at the time. With the temperature trend now in reverse, the permanent presence and expansion of most of these northern birds has failed to be sustained.

Much publicity has been given to the phenomenon of the 'greenhouse effect', which is attributed to carbon dioxide and other emissions emanating from the burning of fossil fuels on a worldwide scale. The implications of this human-induced global warming are as yet uncertain, but the balance of scientific evidence suggests that the west of Scotland can expect a rise in annual mean temperature, further increases in the total amounts of cloud cover and rainfall leading to more frequent flooding of low lying areas. If these predictions prove correct, Loch Lomondside's fragile montane ecosystem is likely to be particularly badly affected, with reduced periods of sunlight in summer and less protective snow cover in winter. The specialised upland plants and animals, already confined to the higher slopes of the region's mountains, would be vulnerable to increased competition from the spread of Lowland species.

Part II

The Influence of Man on the Environment

5

From Nomadic Hunter-Gatherers to Feudal Land Tenure

'The past has no self-imposed boundaries. Prehistory slides into history just as the medieval period merges imperceptibly with the modern.'

Ancient Scotland
Stewart Ross (1991)

When man first left his footprints on the sandy shores of Loch Lomond is unknown, but it is assumed with reasonable certainty that exploration and finally settlement of this thickly forested inland territory came much later than around the more accessible western coastline of Scotland. Archaeologists have problems too in dating the successive periods of prehistory; for although each wave of new colonists added their own distinctive layer of occupation, the traces that have survived in the modern landscape are not only thin on the ground, but subject to overlap in time. Only with the dawning light of written history do events from the past become clearer.

The Mesolithic period

The scant remains uncovered so far of man's earliest appearance on Loch Lomondside have been dated tentatively to around 6,000 years ago, towards the close of the Mesolithic period in Scotland. These Middle Stone Age people were essentially nomadic hunter-gatherers, travelling the waterways by dugout canoe from one temporary encampment to the next, as they followed the migratory movement of wild animals and the seasonal availability of edible plants in these northern climes. For the very first arrivals it is possible that Loch Lomondside only formed a summer hunting-gathering ground, retreating the short distance to the Clyde Estuary coast before the grip of an inland winter set in. In the absence of any remains of dwellings or funerary monuments, their fleeting stopping places have been identified only by the discarded fragments of stone hunting weapons and tools. Just a few of these encampments have been found: Duntreath in Strathblane, Shegarton in Glen Finlas and on one of the larger islands, Inchlonaig. Most of the implements recovered from these sites had been struck from locally obtained hard stone: jasper, lamprophyre, quartz, diorite, etc., but other materials found – flint and pitchstone – were brought in from sources much further afield.

Apart from the limited use of fire, it is generally believed that the Mesolithic people had only a minimal impact on Loch Lomondside's original wildwood; but with their successors came an increasing ability to modify the forest environment.

The Neolithic period

The arrival in the Clyde area about 5,000 years ago of the Neolithic or Late Stone Age people, with their goats, long-horned cattle, primitive sheep and the domesticated young of wild boar (*Sus scrofa*), heralded the earliest beginnings of a more sedentary way of life. Temporary cultivation patches within the more easily cleared upper birch forest were created by slash-and-burn, only to be abandoned within a few years once the natural fertility of the soil was spent. Although scrub would quickly close-in on these shifting agricultural sites, the Loch Lomondside pollen profiles of the period show increases in grasses, bracken and other plants associated with open and disturbed ground. For the first time wild creatures of the forest began to lose ground before the advance of man, some to disappear for ever.

Archaeological evidence is wanting on the wood and turf dwellings of the Neolithic period, which is characterised by more enduring stone-built chambered tombs. These communal burial vaults were covered over with loose stones, the elongated mounds known locally as long or lang cairns (Fig. 5.1). Ten or more chambered tombs have been identified in the southern half of the region, although all have been broken into or robbed of their covering stone. Apart from a very small number of polished stone axe-heads, picked up by chance at various localities throughout the Loch Lomond area, the only other site with possible late Neolithic connections is the Duntreath Standing Stones. Originally in a straight line running from southwest to northeast, the stones' alignment matches up with a notch in the skyline of the Campsie Hills where the rising sun is first seen at the time of the equinox in spring and autumn.

The Bronze Age

The first people with the Celtic knowledge of metal working, initially with copper, but later in bronze, came to Scotland about 4,000 years ago. With the use of metal came the development of offensive weapons, from which can be inferred conflict between the tribes, possibly through competition for the most fertile arable and pasture land. The grouping of hut circles of late Bronze–early Iron Age in upper Strathendrick strongly suggests the increasing need for defence against attack. Yet this war-like race was also capable of producing the finest decorative pieces, especially in precious metals.

Like the preceding Neolithic settlers, the clearest evidence of these new people's presence comes from their method of burying the dead, which evolved during the Bronze Age from communal to individual interment in slab-lined cists (pronounced kists). Above ground, the burial site may be within a circle of set stones or covered over by a rounded cairn of loose stones. Within the cist, the body was placed in a crouching position, often accompanied by handle-less food storage or drinking vessels. This funerary custom has given them the alternative name of the 'Beaker People'. In the latter part of this cultural period, interment of the dead was superseded by cremation, and the ashes of the deceased were stored in a cinerary urn within the cist. At least 20 Bronze Age burial sites have been described for the area, some of them with multi-grouping of stone-covered cists. As agriculture expanded over the centuries, most of these cists were removed as obstacles to ploughing.

Stone carvings in the form of cup and ring markings began in the late Neolithic, but was taken a step further as rock art during the Bronze Age. The

Fig. 5.1 A Neolithic burial cairn on the northern edge of the Kilpatrick Hills.

cup-shaped depressions, which are usually pocked into faces of flat stones, are sometimes surrounded by one or more complete or broken circular grooves. Few in number compared with the neighbouring Menteith area in the Forth Valley, these as yet to be understood symbols are for the most part found on fine-grained lavas and sandstones in the south, but examples are known from Highland rocks in Glen Finlas and near Inverarnan.

The Iron Age

In the wake of workers in copper and bronze came a people with the ability to fashion iron. Exactly when they extended their influence over or settled on Loch Lomondside is again uncertain, but it was probably about 2,500 years ago. For the archaeologist, the Iron Age offers more visual evidence of permanent settlement than just hut circles, burial chambers, standing and carved stones. The advances that took place in domestic and defensive building techniques can be classified into several different types – duns (pronounced doons), hill and peninsular forts, brochs and crannogs.

Duns are low, circular stone defences around individual homesteads, which for their small size have disproportionately thick walls of 3 m or more. For added protection they were frequently sited on steep-sided knolls. Loch Lomondside examples occur at Shemore in Glen Finlas and above Craigton in the Endrick Valley. The walls of Shemore dun are partially vitrified – the inner core of loose stone fused together in a solid mass – showing that the walls' timber lacing has been burned, either by accident or design. Craigton dun is unusual in having been enlarged by the addition of an outer defensive wall. In an Iron Age context the term 'fort' is a misnomer, as it refers to little more than a huddle of dwellings and food stores protected by both inner and outer defences. Dunmore Hill (Fig. 5.2) above Strathendrick and Carman Hill over-

Fig. 5.2 Site of an Iron Age fort on the summit of Dunmore Hill.

looking the lower River Leven are typical high ground sites for such fortified villages. Strathcashell Point on the east side of Loch Lomond is the sole local representative of a peninsular fort, deep water on three sides providing the outer
defence. Iron Age fortifications of increasing architectural sophistication came
to the region with tall circular towers or brochs. Evidence of such a structure
has been found at Craigievern near Drymen, with a confirmed example at
Buchlyvie just outwith the Loch Lomond area. Excavation of the Buchlyvie
broch – popularly known as the Fairy Knowe – has provided invaluable insight
into the diet of Iron Age people in the region. Amongst the carbonised cereal
seeds recovered, the most abundant by far is an early form of barley. Also present were the remains of wild boar and red deer (*Cervus elaphus*); hunting evidently still supplemented the meat from their domestic animals.

Perhaps because of climatic deterioration, farming shifted downhill to the
oak forest-dominated ground, a move made possible because the land could be
cleared with tree-felling axes of iron. With a paucity of natural defensive posi-
tions on the low-lying land, secure refuges were occasionally built in the loch
itself. Known as crannogs, each of these islets of driven timber and sunken
stone supported a platform with its wood and thatch dwelling raised well above
water level. Because of the frequent winter storms experienced on the loch,
most of these structures would have been sited in sheltered locations. Ten
crannogs have been authenticated in the shallow waters of the southern and
central basins of Loch Lomond. Others may have disappeared because they
became convenient sources of stone to build jetties and breakwaters, or
removed as hazards to navigation when deep hulled vessels were introduced to
the loch. The stone base of the large crannog known as Swan Island is above the
water surface for much of the year, but most, such as Strathcashell (Fig. 5.3),
can be seen to advantage only when the loch level is low. At least one – Rossdhu
Isle – continued its defensive role into medieval times, excavations showing that
the crannog was re-used later as the foundations for a small castle. It is only in

Fig. 5.3 Foundations of the Strathcashell crannog exposed at low water.

recent years with the development of new techniques in underwater archaeology that the layers of occupation on these man-made islands are being revealed.

By far the most controversial relic of the period is the Auld Wives Lifts on Craigmaddie Muir. Set in an amphitheatre-like hollow, this weathered rock formation comprises two massive sandstone boulders supporting a flat-topped capstone of immense weight (Fig. 5.4). The name comes from a traditional story that tells of three old women or witches competing with one another over

Fig. 5.4 The mysterious stones of the Auld Wives Lifts on Craigmaddie Muir.

who could carry the largest stone. Even after dismissing the legend, agreement
has yet to be reached on whether the three-stone arrangement is a naturally
occurring glacial erratic, a monument entirely built by early Man, or perhaps
a combination of the two. Even more intriguing are the nine human heads
carved into the surface of the stones, rather curiously a feature unobserved by
archaeologists until as late as 1975. One of the incised heads possibly repre-
sents the druidic horned god Cernunnos. Others suggest something altogether more sinister, the cult of the severed head. The mystery that surrounds the
Craigmaddie Muir stones is still a long way from being solved.

Throughout Britain as a whole, historians consider that this last prehistoric
age was brought to an end by the full-scale Roman invasion of AD43. Iron Age
society north of the Forth–Clyde line (which was only briefly within the influence of Imperial Rome) continued long after that date. Indeed, it could be
argued that the custom of moving home and animals up to the high ground
in summer, which persisted on Loch Lomondside right up to the end of the
eighteenth century, can be traced back to Iron Age pastoral practices.

The Roman occupation during the Flavian period

In AD79, four Roman legions and auxiliary troops under the leadership of
Gnaeus Julius Agricola moved into what is now Scotland, their objective to
extend Rome's claim over the whole island province of Britannia. With the
invasion of North Britannia or Caledonia came the very first written accounts
of actual events, although some of the dates set down in the texts are not always
as precise as historians would like. According to Tacitus, Agricola's son-in-law
and biographer, the invasion force first consolidated its hold over the southern
territories by establishing praesidia (garrisons) across the Forth–Clyde line.
Following a further advance north and a victory of little lasting result against
the gathered tribes in AD83, the Roman army constructed a string of forts just
to the south of the Highland Line. Beyond, so Tacitus tells us, lay 'perilous
depths of woods' – the *Caledonia silva* or Caledonian Forest of the Ptolemy
manuscript map. Strategically, the sites chosen for the forts would have been
on open, defensible ground already cleared of its cover of trees. The loss of
three legions ambushed in Germany's Teutoburg Forest 70 years earlier was
never far from the minds of Roman commanders.

On Loch Lomondside, towards the western end of the new frontier,
Drumquhassle was chosen for building one of the Highland Line forts. The
presence of a Roman fort on Loch Lomondside had been suspected for some
time, but the site at Drumquhassle (which significantly translates into castle or
fortifications on the ridge) was not located until the summer of 1977, when the
outline of the structure was picked up by aerial photography as faint crop
marks in the drying top soil. Sited on a high vantage point to the southeast of
the present village of Drymen, Drumquhassle bears all the hallmarks of Roman
military planning. The size and layout of the fort's inner and outer defences
suggests it was capable of accommodating up to 500 frontline fighting men,
but in practice was probably held by a much smaller force of auxiliary troops
that could be reinforced as required. There is evidence to suggest
Drumquhassle was linked by road to the next fort to the northeast at Malling
near the Lake of Menteith in the Forth Valley and, in the opposite direction,
by a supply route from the probable but yet to be identified base camp overlooking the former Dumbuck ford across the River Clyde. It seems likely these

'Roman roads' were cross-country trade routes or local trackways already ancient before the legions arrived on the scene, although sections of them would have been improved by army engineers.

Whether Drumquhassle (together with the other Highland Line forts) was primarily intended as a containment of the still troublesome Caledonii or as a springboard for the final conquest of the Highlands is uncertain, for in AD86 or 87 the fort was dismantled after only a few years of use, when the occupying Roman forces abandoned much of Scotland to deal with more pressing problems nearer home.

The Roman army did eventually return to the Forth–Clyde line just over a half a century later, completing a more permanent defensive frontier – the Antonine Wall – across the waist of Scotland by AD142. The wall was held against the northern tribes for about 20 years before another and this time final withdrawal south. Although no doubt visited by the occasional forward patrol, the Drumquhassle fort that had once stood sentinel over the furthest flung corner of the Roman Empire, was not re-occupied during the Antonine period.

The three kingdoms

With the abandonment of North Britannia by Rome, there followed a period of several hundred years described by historians as 'the Dark Ages', in which even important events are shrouded from us. What is certain, however, is that the many disparate tribes that had formerly occupied west–central Scotland were superseded by three supra-groupings or 'kingdoms' of old and new peoples – the Britons, Picts and Scots.

The Britons, who were the successors to, if not descendants of, the tribal Damnonii encountered by the Romans, occupied Alcluith or Alclut, their dominion taking its ancient name from the 'Rock of the Clyde'. In the region now referred to as Strathclyde, Loch Lomondside formed the northernmost part of the Britons' territory, and the towering rock at the confluence of the Rivers Leven and Clyde (Fig. 5.5) became known as Dun Breatann – the 'Fortress of the Britons'; a seat of kingship, a centre for ship-borne trade and a place among the larger-than-life Arthurian legends. To the northeast of Loch Lomond stretched the kingdom of the Picts, the direct descendants of the Caledonii who had so stubbornly resisted Roman expansion further north. To the west lay Dalriada – the kingdom of the Scots, a people with cultural links to Ireland. Tradition has it that the Clach nam Breatann (the Stone of Britons) in Glen Falloch formed a boundary between the three kingdoms. If this story has any substance, it seems feasible that the uneasy frontier between the lands of the Britons and the Gaelic-speaking Scots continued southwest from Clach nam Breatann to Cnap na Criche – the boundary hillock – at the head of Glen Sloy, then on to another large stone, Clach a' Breatannaich, near Lochgoilhead in Cowal.

Even as the balance of power ebbed and flowed, the unifying influence of Christianity as it spread throughout the three kingdoms was beginning to make itself felt. The Christian gospel first reached Loch Lomondside through St Kessog from southern Ireland, who settled in the Luss area during the early sixth century. His evangelical mission is commemorated in the name Inchtavannoch or Monks Island. Others of the Celtic Church were to follow in his footsteps in the early eighth century – St Kentergerna and St Ronan – asso-

Fig. 5.5 The Dark Ages settlement on Dumbarton Rock is reputed to have been the northern capital of the legendary King Arthur of the Britons.

ciated with Inchcailloch (island of the cowled women or nuns) and Kilmaronock (Church of St Ronan) respectively. The first step in the emergence of a single nation was the integration of the Picts and Scots, with Kenneth, son of Alpin, becoming ruler over the combined kingdom of Alba by AD842. The two kingdoms had already allied themselves with the Britons against common enemies earlier in the century; and when Malcolm II of Alba died in 1034, he was succeeded by his grandson Duncan (of Shakespeare's *Macbeth*), king of Strathclyde, thereby uniting all three kingdoms for the first time.

There had, of course, been other contenders for dominance over west–central Scotland. On at least one occasion a combined force of Northumbrians and Germanic Angles from the east overcame the defensive heights of Dumbarton Rock, but it was the 'fury of the northmen' that posed the most serious threat to the stability of the region for about 400 years.

Viking raids

History is silent on how many times the Viking longships came up the Clyde Estuary bent on a seaborne raid. On one such assault in the year AD870, Olaf the White, the Norse king of Ireland, laid siege to the Britons' stronghold of Dumbarton Rock. The defenders held out for four months before their capital was overrun and sacked.

Scotland's struggle for national sovereignty and Norse territorial claims for the Northern and Western Isles and elsewhere along the coast came to a head in the mid-thirteenth century. In the autumn of 1263, an assembled fleet of war galleys, under the direct command of King Haakon of Norway, arrived in the Clyde Estuary to deliver a decisive blow. According to the Haakonar Saga, a squadron of the smaller boats broke away from the main fleet and sailed to the head of Loch Long. With their stone ballast removed, the lightweight, shallow-keeled craft were dragged overland on timber rollers across the narrow neck of land (Fig. 5.6) separating the sea from Loch Lomond. Having thus successfully bypassed the heavily defended Dumbarton Rock that protected the only navigable entrance from the sea into Loch Lomond, the raiders put the lochside and island settlements to the fire and sword, before going on to make a strike further east into Scotland's heartland. Laden with plunder, this small invasion force returned to sea the way they had come. Delayed by storms in Loch Long, they arrived too late to play any part in the action between Haakon's main forces and the Scottish army which confronted the invaders at Largs on the Ayrshire coast. A peace treaty between King Haakon's successor and Alexander III of Scotland was signed less than three years later at Perth in July 1266, bringing several centuries of savage onslaught by the Norsemen to an end.

   Probable evidence of the 1263 sacking of Loch Lomondside comes from a Viking warrior burial site discovered in 1851 near the mouth of the River Fruin. Within the burial mound the remains of a Scandinavian-type sword, a spear head and the centre boss of a shield were found. Contrary to popular belief, the so-called Viking stone – a decorated hogback tombstone in Luss kirkyard – has no direct connection with the Haakon raid, most likely representing an outlier of Norse culture from their settlements in southwest Scotland.

The great Earldom of Lennox

Scotland at the time of the Treaty of Perth was quite a different country from the one the Vikings had first encountered during their earliest incursions, the change attributable in part to Anglo–Norman influence from the south. It would be difficult to be precise over the date when the move away from Celtic

Fig. 5.6 The close proximity of Loch Lomond to Loch Long in the Clyde Estuary can best be seen from high ground.

tribal culture began, but an important turning point was the marriage of
Malcolm III to his second wife Margaret, an Anglo-Saxon princess who had
fled to Scotland with her family following the Norman Conquest of England.
Shortly after King Malcolm's death in battle in 1093, the throne was seized by
his exiled brother Donald Ban, who became the last Celtic king of Scotland.
Queen Margaret's half-English sons Edgar, Alexander and David made their
escape to England initially for reasons of personal safety, but by acknowledg-
ing William II (William Rufus) and his successor Henry I as their feudal supe-
riors, they received military backing for regaining the Scottish throne. Donald
Ban was finally overthrown in 1097, all three brothers that had fled to England
becoming kings of Scotland in turn.

The way Scotland was governed changed dramatically during the reign of
David I (1124–1153), who had spent over 30 years in England before succeed-
ing his elder brothers. During this time he had acquired by marriage vast
estates in the east midlands of England, and was well practised in the Norman
feudal system of landownership and patronage.

One of the first great lordships to be established in Scotland on the Norman
principle of land tenure confirmed by charter was the hereditary Earldom of
Levenax or Lennox. Dating from the twelfth century, the Lennox encompassed what was to later become Dunbartonshire and West Stirlingshire, which
included virtually the whole of Loch Lomondside. The early history of the
Lennox is obscure, but among the first of the earls was one of David I's grand-
sons, better known by his later title of Earl David of Huntingdon. Sometime in
the 1190s, the earldom passed to the Scottish line of overlords, who had by
then satisfactorily demonstrated their allegiance to the new regime. The back-
bone to the system was power through force of arms. Although the main
stronghold was the royal castle at Dumbarton, the Loch Lomondside portion
of the Lennox had a network of up to 20 smaller 'castles' that were held by the
Earl's kinsmen and other supporters. The Earl's own castle originally stood in
what is now Balloch Country Park, but at a later date a move was made to a
more easily defended island castle on Inchmurrin. When first built, each of the
smaller fortifications throughout the Lennox comprised a palisaded wooden
tower sited on a natural or artificially raised mound, usually surrounded by a
defensive ditch. Although little more than the earthworks remain, Sir John de
Graham's castle at the head of the Endrick Valley is one such 'motte and bailey' castle. In time these wooded structures evolved into stone-built towers or
keeps; Culcreuch at Fintry and Duntreath in Strathblane (Fig. 5.7) are well-
preserved examples. In addition to the Grahams, some of the oldest family
names connected with landowning on Loch Lomondside can be traced back
to the Earldom of Lennox, including Buchanan, Colquhoun, Cunninghame,
Drummond, Edmonstone, Galbraith, Lindsay, Napier and of course the sur-
name Lennox itself.

Important administrative changes occurred in the Lennox during the reign
of Alexander II (1214–1249). First was the raising of Dumbarton into a royal
burgh in 1222, which conferred on the town's traders and craftsmen certain
privileges and monopolies, exemption from toll and custom charges, and the
right to hold a weekly market or fair. This was followed about 1238 by the setting up of a sheriffdom centred on Dumbarton, considered essential to maintain royal authority and control. From that time onwards, the castle and burgh
of Dumbarton were excluded from the Earldom of Lennox. In addition to act-

Fig. 5.7 A well-preserved medieval defensive tower at Duntreath, Strathblane.

ing as keeper of the castle, the appointed officer was responsible for the military and judicial functions of government in the region, together with collecting the king's revenues. Geographically, the Dumbarton sheriffdom followed much the same boundaries as the Lennox, but during the fourteenth century the western Strathendrick portion, which takes in Buchanan, Drymen, Killearn, Balfron, Strathblane and Fintry, was transferred to the sheriffdom of Stirling. Another tier of administration and revenue raising came from the reorganised church, with the gradual establishment of a diocesan and parochial system from the mid-twelfth century. Payment of teinds or tithes (one tenth of all produce) to the parish church became enforceable by law. Successive Earls of Lennox were particularly generous to the Abbey of Paisley just across the River Clyde, with grants of lands in the Kilpatricks along with specified rights on Loch Lomondside and the River Leven for timber extraction and fishings.

The end of the Lennox dynasty came with the execution of Duncan, the 8th Earl, at Stirling Castle in 1425, because of his allegiance to Regent Albany rather than the absent King James I. The Earl's daughter Countess Isabella (married into the Albany family) was imprisoned for a time, but on release was allowed to live out the rest of her days at the island castle of Inchmurrin. In the absence of male heirs, the break-up of the great Earldom of Lennox began with her death around 1460.

Inheritors of the Lennox

An account of the rise and decline in the fortunes of the Loch Lomondside landowning families after the partition of the Earldom of Lennox would warrant a book in itself; only a very short summary of some of the connecting threads can be given here. The latter part of the period also saw the gradual disappearance of the fortified tower house and the emergence of the country mansion set within its laid out parkland and policy woodlands.

Two ancient Lennox families in their ascendancy were the Colquhouns of Kilpatrick and the Grahams of Mugdock. In the fourteenth century the Colquhouns merged by marriage with the heritors of the lands of Luss, which with their subsequent acquisitions took in virtually the whole of the west side of Loch Lomond. The Grahams, who also adopted the name Montrose from lands granted to them on the east side of Scotland by Robert I, extended their possessions up the east side of the loch by the purchase of the Laird of Buchanan's estate in the late seventeenth century, acquiring almost immediately afterwards what remained of the original Earldom of Lennox. Although Buchanan of Buchanan's extensive estate had been dispersed, another branch of the family – Buchanan of Drumakill – took over the lands of Ross to the south of the loch. Other Lowland families with large estates included the Napiers of Gartness, Ballikinrain and Culcreuch, the Edmonstones of Duntreath and the Smollets of Cameron and Bonhill.

Only one Highland family of the Lennox emerged as a major landowner – the Parlanes or Macfarlanes – who held all the mountainous ground between Inverbeg and Inverarnan. Most of the Macfarlane clan territory was disposed of in 1785, subsequently to be purchased by the Colquhouns in 1821. Just to the north of Loch Lomondside lay the lands of Campbell of Glenorchy, which in time were extended throughout much of Perthshire and Argyll to become the largest feudal landownership in Scotland. It was during the time of Sir Duncan ('Black Duncan') Campbell of Glenorchy that Glen Falloch Estate fell into his family's hands in 1598.

The last hundred years has seen a reversal in the fortunes of Loch Lomondside's long-established estates, as successive inheritors' liability for payment of high death duties on their properties could only be met by selling off tracts of land.

Clan MacGregor

This chapter would not be complete without mention of the brief occupancy of part of Loch Lomondside by Clan MacGregor, not least for the worldwide interest in the romanticised adventures of Rob Roy MacGregor as portrayed by Daniel Defoe, Sir Walter Scott and many others. For centuries the MacGregors had held on fiercely to their ancestral lands in central Scotland, not by feudal charter but by right of sword. But powerful enemies gathered against them, leading to the clan being dispossessed and scattered, and even their very name proscribed. Their support for the royal house of Stewart did see a temporary upturn in the clan's fortunes following the restoration of Charles II in 1660. The first to become a landowner in the Loch Lomond area, Gregor Oig

Fig. 5.8 A garrison of soldiers was established at Inversnaid after the 1715 Jacobite uprising (Author's collection).

MacGregor, acquired Corrie Arklet from the Buchanans about 1661. Then in 1693 the newly installed chief of the clan, Archibald MacGregor of Kilmannan, purchased Craigrostan from the Colquhouns of Luss, turning over the Inversnaid portion to his close kinsman, Rob Roy. By 1706, all of Craigrostan was in Rob Roy's possession. This, together with the acquisition of Ardess in 1711, made him a not inconsiderable property owner on the east side of the loch. Many landless families of the MacGregor clan were encouraged to settle the ground. Local apprehension at the build-up in the number of incoming Highland clansmen loyal to Rob Roy was to prove well founded, for armed parties of MacGregors swooped down to pillage their southern neighbours during the turmoil of the Jacobite uprising of 1715. The government responded by annexing Rob Roy's estate and establishing a permanent military presence at Inversnaid (Fig. 5.8).

6

Forestry, Agriculture and Fisheries

'Over the past two millennia – ever since man began in earnest to
clear the natural vegetation to make way for the crops and animals of
his own choice – our scenery has undergone a process of gradual evolution. The process is still going on, it will continue to go on.'

Man and the Land
L. Dudley Stamp (1955)

Although primarily concerned with describing the economic growth of the
Loch Lomond area, a secondary intention of this and the following two chapters is to provide background information towards understanding the influence that some of these developments have had on the landscape, vegetation
and animal life of the region.

Forest and forest management

The extent of surviving forest confronting the Roman legions when they invaded North Britannia in AD79 has engendered much discussion. With the knowledge gained from the continuing development of pollen analysis techniques,
the general consensus is that the Lowlands of Scotland had already been
denuded of much of its tree cover during the agricultural settlement of the
previous 3,000 years. There can be little doubt too, that another 1,000 years
after the Romans had left, the scarcity of building timber in the most densely
populated areas of west–central Scotland had become acute. Medieval craftsmen's attention inevitably turned to the remaining forests north of the
Highland Line. Loch Lomondside was particularly important, as the River
Leven's link with the Clyde made the movement of heavy timber by water a
practical proposition. Early records are few, but sufficient to show that the
exploitation of the region was well under way by the mid-thirteenth century.
Individual woods are named in documents of the period, which suggests that
first shrinkage followed by fragmentation of the once continuous forest cover
was in progress. Despite the initial piecemeal utilisation of the resource, an
integrated and sustainable system of deciduous woodland management
emerged on Loch Lomondside which became the model for other landed proprietors in the Scottish Highlands.

Free forest and forest law

Forest management from the reign of David I developed as an overlay of
Anglo–Norman practices on an existing system, as all of the king's leading supporters who came north with him to settle in Scotland held estates or came
from landowning families in England. A land grant from the king did not auto-
matically include forest rights; even the Earl of Lennox would have required a

supplementary grant of free forest over his vast estate. Such a grant conveyed to the beneficiary and his appointees all rights to the 'vert [the greenwood and other woodland vegetation] and venison'. In practice, this gave control over all timber products and grazings within the forest, together with the exclusive hunting rights over the 'greater game' – notably red deer, fallow deer (*Dama dama*) and wild boar. Where hunting took precedence, the grazing of domestic animals in the forest was forbidden or restricted as a woodland conservation measure.

A free forest grant included the authority needed to uphold what was embodied in the Scottish forest laws. Administration of these powers was the role of the Head Forester. The position of Head Forester to the Earl of Lennox was a heritable post and one of considerable importance. On taking up this appointment about 1270, one Patrick de Lyndesay not only received all the privileges that went with the post, but additional lands in the Vale of Leven. The duties of office carried out by his staff included supervising and exacting payment for wood-cutting and grazing of domestic stock within the forest boundaries, as well as organising wolf (*Canis lupus*) hunts and safeguarding the greater game. Protection was also extended to birds of prey and their nests in the forest, for the ancient art of hawking was widely practised by the Norman–Scottish nobility. A Head Forester was empowered to bring anyone breaking the forest laws before the courts. Offenders could, however, expect more humane punishment than that reputedly handed out in England, for the Scottish system recognised that a compensatory sum of money or confiscation of goods and chattels was likely to be equally acceptable to the complainant as having the offender imprisoned or maimed. Substantial fines in money or kind became in effect respective payments for licences to carry out what was forbidden by law, and appear to have been a not inconsiderable part of the forest revenues in Scotland.

Very little information on the charters relating to the granting of free forest on Loch Lomondside is readily available. Dundaff in upper Strathendrick was granted to David de Graham as early as 1237. Another, which included the Park of Rossdhu and Glen Mallochan, went to Sir John Colquhoun in 1458. Of considerable interest for the detail it contains is the grant of free forest in Glen Falloch (Fig. 6.1) made to Ure Campbell of Strachur on 31 March 1568 during the regency of the Earl of Murray. What especially catches the woodland historian's eye is an obligation on the recipient to enclose the forest and plant trees – planned re-afforestation that was way ahead of Britain as a whole. But what was gifted could also be taken away, as Ure Campbell and his son found to their cost when they fell out of favour. Denounced as rebels for imprudently failing to pay an expected contribution towards the grandiose baptism of crown prince Henry at Stirling Castle in 1594, they were summoned to surrender their charter into the king's hand.

Documentation relating to the extraction of Loch Lomondside timber

Shortly after Paisley Priory was raised to the dignity of an Abbey in 1245, the *Registrum monasterie de Passalet* records that Donald MacGilchrist, Laird of Tarbet, bestowed on the monks of Paisley the liberty to take whatever building timber they required from the woods on his lands. Similarly, in 1277, the *Glasgow Registrum* tells of Glasgow Cathedral securing a grant of timber from Maurice, Lord of Luss, for reconstruction work on the bell tower and treasury.

Fig. 6.1 A sixteenth-century grant of free forest covering Glen Falloch included provision for woodland conservation.

Included in the grant was pasturage for the horses and draught oxen used during the timber extraction.

Use of local timber is also recorded for secular purposes; the Exchequer Rolls for 1326 lists 100 great boards purchased at Tarbet for repair work at the Levenside manor house and park of Robert I. The reign of James IV (1488–1513) saw many a Scottish oak wood sacrificed in an attempt to transform the country into a maritime power. Loch Lomondside's contribution to this era of boatbuilding came in 1494–95, during preparations for a punitive expedition against the rebellious Lords of the Isles. Accounts kept by the Lord High Treasurer show that several weeks were spent by the carpenters and joiners at Inchcailloch, Sallochy and Luss, selecting, felling and cutting the oak timbers to size. It was not only straight boards that were taken, for the shipwright's experienced eye would be continually assessing every naturally bent or heavily branched oak for the boat's ribs, in fact wherever curved or angled timber was needed. All the roughly hewn pieces were then carried down the River Leven to Dumbarton, where the actual boat construction was taking place. Loch Lomondside could not provide pine masts of sufficient quality, however, the Master of Works being obliged to seek these from other sources. Another entry in the royal account books mentions payment made for oak planks supplied by the Laird of Buchanan to Stirling Castle in 1507. Almost 500 years later history repeated itself, when in 1995 several quality oaks from one of the Buchanan woods were selected for use in the restoration work to the hammer beam roof of the castle's great hall (Fig. 6.2).

Newspaper advertisements from the early nineteenth century reveal a number of standing timber sales in the Loch Lomond area, some drawing attention to the improvements made to the roads or the opportunity of floating the

Fig. 6.2 Some of the oak timbers used in the restoration of Stirling Castle's great hall originated from Loch Lomondside (Norman Tait).

felled trees away as an inducement to purchase. One notice in the *Glasgow Courier* of 3 March 1808 is of special interest, in that it offered for sale no less than 5,000 'scots firs' in Glen Falloch, probably representing the last major stand of Scots pine to be felled on Loch Lomondside.

Woodland use by charcoal burners, iron and lead smelters

Charcoal was very important in early metalworking, for as almost pure carbon it can give twice the heat of an equivalent weight of wood. When charcoal burning first began in the Loch Lomondside woodlands is unknown, but its use in the manufacture of iron from imported ore was apparently well established by the mid-fifteenth century, when the Laird of Buchanan paid part of his taxes due to the crown in what was presumably locally forged iron.

Being compact, iron ore was easier to convey by water transport to the source of the charcoal, than to attempt to move the bulky and easily crushed charcoal from Loch Lomondside to the source of the ore. Charcoal was produced in earth kilns on the levelled forest floor, usually in a position well sheltered from the wind. A number of such platforms have been identified on both the Lomondside mainland and islands. On each platform, peeled coppice poles

Fig. 6.3 A vegetation-covered mound of cinders and slag marks the spot of an on-site iron bloomery.

(the regrowth from the base of a cut tree which was harvested at set intervals) of oak and other tree species were built up into conical stacks. Each stack would be covered over with earth and ash, before set alight and slowly charred over several days. It has been calculated that 1 acre (0.4 ha) of well-managed coppice would be required to furnish enough charcoal to smelt 1 ton (1.02 tonnes) of iron. In contrast to the charcoal kilns, the smelting of iron required a constant blast of air. Fanned by strong winds, the intense heat created by burning charcoal reduced the ore to a 'bloom' of iron. Although very localised, the sites of these temporary woodland furnaces or bloomeries have been found from the Kilpatrick Hills in the south to Glen Falloch in the north. All that can be seen today of this former industry is the occasional heap of discarded cinders and iron slag (Fig. 6.3).

This on-site smelting of iron ore on Loch Lomondside was rendered redundant by the introduction of purpose-built charcoal-fired furnaces – such as at Bonawe in Argyll – followed in turn by the coke-fired blast furnace of the Carron Iron Works. Opened in 1760, the glow from the iron works reflected in the East Stirlingshire night sky heralded the beginning of the industrial age.

Completing the story of metalworking on Loch Lomondside, lead smelting using a fuel mixture of peat and coal at a furnace near Inverarnan lasted only a few years. Following the discovery and opening of a productive lead vein near Tyndrum in 1741, the mined ore was carried by pack horses through Glen Falloch to the furnace at Beinglas; the same boats bringing the coal to the head of the loch were used to carry the ingots of lead down to the Clyde. The mine workings were confiscated by the government after the Jacobite uprising of 1745–46, eventually falling into the hands of a company of mining adventurers who sent the lead ore to their smelting works elsewhere.

Throughout the history of lead extraction at Tyndrum, the only known use of woodland in Glen Falloch was to provide alder and birch for support props in the mine. By the eighteenth century, oak was considered too valuable to be used for such a purpose.

Overall, charcoal and metal production on Loch Lomondside appears to have been carried out on a relatively small scale. There is little evidence to support the popular assertion that the charcoal burners and iron masters were together responsible for the indiscriminate destruction of the area's natural woodland.

Oak coppice and standard management for tan bark and timber

From the mid-seventeenth century, the harvesting of tan bark from the oak woodlands around Loch Lomond had been developing alongside the commercial manufacture of leather products in the west of Scotland, first for the home market and later as exports to North America. Not only was there a growing demand for traditional items such as shoes and horse harness, but eventually for leather belting needed to transmit water and coal-fired steam power to the new manufacturing machines. The high value of £2,000 sterling placed on each cutting of the self-renewing coppice woods when the Buchanan Estate was sold to the Montrose family in 1682, illustrates the early importance of Loch Lomondside to Clydeside's leather industry.

Animal hide tanning by the age-old method, which was a long-drawn-out process involving steeping the cleaned-up skins in progressively stronger solutions of ground-up tree bark and water, made the leather pliant and resistant to decay. Because of its high tannin content, oak reigned supreme over the bark of any other tree, although for some specialist work, such as shoe, glove and bag leather, low tannin birch bark produced a fashionable light-brown shade. Developed from a domestic craft, Dumbarton housed a number of family-run tanning yards. Gradually, however, the industry became centralised in and around Glasgow, which in turn supplied the treated hides to the manufacturers of leather goods.

The concentration of tannin in oak bark is at its peak when the coppice poles are between 20 and 25 years old. To provide a steady supply of top quality material to the tanneries and ensure a regular annual income to the estates, the woodlands were divided into sections or 'hags' equal in number to the number of years making up the cutting interval. Based on surviving records of the Montrose Estate, the hags appear to have been between 28 and 40 ha in size. The rotation period was initially 24 years, but later reduced to 21 years for a quicker turnaround. To increase the yield, tree species of low economic worth ('barren timber') were removed and replaced by planted oak; and in some areas the oak woodlands were extended by enclosing and planting adjoining open ground. Acorns of pedunculate oak (*Quercus robur*) brought up from England were frequently sown, the bark of this species having a slightly higher tannin content than the native sessile oak, resulting in the widespread hybridisation between the two species so evident on the east side of Loch Lomond. Cutting the coppice poles was undertaken in spring, when the tannin concentration was at its highest and the rising sap made the bark easy to peel away. Stripping the bark from the cut oak poles was usually performed by women and children, the latters' involvement inferred from by the seasonal fall in attendance recorded at the local school. The stripped bark was then stacked on platforms to catch the sun and wind, the drying process taking at least three weeks before the bark was considered sufficiently 'cured'. After loading aboard the waiting gabbarts – the all-purpose shallow draughted work boats on the loch – the dried bark was transported to the Dumbarton and Glasgow leather tanneries via the River Leven.

As coppicing techniques developed, it became the practice on the Montrose Estate for the stumps of the cut oaks to be trimmed as low to the ground as practicably possible, to encourage the new shoots that appeared to put down independent roots of their own. So effective was this method of stimulating fresh growth from the base of the cut tree compared to the old-style stump regrowth, it can be difficult a century or so after the practice ceased to distinguish a well-grown coppice oak of root stock origin from a 'maiden' tree that has never been cut at all. Thinning out of the weakest and most crooked new shoots arising was carried out at pre-determined intervals, ensuring only the most vigorous poles grew on to the next rotational cut. As the older stocks produced rather poor coppice growth in their latter years, it was considered worthwhile to periodically replace each one with a fresh sapling from the estate's tree nursery. Where there was no permanent enclosure wall, priority would be given to protecting the oak's new growth from the attentions of domestic grazing animals and deer. Using little more than peeled coppice poles as stakes interwoven with branchwood, these quickly assembled 'stob and ramble' fences (Fig. 6.4) were expected to last for about six years, by which time the leading shoots were beyond the reach of most browsing animals. On the islands where the woodlands were unfenced, deer numbers would be kept down by organised shoots to protect the young coppice. As an added precaution, the keeping of goats was forbidden under the terms of the leases granted for farms situated within the wooded areas.

Not every coppice pole was harvested at each cutting, as some of the straightest were selected to grow on as 'reserves' through two or more rotations, when it would be referred to as 'measurable' timber. The following example of oak coppice management is taken from a pocket book kept by a nineteenth-century head forester to the Montrose Estate, his entry recording the cutting of the first of four hags in Sallochy Wood in 1837. From this hag (of unspecified size) was obtained oak bark from 463 first rotation poles growing from the parent stocks, plus 174 second rotation young trees and 46 third or more rotation 'old growth' trees, the wood from the latter two classes being needed to meet the estate's requirements for different sizes of building timber. According to anticipated future timber requirements, a number of first rotation poles and second rotation young trees would have been held over as reserves.

Prices obtained for tan bark in Scotland reached their peak during the Napoleonic Wars as imports from the Continent dried up. The inflated value of the home-grown bark fell back again once foreign imports were resumed, Luss Estate turning instead to the establishment of conifer plantations. Sir James Colquhoun of Luss was not Loch Lomondside's only nineteenth-century 'planting laird'. In 1822, Hector Buchanan of Ross Priory was awarded a prize by the Highland and Agricultural Society of Scotland for planting 261,000 trees on his estate in less than two years. The proprietor of Arden and Auchindennan Estates planted upwards of a million trees.

The Montrose Estate persevered with the management of its oak woodlands; the export of bark in the early 1840s stated to be 500 tons (508 tonnes) per

Fig. 6.4 A local example of a stob and ramble fence, which protected the young oak coppice from browsing animals (Mary Bruce collection).

annum. It was the development of much quicker acting synthetic tanning agents in the 1880s which was to bring the utilisation of oak coppice for tan bark to its eventual end. With the steady fall in prices obtained for bark came an increase in the number of first rotation oaks being 'singled' (all but the straightest pole removed) and these left to grow on to measurable timber. When the older trees were eventually felled, they were no longer replaced by oak saplings, the gaps being filled with quick-growing conifers. Overshadowed by the larger number of maturing oaks and the introduced conifers, a loss in vigour of the remaining root stocks and in the quality of bark the coppice produced hastened the industry's decline. There appear to be no surviving Montrose Estate papers relating to coppice management after about 1870, but, although the market demand for tan bark had all but gone, eyewitness statements combined with annual ring counts of trees from the last coppice cycle show that some oak coppice management continued on the east side of the loch right up to the First World War (1914–18).

Coppice woodland management on the Montrose Estate had continued long after it had been abandoned as uneconomic by other estates in the Highlands of Scotland. The reasons for this were its close proximity to the Glasgow tanneries and leather finishing factories, the availability of cheap water transport and the advantage of a local wood distillation works which was capable of turning small wood with little more than firewood value into a worthwhile profit. Several tons of oak were required to produce one ton of bark, so there was no shortage of raw material. Initially established in the Vale of Leven in the 1790s, Millburn wood distillation works claimed to be the first of its kind in the country. The same firm then set up additional premises at Balmaha, known locally as the 'Liquor Works' (Fig. 6.5), which could handle 700 tons (711 tonnes) of

Fig. 6.5 The pyroligneous acid works at Balmaha before its closure in the early twentieth century (Mary Bruce collection).

non-measurable wood a year. Apart from the principal distillate – pyroligneous acid (crude acetic acid) – there were residual products such as charcoal and wood tar, the latter being used as a wood preservative and for treating roofing felt. Even the inflammable gases given off during the process were piped into the furnaces below the retorts, effecting a saving in fuel. Most of the pyroligneous acid was destined for the textile factories in Glasgow and the Vale of Leven, where it was used in the manufacture of mordants (colour-fixing agents) essential for preparing calico and cotton to accept permanent dyes. When this market was lost through the introduction of new direct colours that did not require mordants, the wood distillation was closed down.

The closure of the Balmaha works in the early 1920s finally brought to an end between 250 and 300 years of partnership between Loch Lomondside's managed oak coppice and the urban manufacturing industries. With the Montrose Estate's woodland economy all but gone, the coppice growth on each of the root stocks was expertly 'singled' and the remaining vigorous leader allowed uninterrupted growth to eventually take its place in the canopy of the gradually appearing semi-natural high forest (Fig. 6.6).

Other woodland products

As part of Loch Lomondside's former woodland management, tree species other than oak which had commercial value included birch, holly, alder, ash, hazel and willow.

Birch bark has already been mentioned in connection with the leather industry. With the wood fine-grained and easily turned, birch was also much in demand for thread bobbins used in the textile industries at Paisley and in the Vale. In addition, birch logs were specifically chosen for the drying of malt in the production of whisky, the burning wood not imparting any disagreeable flavours to the finished product. The wood of holly, which is both fine-grained

Fig. 6.6 Former oak coppice
of different age classes
reverting to semi-natural
high forest.

and relatively hard-wearing, fetched exceptionally high prices for making the
patterned wooden blocks used in hand-printing elaborate designs on cloth. A
lightweight wood that could withstand repeated wetting and drying, alder was
particularly sought after by the makers of cheap and durable footwear. Loch
Lomondside's alder groves attracted 'cloggers' – itinerant cutters of roughly
prepared wooden soles – from both Glasgow and further afield. Initially they
worked from on-site encampments, but later seasonal workshops were set up
beside the sawmill at Croftamie. Burned carefully, alder wood converted into
top-grade charcoal suitable for the manufacture of gunpowder. Ash poles provided most tool handles, with hazel poles used for a variety of purposes, most
notably woven hurdles. The moribund remains of two willow plantations laid
out beside the lower River Endrick show that willow wands were once regularly supplied to the basketwork trade.

Never managed in a sustainable way like the tree species above, juniper was
exploited almost to the point of local extinction, the kindling properties of this
coniferous shrub being greatly valued in the smoking of fish and in the process
of distilling illicit whisky. Local tradition has it that juniper was also burned in
the belief that its aromatic smoke warded off infectious diseases.

Twentieth-century afforestation

Once Glasgow had begun to expand from a small medieval town, the dwindling timber resources of the Highland forests could not meet its increasing demands. Additional supplies had to be brought in from abroad. A register of ships kept at Dumbarton for the period 1595–1658 shows that one in every four entering the River Clyde was carrying a cargo of wood.

Just how dependent the country was on imports of timber from Scandinavia, Russia and North America became evident when essential supplies were cut off by enemy blockade during the First World War. Large areas of both native woodlands and conifer plantations were clear felled, Scotland providing more timber throughout the crisis than the rest of the United Kingdom put together. It has been suggested that if the war had been prolonged for another two years, most of the remaining Scottish woodlands would have been swept away before the axe and saw. Immediately after the end of hostilities, the newly created Forestry Commission was charged by Government with replenishing the nation's home-grown timber stocks as quickly as possible. Yet the first state forests were not even 20 years old when timber supplies were again disrupted, with the outbreak of the Second World War (1939–45). Scotland's timber reserves were depleted still further, providing the impetus for an expanded programme of post-war planting from 1947.

Earlier, in 1931, the Forestry Commission had purchased from the Montrose Estate its first Loch Lomondside holding – Garadhban Forest – formed from the amalgamation and extension of several existing plantations between Drymen and Balmaha. This was followed by the Commission's acquisition in 1951 of a large proportion of the former oak coppice woodland and other plantable land between Milarrochy and Cailness. Named Rowardennan Forest, almost all of the planting was of non-indigenous conifers, especially the fast-growing Sitka spruce (*Picea sitchensis*) from the west coastal region of North America, which offered a high yield for a short rotation period. Rowardennan and Garadhban Forests were combined in 1971 to form the Buchanan Forest. The now mature plantations help sustain the pulpwood, chipboard and saw log industries. From the mid-1960s, the Forestry Commission began extensive planting of high-level sheep walk on the Kilpatrick Hills (Fig. 6.7). Drainage of the wet ground was made possible by the development of new techniques in upland ploughing. All the new large-scale conifer planting on Loch Lomondside's hill ground since then has been carried out by private forestry companies.

Up-to-date figures on the extent of both Commission and privately owned coniferous forest in the region are not readily available, but even a casual perusal of the relevant Ordnance Survey maps will confirm that, by the late 1980s – which marked the end of the peak period in planting – total coverage by non-indigenous conifer plantations in the Loch Lomond area exceeded that of existing semi-natural deciduous woodland several times over.

Agriculture and the community

The Normanisation of Scotland had fundamentally altered the pattern of land ownership on Loch Lomondside, but there is little to suggest that the methods of farming changed in any significant way. Soil types and climate determined what use could be made of the land. Still following the old Celtic way of life,

Fig. 6.7 Traditional sheep walk afforested up to 300 m in the northern Kilpatrick Hills.

the tenant farmers clustered together in small 'farm-towns' that comprised a sufficient number of families to provide the manpower required to carry out the heavy work and to act in mutual defence should the need arise.

Early farming practices

To ensure equal shares over the most fertile soils, the most productive arable land – the farm-town's 'infield', which received all the available byre manure – was divided into a series of strips or 'rigs' that would be allocated in turn to each of the joint tenants. In contrast, the undivided pasture land of the 'outfield' was managed in a more communal manner. During the day, the townships' cattle were entrusted to the care of the common herdsman, who ensured that the animals did not stray into any part of the unenclosed infield, which in season was kept permanently under crops. The outfield was primarily semi-rough grazings, although some parts were intermittently brought into cultivation. Prior to ploughing and sowing any part of the outfield, cattle were regularly folded overnight on the selected plot until it was considered sufficiently broken up and manured. After the crop was gathered in, these temporary cultivation patches were allowed to lie fallow until the fertility of the soil was restored. At the top end of the outfield lay the head dyke. Usually a stone wall topped by turf, the head dyke separated the infield and outfield from the moorland and hill ground beyond. Today, many of the old head dykes are just tumbledown lines of stones, but where this important demarcation line between the cultivated and uncultivable land can be traced on Loch Lomondside, it barely reaches an average of 150 m OD. This suggests that it would require only a relatively small deterioration in the climate to create unfavourable crop-growing conditions over a greater part of the region.

Of sturdy construction, the old Scots plough was well suited to the task of turning over rough ground littered with tree roots and loose stones. But being both heavy and cumbersome, the plough required a team of up to eight oxen under the guidance of two or three men. Such a long train needed a wide turn-ing circle, often leading to the furrows assuming a serpentine shape; and with the plough-share cuts always turned towards the centre of each cultivation strip, the rigs or ridges gradually increased in height over time. Raising the crown height of the crop-bearing ground not only achieved rapid run off of excess rainwater to the wide furrows (in effect, open drains) on either side, but less back-bending was required when using a sickle to harvest the ripened grain. The subsistence cereal was oats, with smaller amounts of a barley known as bear or bere grown as a cash crop to help meet the monetary part of the rent. Very unpopular with the farming tenants was the custom of being 'thirled' (tied) to the landowner's corn mill for grinding their grain, with an unnegotiable percentage of the meal handed over to the miller in return. Equally resented was having to pay the remainder of the rent in stipulated ser-vices to the landowner's estate.

To rest the home grass and help prevent outbreaks of disease amongst the stock caused by continuous use of the same ground, the cattle and goats were driven each summer beyond the head dyke to be tended at the shieling graz-ings in the surrounding glens and hills (Fig. 6.8). Initially this is likely to have been wood pasture, but over the centuries the browsed trees and montane shrubs slowly gave way to open grassland and ericaceous heath on the upper slopes. The approach of the grain harvest and the need for extra hands back at the farm-town signalled the return home.

The age of agricultural improvement

As late as the eighteenth century, travellers from the south were unanimous in condemning what they saw as outdated farming practices, which provided lit-tle more than the needs of each household rather than a surplus of produce

Fig. 6.8 High-level shieling grazings in the Arrochar Hills.

for sale in Scotland's rapidly expanding market towns. Yet changes were on the way. Tenancy periods were being extended, while thirlage to the mill and services to the landlord's estate were about to become a thing of the past. Throughout the low ground, the open infield and outfield was gradually enclosed in a patchwork pattern that can still be recognised today. The advent of underground tiled drains brought an end to the open furrow drain and the opportunity of levelling the ridged fields, which was achieved by first dividing each rig into two narrower and lower strips, before cross ploughing the entire field. With improved drainage techniques came a concerted effort to bring the 'wastes' into cultivation. Factory-produced farm implements of increasingly advanced design became available, including the innovative Smith's light-weight plough. Compared to the old Scots plough, its replacement could be drawn by just a pair of horses and rein-controlled by one man, although any large stones lying about the field had to be first cleared by hand. With the once-ridged fields effectively levelled, utilisation of the newly developed agricultural machines became possible, such as Bell's reaper which was able to replace an entire line of hand cutters with scythes. Heavier yields proved possible by the use of supplementary mineral fertilizers (principally lime), the region's upgraded roads facilitating its distribution to all but the remotest farms. New crops and improved breeds of farm animals were introduced by the more progressive landowners, their lead eventually followed by the rest.

It should not be inferred from the above that Loch Lomondside underwent an 'overnight' agricultural revolution, for the improvements in soil, crop and animal husbandry were initially slow to take hold. At the time of Scotland's first agricultural survey undertaken in the 1770s, all stages in the evolution from the old to the new husbandry were still working side by side. On the fertile flood plain either side of the lower Endrick, the Aber farm-town folk to the west of the river still clung to their forefathers' open field system, whereas the smaller holdings on the Duke of Montrose's estate to the east had already been amalgamated into larger farms under long-term leases, with the division and enclosure of individual fields well advanced. Even by the end of the eighteenth century, of the 13 parishes within the Loch Lomond catchment area, only Strathblane nearest the Glasgow markets could report in the *Statistical Account of Scotland* that the landowners and tenants had fully embraced the concept of rotational farming, which included the introduction of new strains of cultivated grass. With increased mechanisation and the stimulus of high prices for home produce during the prolonged French wars, the pace of change noticeably quickened. By the time of publication of the second *Statistical Account* (1834–45), the adoption of a six year rotation – oats, green crop (as often as not potatoes, which gradually replaced oats in the staple diet), grain crop (usually barley undersown with grass), hay, followed by two years of pasture – was almost universal on the more fertile soils throughout the Lowland region.

Farming in the uplands on the other hand was severely limited by an uncertain climate and poor soils. On this less favoured ground there was an almost total shift away from mixed agriculture to an almost exclusive hill sheep regime. Loch Lomondside, in fact, has the longest history of intensive sheep rearing north of the Highland Line. As a hardy animal that could withstand the demanding conditions of an upland winter, the Linton or blackface breed of sheep was first introduced from the Scottish Border counties into Glen Mallochan above Luss about 1747. The new prosperity brought to this mar-

ginal farming area is commemorated by a carved ram's head on the Tup
Bridge over the Mallochan Burn (Fig. 6.9). Encouraged by the opportunity of
long leases made available for hill pastures blessed with a fertility bequeathed
by generations of summering cattle, other flock masters from the south soon
followed suit. By the end of the century some 50,000 sheep were being run on
the Loch Lomondside hills, although this initial high stocking rate proved
unsustainable once the legacy of fertility had been consumed. Heavy grazing
of the uplands combined with the practice of heath burning to provide an
early bite of spring grass resulted in the natural vegetation cover of heather
and other dwarf shrubs on the rain-sodden hills rapidly receding. Bracken,
which was formerly held in check by trampling cattle and harvesting the fern
for the animals' winter bedding, began to dominate the lower slopes. Golden
eagles (*Aquila chrysaetos*) and ravens (*Corves corax*), hitherto ignored by the cattle graziers, became subject to persecution as a precaution against the possibility of the birds killing live lambs. Despite occasional periods of low prof-
itability, caused in most cases by the importation into Britain of large quantities of mutton and wool from abroad, sheep have remained the mainstay of
farming on Loch Lomondside's hill ground right up to the present day.

Fig. 6.9 The Tup or Ram's
Head Bridge at Glen
Mallochan.

The establishment of a railway network in the mid-nineteenth century, which linked the fertile agricultural land of southern Loch Lomondside with the growing urban centres of Scotland's central belt, encouraged a swing towards dairy products in the now market-driven farming economy. With the increase in dairy herds came an expansion of improved grassland, together with supplementary forage crops needed as the animals' winter feed. In common with the problems faced by Highland sheep farmers, a flood of cheaply produced food from abroad – in this case of grain from the newly opened-up wheatlands of the world – saw a decline in home-grown cereal production. This move away from arable farming in the southern half of the region was only halted by the two World Wars, which brought severe restrictions on essential food imports reaching Britain by sea. These two peaks in land put back under the plough were, however, both of a temporary duration.

Agricultural development in the Lowland region during the second half of the twentieth century was one of continuous change; more efficient farm machinery – to the total exclusion of the working horse – new fertilizers and pesticides, a move away from dairy to beef cattle and a decline in growing oats in favour of barley, which can be harvested earlier and produces a better quality straw. Less dependent on dry weather for successful harvesting, silage production (grass preserved by fermentation) has taken over a large share of the grassland formerly saved for hay. Together with root crops, silage is now used as the main feed for overwintered stock.

The drift from the land during the eighteenth and nineteenth centuries

A consequence of the agricultural reforms and less labour-intensive work practices gradually introduced from the eighteenth century was the displacement of a significant proportion of Loch Lomondside's rural population. Loss of all common land through enclosure by contiguous landowners deprived many people of a livelihood by self-sufficiency; yet at the same time amalgamation and mechanisation of farms was cutting back on the number of agricultural workers and casual wage-earners required. In the uplands, many of the long-standing farming tenants were obliged to vacate their holdings to allow the incoming flock masters to run enough sheep in the emptied glens to meet the increased rents.

Parishes on the east side of the loch experienced the greatest exodus of people. Drymen and Buchanan both lost more than a third of their inhabitants during the second half of the eighteenth century, and the mainly Gaelic-speaking population of Buchanan declined by a similar number again over the next 30 years. One part of this Highland parish was entirely denuded of its residents, the kirk session records showing that where 63 families had once lived, the land was entirely given over to sheep. Under the terms of the new leases coming into effect, it was not unusual to have stipulated that every abandoned steading be dismantled or at least rendered uninhabitable by removing the roof. The ruins of some of these homesteads can still be seen (Fig. 6.10), providing a poignant reminder of a way of life that has disappeared.

Compared to the national outcry that followed the enforced removal of rural people in favour of sheep elsewhere in the Highlands and Islands of Scotland, this precursor to the notorious 'Highland Clearances' attracted remarkably little public attention and critical comment. One explanation for this is that the 'pull' factor appears to have been equally as strong as the 'push'. Attracted by

Fig. 6.10 The ruins of just one of many deserted steadings on Loch Lomondside.

the waged labour and housing opportunities, many of the younger people left the land of their own accord for the rapidly developing textile villages of Fintry, Balfron, Blanefield and those in the Vale of Leven. The population of Bonhill in the Vale, for example, increased from less than 1,000 in 1755 to almost 4,000 by 1831. Despite the short distance of this human migration, the overall effect was a breakdown in the old social order and a diminishing of the cultural and linguistic differences that had for so long separated Loch Lomondside's Highland and Lowland communities.

Monastic and commercial fisheries

Records of organised fish-catching in the area date back to the thirteenth century. From 1224, a succession of grants bestowed on the Abbey of Paisley by the Earls of Lennox gave those in service to the abbey the right to build and operate yairs (permanent funnel-mouthed fish traps) on both sides of the River Leven. Initially sited in the brackish lower reaches of the river to take advantage of the incoming and outgoing tide, the yair system was later adapted to the upper freshwater stretch for the trapping of Atlantic salmon and sea trout swimming upstream to spawn. The charters also show that as yairs gave way to nets, grants from other Loch Lomondside landowners entitled the abbey to fish the loch, as well as giving them the liberty to erect bothies and to dry their nets on both the mainland and island shores.

With the dissolution of abbey lands and privileges at the time of the Reformation, the rights to net the Leven were passed by the Crown to the Burgh of Dumbarton. However, other riparian landowners, notably the Colquhouns of Luss, also laid claim to various stretches of the river. The disputed ownership was only resolved when Dumbarton sold the burgh fishing rights to the Luss Estate in 1862, although bringing to an end the overfishing

Fig. 6.11 Evening netting for salmon and sea trout in Loch Lomond (William Simpson).

of Loch Lomond's migrating salmonid stock by professional netsmen operating under lease in the River Leven took until 1895. Riparian landowners with netting rights still occasionally exercise these in a limited way (Fig. 6.11), but compared to sport angling with rod and line (see Chapter 8), the number of salmon and sea trout removed from the water by nets is extremely small.

Because of their abundance in Loch Lomond, powan (*Coregonus lavaretus*) have probably been fished ever since the first nets were cast in the loch waters, although not until a descriptive account dated 1724 is it positively stated that they were caught in nets like shoals of herring. The two methods employed were sweep netting, where the net is drawn into the shore, and ring netting, where the net is cast in a circle out in the open loch. Powan netting in Loch Lomond has been practised only intermittently during the last hundred years, most intensively as the result of food shortages during the two World Wars.

Other species have been commercially fished in Loch Lomond and the River Endrick from time to time, including the roach (*Rutilus rutilus*) and European eel (*Anguilla anguilla*). At one time, roach in the middle reaches of the Endrick were netted in their thousands; and when water mills operated on the river their inlet lades would have been furnished with traps for eels. Today, only a scattering of eel cages around the Endrick Bank and hinterland are still in use, the catch destined for the London or continental restaurants as a gourmet dish.

The intensive rearing of salmonids by cage culture in Loch Lomond was briefly considered and several prime sites identified. An environmental assessment report on the potential impact of fish farming, which was prepared in 1981–82, recommended against any such development in the loch, primarily on the grounds of deterioration in the quality of the public water supply. Loch Lomond is not immune from fish farming activities elsewhere, however. In September 1998, several hundred farm-bred salmon of a different genetic strain to the wild stock of Atlantic salmon entered the River Leven during the autumn spawning run following their escape from a damaged fish cage in the Clyde Estuary.

7

Industry, Water Supply and Hydro-electric Power

'No sound of wheel
Turning with flash of spray comes from the mill,
Its voice of toiling now is hushed and still.
The window panes
Are broken, and the oaken doors
Stand open to the rains,
And moss grows green upon the rotting floors.'

Newton Mill
Anon (1928)

From earliest times the inhabitants of Loch Lomondside had made use of its land and water resources to meet little more than their own requirements. This way of life was to change forever with the advent of mechanisation and the ability to mass produce. Improved communications opened up new markets for mill and factory-made products, some of them worldwide. With industrial growth came the concentration of a large proportion of the local population into towns and textile mill villages, paradoxically creating new pressures on the surrounding countryside, in particular as a dependable provider of clean water on demand. Despite the high annual rainfall in the region, this need could only be met by the construction of storage reservoirs. Energy consumption rose in parallel, progressing from water power to fossil fuels; and, in the second half of the twentieth century, to hydro-electricity, which necessitated further water diversion and storage on a large scale.

The industrial era

Textile manufacturing
Until the eighteenth century, the rural textile industry on Loch Lomondside served only local needs, producing linen (from home-grown flax) and woollen cloth. The first sign of change came in the 1720s, with government premiums available to perfect machinery for separating out the flax fibres, which were then combed and spun into linen thread. Grants were also made available to set up the large open bleachfields needed to whiten the greenish-grey cloth that the flax produced. Thereafter the picture was one of continuous development and expansion using imported raw materials, linen manufacturing slowly being replaced by cotton.

From 1707, the Treaty of Union between Scotland and England had greatly facilitated Scottish trade with the English colonies in North America and the

West Indies, with the Glasgow merchants taking full advantage of their west coast proximity to the direct Atlantic routes. Fortunes were made by importing tobacco and sugar, and much of the new capital created was used to diversify into textile production. There was a number of good reasons for establishing the new textile manufactories away from Glasgow itself, not least the available labour pool made up of those displaced by the sweeping changes in rural land management and tenure. Fast-flowing upland rivers and streams could be harnessed to power the spinning, weaving and later, cloth-printing machines, as well as provide the copious supply of soft water needed to both bleach and dye. There was yet another benefit to be gained from the region's wet climate, for the high humidity encouraged the cotton fibres to cling together during the spinning stage, reducing the risk of breakage when the yarn was under strain.

The first of several commercial bleachfields on the River Leven's flood meadows was established in 1715. Unbleached linen cloth was soaked with water from a network of channels before being laid out to dry in the sun, the process repeated at regular intervals over the course of several weeks. Long after open-air bleaching was abandoned in favour of synthetic agents, which could whiten the linen cloth indoors in a matter of days, the word 'field' persisted in the names of the Vale's dye and print works. Although spinning and dyeing of linen thread had been mechanised, it was to be some years before techniques became available for the factory dyeing of already woven cloth. The first printworks able successfully to apply colour to cloth became operational in 1768. This period of textile dyeing and printing also produced the first reported incidents of industrial pollutants discharged into the River Leven, seriously damaging the fishings. On the east side of the region, releases of industrial effluent from a print works established beside the River Blane also proved harmful to fish stocks.

By the turn of the nineteenth century there were up to six print works and five bleachfields concentrated in a 5 km stretch of the River Leven, between them employing some 3,000 men, women and children, their output confined almost exclusively to the finishing stages in the treatment of bought-in cloth. Strathendrick's textile industry revolved more around the initial processes of spinning and weaving. With the price of linen steadily rising and the repeal of protectionist legislation that had acted against cotton cloth, by the mid-eighteenth century the latter had become the cheaper of the two materials. To meet this new opportunity, cotton-spinning mills were erected during the 1790s at Balfron and Fintry (Fig. 7.1) alongside the River Endrick, with reservoirs constructed to provide additional headwater during the drier summer months. In both locations, company houses were specially built to house the influx of workers. Balfron, the largest concern, employed 400 factory workers engaged in spinning, with an equal number of outworking hand-loom weavers producing the cloth in their own homes. But barely had these water-powered mills become fully operational, than cotton processing by coal-fired steam power was introduced elsewhere. Conversion to steam power was not a practical proposition in the Endrick Valley because of the distance from the nearest source of coal. It was these same enterprises that were hardest hit by the general trade depression that followed the end of the Napoleonic Wars and the adoption of power loom weaving in other parts of industrialised Scotland. The cotton famine brought about by the American Civil War (1861–65) was to prove the last straw, and by the end of the century all of the outlying mills had closed down. One lasting

Fig. 7.1 An abandoned cotton mill at Fintry in Strathendrick (Author's collection).

legacy of this rural industrial age, however, was the improvements carried out on what had been up to then very rough country roads.

Although the Vale of Leven's dyeing and printing industries had been similarly depressed by the American cotton shortage, they quickly recovered once supplies were restored, at peak production employing between them some 6,000 people. With auxiliary steam power installed and mechanical cylinder printing replacing all but specialised block printing by hand, the output of finished cloth greatly increased. The Vale printworks became the country's leading exponents in the use of Turkey red, a dye noted for its vividness and ability to withstand strong sunshine without fading, essential qualities needed for the intended markets in the Far East. By the end of the nineteenth century, however, the various dyeing and printing works in the area found themselves struggling against increasing competition from abroad and technical advances made by rival concerns in the north of England. Even with a rail transport link, the last outlying printworks at Blanefield had ceased production by 1898. In the Vale, amalgamation into one large company slowed down the decline for a time, but one by one the Vale works closed their doors. A brief respite came with the opening of a silk-dyeing factory at Balloch in the early 1930s, but when this was wound up in 1980, it brought to an end the textile industry which had been the mainstay of the Vale of Leven's economy for some 250 years.

Glass-making and ship building at Dumbarton

Dumbarton's early history as a seaport trading with England and the Continent owed much to the presence of a gravel encrusted shoal that stretched across the Clyde Estuary just upstream of the town, preventing the further passage of all but the smallest boats. But once a navigable channel had been dredged through 'the grand obstacle' in the 1780s, giving fully laden sea-going vessels

Fig. 7.2 Seen from above the town, the Dumbarton glass works in full production
(Dumbarton Libraries collection).

access to the very heart of Glasgow, Dumbarton's importance for handling overseas trade went into decline. With the lower tidal reaches of the River Leven too
saline and turbid to be of use in the textile industry, Dumbarton instead turned
to the manufacture of glass and the building of ships.

The setting up of a glass-making company in Dumbarton took place in 1776,
making use of a large sandbank near the mouth of the Leven for its raw material. The necessary potash came from burnt seaweed imported from the
Western Isles. Three cone-shaped glass furnaces, which were said to have been
the largest in Scotland, were a conspicuous feature of the town's skyline (Fig.
7.2), often remarked upon in travellers' accounts. Dumbarton specialised in
high quality crown glass, produced by revolving the molten material into circular discs from which small window panes were then cut. Apart from a short
break in the 1830s, glass-making at Dumbarton continued until about 1850,
when closure of the works followed the removal of the duty on cheaper glass
imported from abroad.

Ship building on the lower River Leven dated back at least to the time of
Robert I, the Loch Lomondside woods meeting much of the early industry's
requirements for timber. It was not until the transition from wood to iron in
the nineteenth century that the Dumbarton yards really came into their own,
to their credit introducing several 'firsts' in ship design and construction as sail
power gradually gave way to steam. Pioneering in service too, for it was the
locally built *Margery* that became the first ever steamship to cross the English
Channel. Some idea of the upsurge in ship building activity at Dumbarton can
be gauged from a published list of more than 360 vessels built during a 20 year
period between 1839 and 1859. Over the next two decades, 16 different yards
were engaged in building and refitting ships, with allied trades such as
foundries, rope works, sail and boiler makers giving further employment in the
town. Whereas the textile factories in the Vale lost out as a result of the

American Civil War, ship building on the Leven was given an additional boost with orders for fast blockade runners from the southern states. The local yards played an important role in the creation of the largest inland waterway fleet ever assembled – the Irrawaddy Flotilla in Burma, immortalised in verse by Rudyard Kipling in his *Road to Mandalay*. The venture earned Dumbarton a permanent place in the annals of ship construction, with well over 400 shallow draft vessels destined for the riverboat trade built in kit form by one company alone. An individual inland steamer worthy of special mention is the *Coya*, which was built at Dumbarton in 1891 before being taken apart and the sections shipped off to South America. There it was reassembled and launched on Lake Titicaca, 3,960 m up in the Peruvian Andes, the vessel giving service for over 80 years.

The prosperity that ship building brought to the town was not to last, a gradual closure of the Dumbarton yards reflecting a national decline in the industry. Despite having diversified into roll-on/roll-off ferries and hovercraft, the last surviving large company – Dennys – ceased trading in 1963, but with an outstanding record of having built some 1,500 passenger, merchant and warships. The most celebrated vessel to come from a Dumbarton ship building yard is undoubtedly the fast tea clipper *Cutty Sark* (Fig. 7.3), which was launched in November 1869. After falling on hard times, this now restored merchantman is exhibited at Greenwich in London, an evocative reminder of the last great days of sail.

The motor, munitions and aircraft industries

At the height of industrialisation, there were, of course, other major manufacturies in Dumbarton and the Vale of Leven apart from textiles, glass-making

Fig. 7.3 The famous *Cutty Sark* was just one of hundreds of ships built on the River Leven (Dumbarton Libraries collection).

and the building of ships. Vintage motor enthusiasts will not need reminding
of the Vale's connection with the renowned Argyll car. Within a year of com-
mencing production in 1906, the Argyll works in Alexandria were turning out
more cars per year than any of their competitors outside of the United States
– going on to introduce a range of models and to take several long distance
and speed records, all of which added to the car's prestige. Success was short-
lived, for high overheads eventually forced the company into liquidation in
1914. With the outbreak of war in the same year, the Vale car factory immediately turned over to the production of munitions, with an enlarged but temporary workforce of nearly 3,000. As Britain began to rearm in the 1930s, the
empty premises were taken over once more, this time for torpedo manufacture
until 1969. The ship building yard of Dennys had flirted with aeroplane design
from the earliest days of powered flight, including the development of an aircraft capable of vertical take-off which was flown for the first time in 1912. With
war clouds gathering in Europe, the Blackburn Aircraft Company came to
Dumbarton in the late 1930s, employing at its peak up to 4,000 workers.
Several different types of aircraft were produced at the Blackburn factory, but
the best remembered is the famous Sunderland Flying Boat. Some 250 that
were built at Dumbarton went into service all over the world in the dual role
of an anti-submarine and transport plane. Aircraft production in the town
ceased soon after the end of the war.

Much less dependent today on just a few large companies providing employment for a substantial proportion of the local workforce, both Dumbarton and
the Vale of Leven have overcome their disappearance by diversifying into a
much wider range of light and service industries. Employment opportunities
elsewhere on southern Loch Lomondside are very limited, and the villages in
the Endrick and Blane Valleys are largely reliant on Greater Glasgow for work.

Water storage and supply

The water demands of an ever-growing population in central Scotland has
meant that Loch Lomondside, with its high annual rainfall, has been at the
very forefront of schemes for water storage and supply for both domestic and
industrial use (Fig. 7.4).

Before 1855, when the Corporation of Glasgow finally decided on developing Loch Katrine in the Trossachs as a gravity feed water supply to the city, a
number of other options had been under consideration. Amongst the schemes
proposed was one to be sited in upper Strathendrick, which apart from a reservoir, would have included a conduit encircling the Campsie Hills via
Strathblane and the Glazert Valley, intercepting many of the Campsie streams
en route. Loch Lomondside was affected by Glasgow's choice of Loch Katrine,
however, first by its pipelines to the Milngavie holding reservoirs and later by
the inclusion of Loch Arklet near Inversnaid into the scheme. In 1914 a dam
was built across Glen Arklet's western end, raising the surface height of a small
existing loch by 6.7 m. Arklet Reservoir is connected to Loch Katrine by a tunnel through the Lomondside–Glen Gyle watershed.

Water engineers had not lost sight of the upper Endrick Valley. The completion in 1939 of the Carron Reservoir was an unusual undertaking in that it
straddled both sides of the Endrick–Carron watershed, requiring a dam at
either end. When the valley was flooded, several farms with good quality agricultural land were submerged. In addition to east Stirlingshire, all of south-

Fig. 7.4 An early nineteenth-century cotton mill dam in the upper Endrick Valley is dwarfed by the twentieth-century Carron Reservoir in the distance.

eastern Loch Lomondside is now served by the Carron Reservoir, the fourth largest source of domestic and industrial water in Scotland.

Faced with a need for additional water supplies to the rapidly industrialising Vale of Leven, Renton extended a small lochan on Carman Muir, while the other townships turned to a Loch Lomond water pumping station near Balloch. In practice, pollution of the pumped water from the loch's steamers and sewage discharge proved a constant problem, and the scheme was abandoned when a new reservoir in Glen Finlas in the Luss Hills became operational in 1909. The Finlas supply was later extended to Kilmaronock, covering all of the south side of the loch.

With both Dumbarton and neighbouring Clydebank having fully exploited the water gathering grounds of the southern Kilpatrick Hills, the last Clydebank reservoir to be built was sited some distance away from the town in the then untapped northern half of the hills. Opened in 1914, the Burncrooks Reservoir was constructed around one of the feeder streams to the River Endrick. About the same time as the Burncrooks scheme was being planned, Dumbarton Burgh was investigating the possibilities of enlarging Loch Sloy, some 32 km away in the Highlands. When this plan was turned down by a parliamentary commission of enquiry, the feasibility of reservoirs in Glen Luss and elsewhere was examined, but both cost and distance from the town became contributory factors in all the sites' eventual rejection. Finally, spurred on by the summer drought of 1955 which left the town acutely short of water, Dumbarton turned to Loch Lomond. In June 1960, a small pumping station was opened on the lochside at Auchendennan, well away from the sources of pollution that had blighted the earlier pumping scheme at Balloch.

The *Water (Scotland) Act 1967* brought into being the Central Scotland Water Development Board, whose remit was to initiate schemes to provide water in

Fig. 7.5 The barrage constructed across the River Leven at Dalvait ford has controlled the discharge of water from Loch Lomond since 1971.

bulk throughout the densely populated and industrialised central belt of Scotland. Loch Lomond's massive storage capacity made it a tempting choice. The Loch Lomond Water Scheme, which involved controlling the natural discharge from the loch by means of a barrage across the River Leven (Fig. 7.5), was officially opened on 29 June 1971. Through its pumping station at Ross Priory on the loch's southern shore, the Board was given the authority to abstract up to 455 megalitres (100 million gallons) of water per day, providing the level of the loch does not fall below 6.7 m (22 ft) OD. To counter the loch's falling water level in the driest summer months, additional storage capacity by the provision of supplementary reservoirs in Glen Fruin, Glen Luss and Glen Douglas was an option, but in the event not carried out. Anticipated rising water demand in the new millennium has necessitated further development of the Loch Lomond Water Scheme to increase the rate of abstraction.

The provision of hydro-electric power

Right up to the Second World War, the use of hydro-electric power in Scotland had been very low key. The Loch Sloy hydro-electric scheme on the west side of Loch Lomond, which was formally opened on 18 October 1950, was one of the great civil engineering achievements of the immediate post-war years, and the first of the newly formed North of Scotland Hydro-Electric Board's large-scale projects to be completed. By the construction of a dam linking Ben Vorlich with Ben Vane (Fig. 7.6) and increasing the loch's natural water gathering ground by almost five times through a system of incoming aqueducts and tunnels from neighbouring catchments as far afield as Ben Lui, the water level of Loch Sloy was raised by a massive 47 m. From the reservoir, a 3.2 km tunnel was driven through the heart of Ben Vorlich to a 130 megawatt capacity gen-

Fig. 7.6 The Loch Sloy hydro-electric scheme opened up former remote country.

erating station at Inveruglas overlooking Loch Lomond. Output was increased to 160 megawatts in 1999.

Other projects have been proposed from time to time. Both conventional and pumped storage hydro-electric reservoirs on the headwaters of the Mar Burn above Balmaha were investigated, although neither of these schemes progressed further than the drawing board. The upgrading of Loch Sloy to pumped storage was also looked into, but the concept was eventually dropped. Finally, in 1976 the Hydro-Electric Board put forward their case for a pumped storage scheme at Craigrostan on the slopes of Ben Lomond, the upper reservoir sited on the headwaters of the Cailness Burn. As envisaged, it would initially have a capacity of 1,600 megawatts, but with the potential for upgrading to 3,200 megawatts. For reasons discussed in Chapter 13, the scheme was put in abeyance, and vastly increased costs in the future seem likely to prevent the project remaining a viable option in the North of Scotland Hydro-Electric Board's successor's long-term plan.

From everything outlined above, it can be seen that there is scarcely a valley or glen, river or standing water in the region that has not been drawn into or at least considered for one water utilisation scheme or another. From the very first small water bodies constructed to keep the water wheels of the local corn mills turning in summer to the regulating of Loch Lomond itself for urban and industrial needs over a wide area of central Scotland, the spread of dams and reservoirs, power and pumping stations, electric pylons and water pipelines has, within a comparatively short space of time, had an accumulative impact on the face of Loch Lomondside equal to that of much longer standing rural land uses.

8

Field Sports and other Recreational Activities

'Loch Lomondside ... I think this part of the Highlands is as wild as any I have seen. We are upon the side of a great lake, bordered round with exceedingly high mountains ... A man in health might find a good deal of entertainment in fair weather, provided he has strength to climb up the mountains and has keenness to pursue the game they produce.'

Correspondence of Lieutenant Colonel James Wolfe
(25 June 1753)

The transition from killing wild animals for essential protein to the ritualistic hunting of fur, feather and fin for the excitement of the chase was a gradual process. At Govan Parish Church further upstream on the River Clyde, there is a sarcophagus with a carved depiction of red deer and wild boar closely pursued by a mounted nobleman, possibly representing one of the kings of Strathclyde. The sarcophagus appears to be of late ninth-century design, although similar scenes on earlier Pictish symbol stones elsewhere in Scotland suggest that participation in the hunt just for pleasure was commonplace before then. Such field sports evolved from the need to control wild beasts of the forest which posed a threat to livestock and crops, but hunting dangerous animals from horseback was further encouraged in gaining skills with weapons of war.

The hunting grounds of Robert the Bruce

The earliest documentary source on the royal passion for the hunt are the Scottish Exchequer Rolls, which show that in his latter years between 1326 and 1329 Robert I created an 80 ha palisaded deer park and falconry mews beside his manor house on the west bank of the River Leven, believed to be the same place now known as Mains of Cardross at Dalmoak. Outside the enclosed park lay the king's hunting preserve on the edge of the Highlands, where the fourteenth-century chronicler John Fordum tells us: 'along the foot of these mountains are vast woods, full of stags, roe-deer and other wild animals and beasts of various kinds'. With most of the hunt servants on foot, unleashed dogs were used to chase and hold the quarry at bay until the king's party caught up. The pack kept by Bruce are said to have been large white hounds first brought over from France at the time of the Norman Conquest.

According to the historian Boethius, on one of King Robert's hunting expeditions he narrowly escaped with his life when a wild white bull (*Bos taurus*) turned on his pursuers, such a moment vividly captured by Sir Walter Scott:

'Mightiest of all the beasts of chase,
That roam in woody Caledon,
Crashing the forest in his race,
The Mountain Bull comes thundering on'.

As the forest cover receded, the last of these ancient white cattle were herded into parks at Cumbernauld (East Dunbartonshire) and Stirling, where the fierceness for which they were renown was gradually bred out. Their descendants, with their distinctive black ears and muzzles (Fig. 8.1), can still be seen at Chatelherault, a former hunting lodge of the Dukes of Hamilton in Lanarkshire and at Cumbernauld's Palacerigg Country Park.

Deer parks

Robert the Bruce was probably the first to introduce fallow deer to Loch Lomondside, this favourite beast of the chase of the Norman–Scottish nobility having been kept in the Kings Park at Stirling since at least 1290. After Levenside, the next deer park to be created in the area was on Inchmurrin, the old castle at the west end of the island serving as a hunting lodge for the lairds of Lennox and their royal guests. Again, the species of deer introduced is not mentioned in the earlier records, and it is left to the sixteenth-century map maker Timothy Pont to note: 'in this yle ar many fallow deer, whair the kings used hunting sumtyme'. In 1663 the Colquhouns laid waste to Inchlonaig for the sole use of fallow deer. Between them, the two island deer parks supported some 450 head of fallow, a high stocking rate that could only be sustained during the lean months of winter by supplementary feeding. The last fallow deer herd to be established on Loch Lomondside was in the Colquhoun's pleasure grounds of Rossdhu House in the mid-nineteenth century. On Inchlonaig and in the deer park at Rossdhu, metal tree guards were placed around many of the trees to prevent damage to them by the deer. As management of these herds declined, the park-bred fallow deer began to escape from their confinement and establish themselves in the wild.

Fig. 8.1 Descendants of an ancient breed of white cattle that once roamed wild in Scotland's forests.

Deer forests

In the social upheaval that followed the Jacobite uprising of 1745–46, red deer numbers in Scotland were reduced to an extremely low ebb by indiscriminate killing, so much so that on Loch Lomondside the incoming blackface sheep initially had the uplands to themselves. The first sign of a change in the fortunes of the red deer came with the creation of deer 'forests' — more often than not, just open hill ground – entirely for sporting purposes. Throughout the first half of the nineteenth century, wandering animals from newly established deer forests at Blackmount and Glen Artney (both outwith the Loch Lomond area) did occasionally put in an appearance, but because of their potential for damaging the oak coppice woodlands still in full production, the deer were not encouraged to settle.

Attitudes changed dramatically from about 1880, when the rental value of the hill sheep grazings plummeted to an uneconomic level, as large-scale imports of colonial wool and mutton undermined market prices. Yet at the same time the demand for sporting lets in Scotland had never been higher, spurred on not only by a significant reduction in travelling time from England with the coming of the railway, but the sovereign seal of approval bestowed upon deer stalking in the Highlands by Queen Victoria and Prince Albert at Balmoral. In line with this new sporting fashion, a number of sheep walks on Loch Lomondside were converted to deer forest. These included Glen Falloch, Loch Sloy (Ben Vorlich and Ben Vane), Inversnaid and Rowardennan (Ben Lomond) forests. Hunting lodges – some in the pseudo-baronial style (Fig. 8.2) – were specially built to accommodate the proprietor's guests and sporting tenants, together with their retinue of domestic staff. Shot beasts were brought down off the hill by sure-footed Highland ponies, a task entirely taken over today by all-terrain vehicles. Overall, the quality of the stags killed on Loch Lomondside has not been exceptional, although included among the trophy heads have been several much coveted 12 pointers or 'royals'.

Fig. 8.2 A former purpose-built hunting lodge at Rowardennan is now a popular youth hostel.

This peak in the management of several Loch Lomondside estates for red deer was cut short by the outbreak of the First World War. Prices for home-produced wool and mutton rapidly recovered and all able-bodied sportsmen and professional deer stalkers found themselves fully occupied with the British expeditionary forces abroad. Subsequent organised stalking in the district has been far less intensive which, together with the extensive cover provided by recent afforestation of the hills, has led to a marked increase in the Lomondside red deer population – currently estimated at between 1,500 and 2,000 animals – their range extending southwards well below the Highland Line.

Grouse moors and pheasant coverts

When the only available firearm was the heavy, muzzle-loading flintlock, the hunting of red grouse and pheasant (*Phasianus colchicus*) – the latter introduced locally as a sporting bird in the early nineteenth century – could be a very arduous affair. Walking the woods and moors with dogs trained for pointing or flushing out the concealed game usually meant a long, tiring day for only a modest return. The sport was transformed by the development of the breech-loaded waterproof cartridge, with its speed in reloading and ability to perform in all weathers. This led in turn to the emergence of the sporting estate. Shoots became organised with military precision, the grouse or pheasants driven by a line of beaters towards the waiting guns, enabling for the first time huge numbers of birds to be killed. Every estate owner competed with his neighbours to produce the largest head of game for the season for, apart from social prestige, where the shoot was let, the greater the number of birds shot the higher the sporting rent which could be asked the following year. Records kept for the Buchanan grouse moors show that the most productive period occurred just before the First World War, the number of grouse shot peaking at over 1,800 birds in the 1911 season, 480 on 6 September alone. The best season for pheasants in the Buchanan coverts and coppice woodlands was the winter of 1909–10, with nearly 2,000 birds killed, a single day's shooting on 16 November accounting for almost half of the total bag.

The presenting of such artificially high numbers of grouse and pheasants to the waiting guns had only been achieved by the almost total elimination of all predatory mammals and birds by gamekeepers engaged for this purpose. Some proprietors initiated a bounty system, a specified payment made for each carnivore or bird of prey destroyed. Recalling the former abundance of natural predators on the Luss Estate before their ruthless slaughter began, the mid-nineteenth-century sportsman/naturalist John Colquhoun wrote:

> ' The golden eagle built in Luss Glen, so did several pairs of peregrines in the wilder cliffs. I have myself seen, in one season, three nests of that sylvan ornament the kite – one in an oak tree on Rossdhu lawn, and the other two in the pine wood of an adjacent mountain. The marten was constantly flushed in the same pine wood, nay, even in the lower grounds; and the wildcat was far from rare. In the course of time my brother engaged a first-rate lowland gamekeeper, whose trapping feats on the carnivora were even more exciting than anything the game could show; and the rarer, wilder, predatory birds and beasts rapidly disappeared.'

Displaying the grisly corpses of these animals on a gibbet (Fig. 8.3) was widely practised by gamekeepers, for it showed to their employers that they were
conscientiously carrying out their appointed task. The following contemporary
description of one such gibbet on a Loch Lomondside estate exemplifies the
single-minded onslaught against all known and suspected predators of game:

> 'Vermin of all kinds and degrees are here treated with well-merited
> rigour. The toad that plunders the hen-roost, the sleeky weasel, and
> the stoat – egg suckers by habit and repute from time immemorial –
> with the hoodie-craw, the hawk and the owl – all birds of evil omen to
> the game – are here sacrificed with the shortest possible shrift. Look at
> these relics of departed reivers (thieves) nailed on the rafters of the
> kennel, and think what a salvation of innocent partridges and grouse
> has been effected by their destruction.'

The predators of game fish were similarly dispatched, Colquhoun going on
to describe how otters (*Lutra lutra*) were trapped on the loch. Goosanders
(*Mergus merganser*) and red-breasted mergansers (*M. serrator*) were shot on
sight as a matter of course, but the Montrose Estate gamekeepers did at least
spare the breeding colony of grey herons on the lower reaches of the Endrick
on account that 'herons' formed part of the Montrose family's coat of arms. In
John Colquhoun's own words, the fish-eating ospreys (*Pandion haliaetus*) nesting on Inchgalbraith, part of Luss Estate, were destroyed during a 'vermin cru-
sade'. The rarer creatures killed in the interests of game preservation were sent
to taxidermists' establishments in Glasgow, Edinburgh and Perth, the
Victorians' passion for stuffed birds and mammals in the parlour or trophy
room placing an additional price on these animals' heads.

The impact of this wanton persecution by gun, trap and snare was such that
a number of native animals, notably the pine marten (*Martes martes*), polecat
(*Putorius putorious*), wildcat (*Felis catus*), red kite (*Milvus milvus*), hen harrier
(*Circus cyaneus*) and osprey were totally banished from the area. Well over a
century later, the polecat and red kite
have yet to re-establish themselves,
and even the others are still very
scarce. Apart from the local extinction of several species of predator,
another unfortunate legacy of the
game bird culture during the
Victorian and Edwardian periods was
the widespread planting of rhododendron as cover for the pheasants.
Now thoroughly naturalised, this all
too successful shrub has invaded
many of the Loch Lomondside woodlands, its dense evergreen foliage
totally shading out the native ground
flora and preventing regeneration of

Fig. 8.3 A row of illegally killed buzzards
on a modern day gamekeeper's gibbet
(Robert Pollock).

indigenous trees. To date, all attempts to bring rhododendron under control have all been on a small scale and consequently had little overall effect.

After the First World War, the returning sportsmen and gamekeepers picked up where they had left off. For red grouse, 1934 with its fine summer weather was a particularly good year on most of the local estates, the Buchanan moors yielding 1,800 birds in nine days of driving. As the acreage of good heather moor receded from a gradual run down in moorland management, overgrazing by sheep, bracken infestation and the advent of upland afforestation, red grouse numbers on Loch Lomondside went into a steep decline. On formerly well-stocked moors where the seasonal bag of grouse was once counted in hundreds, hardly a bird can now be seen. Pheasant shooting, on the other hand, has generally held its ground, although it is maintained only through the buying-in and releasing of large numbers of hand-reared birds each autumn to supplement the small breeding stock. Attempts have been made to introduce the red-legged partridge (*Alectoris rufa*) from time to time, but this predominantly southern European species appears unable to acclimatise to the region's cool and wet climate. Even the North American wild turkey (*Meleagris gallopavo*) was tried out in Rossdhu Park for a while.

Wildfowling and snipe shooting

Most of the wildfowling on Loch Lomondside is concentrated in and around the Endrick Marshes, where the largest number of birds feed and roost. Estate game books covering the late nineteenth– early twentieth centuries show that duck were a favourite quarry, but the almost complete absence of goose entries confirms that today's high numbers of wintering geese in the area is a fairly recent phenomenon. The winter-flooded Wards Low Ground is a legacy of the heyday of wildfowling on the Endrick Marshes, with the abandonment of badly drained arable ground in favour of flighting ponds to attract wild duck towards the concealed guns.

Marsh hay meadows after cutting in late summer gave the opportunity of large bags of common snipe (*Gallinago gallinago*). In the 1873–74 season, one of the landed proprietors of the Endrick Marshes – Sir George H. Leith Buchanan – shot a record total of 350 snipe on his ground.

Angling

A dedicated angler has by nature to be an unshakeable optimist. The Loch Lomond fisherman's lament says it all – 'washed off by rain, blown off by wind, driven off by despair' – yet still he returns time after time to try his luck once more in a favourite drift.

Much is owed to visiting anglers for our knowledge of the early development of sport fishing on Loch Lomond and its tributary rivers. To be expected considering the unsettled times, all concerned were military men. The first was Richard Franck, a lieutenant quartermaster in the Cromwellian army during the Civil War. It was a second tour of duty to a more peaceful Scotland in 1658 which gave Franck and his travelling companion the opportunity of casting their rods over the River Leven. Catching both salmon and sea trout, it was the first locally recorded instance of use of an artificial fly. Lieutenant Colonel James Wolfe (later in life to become a national hero as General Wolfe of Quebec) must have noted the angling potential of the area while temporarily stationed at Inversnaid garrison after the Battle of Culloden, for he made sure to bring along his fly-fishing rods when posted again to Loch Lomondside with five companies of soldiers from the 20th Regiment for military road building in the summer of 1753. The account of Colonel Thomas Thornton's highly successful sporting tour of Scotland undertaken ca. 1786 is especially instructive, particularly for the wealth of detail on eighteenth-century angling techniques and tackle.

Then as now, the special attraction of Loch Lomond was the chance of landing a large specimen fish. Thomas Thornton's record fish was a 7 lb 7 oz (3.3 kg) perch (*Perca fluviatilis*), which he carefully weighed on his portable scales. Even today, this weight remains unchallenged for a Scottish rod-caught perch. And again, a 41 lb (18.6 kg) Atlantic salmon taken from the loch by Thornton was not beaten for 126 years, when a remarkably good fish was successfully played by Mr Edward Cochran on 15 April 1930. Weighing in at 44 lb (20 kg), this once-in-a-lifetime salmon (Fig. 8.4) is a record for Loch Lomond yet to be surpassed. In more recent years a 22 lb 7 oz (10.2 kg) sea trout, caught in the River Leven on 22 July 1989, became the new British record for the species.

If a really gigantic fish is going to be taken from the loch, it will undoubtedly be the predatory pike (*Esox lucius*), a fully-grown specimen capable of

Fig. 8.4 Mr Edward Cochran with his record-breaking salmon from Loch Lomond (Author's collection).

putting up a fight to test the mettle of even the most seasoned angler. Loch Lomond abounds with enormous-pike-that-got-away stories, but one that did not in July 1947 was found to weigh 47 lb 11 oz (21.6 kg). This British rod-caught record was by no means the first big pike to be encountered locally, for a massive specimen was found marooned in a lagoon near the Endrick Mouth ca.1934, its weight estimated at 50 lb (22.7 kg) or more. The creature's fear-some-looking head is preserved in Glasgow's Kelvingrove Museum. Based on stories of monster pike from the early days of angling, the distinguished nine-teenth-century zoologist William Yarrell was convinced that the productive waters of Loch Lomond were capable of producing a colossus well in excess of 70 lb (32 kg). He might yet be proved right.

Regrettably, some visiting anglers have not been content with pitting their piscatorial skills against Loch Lomond's indigenous fish, irresponsibly intro-ducing a number of southern species (see Chapter 9) with the potential for unstabilising the loch's ecological balance evolved over thousands of years. The deleterious effects of industrial effluent discharged into the Rivers Leven and Blane has already been mentioned. It was this together with over-netting of migrating salmonids moving up river to their traditional spawning grounds which led to the setting up of an organised body in the mid-nineteenth cen-tury to combat these particular problems. After overcoming several setbacks, the Loch Lomond Angling Improvement Association in its present form was established in 1901. With a large membership, the LLAIA employs full-time water bailiffs and maintains its own salmon and sea trout hatchery for restock-ing purposes.

Mountaineering and rambling

Of all Loch Lomondside's outdoor recreational pursuits, 'mountaineering' attracts the largest number of devotees. Most would modestly describe them-selves as hill walkers, but there is a small hard core of rock and ice climbers, together with downhill skiers in winters with sufficient snow.

In the early days of travel, the Scottish mountains were regarded by visitors from the south as both desolate and frightening, places to go out of one's way to avoid. A gradual change in perception can be seen in the journal of the lit-erary figure Thomas Gray, who, during his first visit to Scotland in 1764, enthused over the mountain landscape around Loch Lomond which he thought exquisite. But if the followers of the 'picturesque' movement who came hard on his heels found the serenity of mountains reflected in the still surface of the loch an uplifting spiritual experience, most still detested the sight of peatbog and moor. As one early guide book to the area described the Muirpark route between Drymen and Gartmore: 'nothing can be bleaker than the scene which presents itself at the summit of the hill'.

Shepherds and fox-hunters regularly crisscrossed the region's hills in the course of their duties, but actually going up a mountain just for the pleasure of standing on its summit to take in the view was unheard of until the mid-eigh-teenth century. Loch Lomondside's first recorded touristic ascent took place in the year of 1756, when a Cambridge University graduate William Burrell and sev-eral of his friends set their caps at scaling Ben Lomond. According to his diary, Burrell was overcome with vertigo on the final approach to the top and had to descend, but his unheeding companions forged ahead to 'feast very heartily' on the summit. Initially only an intrepid few followed their example, but by 1804

James Denholm in his *Tour to the Principal Scotch and English Lakes* observed that
'the greatest part of travellers who visit Loch Lomond upon a pleasure excursion
take advantage of the ferry at Inveruglas [Inverbeg], and cross the lake to ascend
Ben Lomond'. Colonel Peter Hawker, who is credited with the first winter ice
climb on the Ben, added that in summer 'ladies very commonly go up, and
sometimes take with them a piper and other apparatus for dancing'. A new
breed of professional mountain guide emerged, with horses for hire to carry the
less energetic to the summit. Visitor numbers to Loch Lomond did temporarily
fall away with the appearance in 1810 of Sir Walter Scott's poetical work *Lady of
the Lake*, which drew the tourists clutching their copies of the book more towards
Loch Katrine, but the popularity of Loch Lomondside fully recovered seven
years later after Scott published his locally set novel *Rob Roy*.

What began as a gentleman's leisure pursuit, to be followed in turn by the
professional classes, gradually encompassed a wide range of Scotland's social
spectrum as Saturday afternoons off from work became commonplace and the
rigid Sabbath observance customs were relaxed. As the second half of the nineteenth century progressed, the improved rail and steamer services allowed the
new excursionists – who were intent on cramming as much as possible into a
one day trip – to reach Loch Lomond in ever increasing numbers. Railway
engineers from Snowdonia in North Wales even investigated the possibility of
a mountain railway to the top of Ben Lomond, but the idea came to nothing.
The Campsies too proved extremely popular. Hugh MacDonald's *Rambles
Round Glasgow* (1854), which included described walks over Loch
Lomondside's southern foothills, went through several editions to meet the
new demand. By the early 1890s, at least ten different rambling clubs were
operating out of Glasgow alone.

Others in the pursuit of some scientific enquiry or other were afoot in the
Loch Lomondside hills right from the beginning. The Reverend John
Lightfoot and George Don are just two from a long list of distinguished
botanists whose early explorations of the high tops contributed to our knowledge of the region's montane flora. Amongst a rash of natural history bodies
founded in the mid-nineteenth century was the Perthshire Mountain Club,
which, in the Loch Lomond area, directed its attention to the Glen Falloch
Hills. Eligibility to the club was restricted to those members of the Perthshire
Society of Natural Science who could claim to have botanised in the county at
altitudes of over 3,000 ft (914 m).

The very first mountaineering organisation in Scotland was formed in 1866
at Glasgow's Old College – the forerunner of the present University. Known as
the Cobbler Club, after the Arrochar area's best known summit, its stated aim
was to promote the climbing of every worthy hill that could be reached from
Glasgow in the course of a Saturday excursion; and 'to crown the labours of
the day by such an evening of social enjoyment as can only be spent by those
who have had a sniff of true mountain air'. From these early beginnings came
the Scottish Mountaineering Club (Fig. 8.5), formally constituted in Glasgow
on 11 March 1889, publishing the first issue of the club journal in January of
the following year. From the very start, the SMC's journal enthusiastically
pointed the way to rock outcrops near to hand such as the Whangie in the
Kilpatrick Hills, still a popular climbing spot. Newly described routes on the
higher rock faces of the southern Highlands came thick and fast and there is
even an account of a 600 ft (185 m) winter snow glissade made down Ben

Fig. 8.5 A Scottish Mountaineering Club meet at Tarbet in 1895 (S.M.C. collection).

Lomond's northeast corrie. A milestone in Volume I of the journal was the publication of Sir Hugh Munro's 'Tables giving all the Scottish Mountains exceeding 3,000 ft in height'. A total of 538 tops of 3,000 ft (914 m) or over were listed, including 283 given the status of separate mountains. The latter almost immediately became known as 'Munros', and reaching the summits of them all presented a challenge to many club members. There had been the occasional peak collector before, such as the geologist John MacCulloch in the early part of the century, but now 'peak-bagging' as a sport was pursued in earnest. The first person to complete an ascent of all the listed Munros and subsidiary tops was the Reverend A.R.G. Burn, realising his objective on 20 July 1923 having saved the twin-topped Beinn a' Chroin at the head of Glen Falloch for his celebratory final one. Although peak-collecting aimed at making a high personal score was initially frowned upon by the club elders, hundreds of dedicated Munroists have followed the Reverend Burn's example.

It was one of the founder members of the Scottish Mountaineering Club, W.W. Naismith, who first introduced Norwegian skis into the country, giving them a trial run on the snow-covered Campsie Hills in March 1892. Despite coming to grief several times, Naismith concluded his assessment of the future of skiing in Scotland with what proved to be a prophetic statement: 'it is not unlikely that the sport may eventually become popular'. Ice skating on the loch is the one winter sport that has dramatically declined. Prolonged periods of intense frost producing weight-bearing ice have become so infrequent that the once familiar spectacle of hundreds of skaters besporting themselves on the loch's frozen surface is no longer within living memory.

Numbers participating in hill walking continued at a high level throughout the latter years of the nineteenth century and up to the outbreak of the First

World War in 1914. This period was to witness serious clashes between ramblers who wished to exercise their much cherished freedom to walk unhindered over open countryside, and landowners attempting to impose exclusivity over Loch Lomondside's newly created deer forests and grouse moors by closing paths and tracks used from time immemorial. As W. C. Paterson commented on the land closures in his collection of poems *Echoes of Endrickvale*, published in 1902:

> 'They're kept for deer an' whirrin' grouse,
> By rich sportsmen executed,
> So sacred is the shrine of sport,
> Trespassers Prosecuted.'

When James Bryce MP secured a debate on his *Access to Mountains (Scotland)* bill, which was brought before Parliament but without success in March 1892, he specifically referred to the extreme measures taken by the sporting proprietors of the Kilpatrick Hills. Prevented from setting foot on these hills by prohibitive signs, barbed wire, threat of litigation and even physical violence, the people of Dumbarton finally became so incensed that in May 1911 a mass demonstration took place on the Overtoun Estate, where a locked gate across the road was torn from its hinges. Demonstrations against path closures also took place in Balloch, after walkers found the southern shores of Loch Lomond closed to them. Despite the outcry, the public only fully regained their traditional right of access to Loch Lomond when Balloch Castle and its grounds were purchased by the Corporation of Glasgow in 1915.

After the inevitable lapse of support for organised outdoor pursuits during the First World War, a resurgence of interest led to the formation of the Glasgow and West of Scotland Ramblers Federation, who, by chartering trains and steamers, could assemble parties of up to 500 members at Rowardennan to walk en masse up Ben Lomond. Glasgow again led the way with the Rucksack Club of Scotland, pioneering the providing of hut accommodation for the use of its members. The Rucksack Club gave way in turn to the Scottish Youth Hostel Association, and Inverbeg was chosen in 1931 for the organisation's first hostel on Loch Lomondside. When the SYHA formally opened Auchendennan House near Balloch on 6 April 1946, it was claimed to be the largest outdoor activities centre in the world.

As found elsewhere, such as in the Lake District of England, the over popularity of certain parts of Loch Lomondside with those seeking the outdoor experience has left its mark. Clearly seen from miles away, the disfiguring linear scar leading up the southern shoulder of Ben Lomond bears witness to the cumulative effect of countless trampling boots. On its severely eroded summit, the botanist will look in vain for the covering of moss heath with its cushions of pink-flowered moss campion (*Silene acaulis*) that so delighted the early visitors to the top. Even on the low ground, some sections of a once secluded and little used woodland path on the east side of the loch become churned into quagmires in wet weather since it was linked into the West Highland Way (Fig. 8.6), a well-publicised long distance walkers' route from Milngavie to Fort William that is completed by over 50,000 participants each year.

Fig. 8.6 Long distance walkers on the Inversnaid to Inverarnan stretch of the West Highland Way.

Powerboating

No outdoor recreational pursuit on Loch Lomondside has altered more in character than boating. Although sedate pleasure cruising, yachting and canoeing on the loch still attract their devotees, others are drawn by the excitement of fast water sports such as water-skiing, jet-skiing and the like. This change in emphasis was made possible by massive upgrading in engine size and power, compared to the older outboard motors that were capable of achieving only a few knots per hour. Fast water sports exercise a hugely disproportionate intrusion on the tranquillity of the loch for the comparatively small number of participants involved. Quite apart from assailing the ears of those who come to Loch Lomond for the quiet contemplation of the magnificent lakeland scenery, or frustrating the salmon angler as he sees the waters around favoured fishing banks repeatedly churned over, the recent influx of speedboat, water- and jet-ski enthusiasts give little respite to the loch's summer wildfowl with their young broods which depend on sheltered and undisturbed feeding waters to survive. In these same shallow waters, the underwater aquatic plant growth and its dependent invertebrate fauna can be badly affected by both propeller damage and increased turbidity from the stirring-up of the loch bed. In addition, ever-increasing levels of toxic residues from engine fuel are being detected at peak periods in the most frequented areas. Well in excess of 5,000 power craft are registered for use on Loch Lomond, a recent census figure showing that over 1,000 can be out and about on fine summer days.

Hand in hand with the expansion in powerboat usage on the loch has been an upsurge in the number of day-trippers to the islands, especially to those with attractive beaches. Inchmoan with its long stretches of fine sandy shores was once noted for the birds nesting at its water's edge, but these have all but disappeared in the face of increased recreational pressure.

Part III

Wildlife Habitats, Communities and Species

9

The Loch and its Surrounds

'Loch Lomond ... the white pebbled shores on which
its gentle billows murmur, like a miniature ocean,
its rocky promontories rising from the deep water,
rich in wild flowers and ferns.'

The Highlands and Western Islands of Scotland
John MacCulloch (1824)

Loch Lomond has been under continuous study longer than any other large
body of fresh water in Scotland. In 1938 the University of Glasgow initiated a
course in freshwater biology, opening its first lochside field station at Rossdhu
eight years later, and moving to the present site near Rowardennan in 1964.
One of the fruits of this long-term investigation was the unravelling of the
loch's pyramid of energy, which has at its broad base countless millions of
microscopic water plants or phytoplankton, progressing upwards by successive
stages to comparatively small numbers of fish-eating birds and even fewer
mammals. Much of the University Field Station's research on Loch Lomond,
the River Endrick and some of the smaller water bodies in the area is beyond
the scope of the present work, but a number of relevant publications are
included in the bibliography for further reading.

The underwater environment

The dual nature of Highland and Lowland Loch Lomond is shown clearly in
the two portions' differing response to heat and light from solar radiation. In
the fjord-like northern basin (Fig. 9.1) the effect of heat radiation from the sun
during the summer months brings about the seasonal phenomenon of thermal
stratification. As the slowly warming surface water (the epilimnion) becomes
less dense than the cold water below (the hypolimnion), from late spring to late
autumn the two layers are effectively separated by an intermediate zone of
rapidly lowering temperature known as the thermocline. This invisible barrier
severely inhibits any exchange between the wind-circulating surface water
above and the still, deep water below. First forming at about 15 m below the surface, where there is sufficient depth of water the thermocline slowly descends
to about 30 m, reaching its maximum development by the end of the summer.
With the onset of falling surface temperatures and frequent strong winds in late
autumn, the stratification breaks down, with remixing of the upper and lower
water layers. The separation of warm and cold water in the expansive southern
basin during the summer tends to be very transitory. With minimum wind shelter from the much lower surrounding hills, together with the buildup of wave
strength over greater distances, any layering that does develop in the relatively
shallow water of the southern basin is unstable and readily overturned.

Fig. 9.1 The over-steepened sides to the northern half of the loch plunge to a depth greater than the North Sea.

Light from the sun dictates the potential depth of the euphotic zone; that is from the loch surface to the lowest level where daytime photosynthetic activity in the drifting phytoplankton is sufficient to sustain life during the hours of night-time darkness. Light penetration of the loch's water depends not only on the intensity and duration of sunlight reaching its surface according to season and cloud cover – the latter having the greatest effect in the high rainfall mountainous region – but also on the amount of light absorbed by dissolved and suspended particle matter within the water itself. Light absorption by peat particles in the loch's waters is at its highest in the northern basin, especially following a rapid runoff of surface water from the surrounding upland catchment area after a period of heavy rain. Overall, the lower limit of the euphotic zone in Loch Lomond varies between 6 and 9 m below the water surface. Within the euphotic zone lies the upper phytal zone, which is where sufficient light reaches the loch bed to permit the growth of rooted aquatic plants. Throughout Loch Lomond this zone rarely exceeds 4 m below the water surface. At mean loch level, water depth from zero to 4 m makes up only about 10 per cent of the total surface area of Loch Lomond, by far the largest proportion of these shallows in the southern and central basins. However, with the unstabilising effect of wave movement on the loch bed (Fig. 9.2), it is only in areas sheltered from the prevailing westerly winds that these well-lit waters in the phytal zone reach anything like their full potential for plant and animal life. Below the euphotic zone and the maximum depth of light penetration lies the profundal zone, where no plant growth is possible and only a few specialised deep water animals can exist.

Both plant and animal productivity also depend on the total amounts of mineral and organic nutrients fed into the loch by inflowing rivers and streams.

Fig. 9.2 The unstabilising effect of wave movement on exposed shores prevents the establishment of many plants and animals.

Compared with the soft sedimentary rocks and fertile soils that make up the loch's southern catchment, the hard and often peat-covered metamorphic rocks around the loch's northern basin yield very little in the way of soluble minerals. This means that the waters in the Highland part of the loch are oligotrophic (poor in nutrients), whereas those in the Lowland portion are for the most part mesotrophic (moderately enriched with nutrients). Disparity between the upper and lower loch, originating from their differing geology and soil types, is further enhanced by mineral fertilizers used in agriculture and organic matter (silage effluent, treated sewage, etc.) discharging into the southern basin by natural drainage and waste-water drains from the more intensively farmed and densely populated Lowland region. Some watercourses entering along the loch's southern margin carry sufficient mineral and organic material to create locally eutrophic conditions (rich in nutrients). This unusually wide range of nutrient loading and productivity in the same water body goes some way to explaining Loch Lomond's exceptional diversity of plant and animal life.

Aquatic life of the loch and lochside edge

Beyond the limit of solar penetration, the profundal zone is a world of darkness and cold but stable temperatures. At these depths the accumulated fine silts and clays that make up the bed of the loch support a very limited fauna, comprising mainly of tube worms (Tubificidae), tiny pea-shell cockles (Lamellibranchiata) and the larvae of dancing (non-biting) midges (Chironomidae), all of which are dependent for food on organic debris 'raining' down from the euphotic zone above. The number of different profundal species is small, but amongst them are two which deserve individual mention.

Arcteonais lomondi is a mud-burrowing worm that was new to science when first described from the northern basin of the loch; even now it is known elsewhere only in the deep waters of Loch Morar. The other is the bivalve mollusc *Pisidium conventus*, a surviving arctic relict from a considerably colder period in Britain's past, which occurs right down to the deepest parts of the Loch Lomond trench.

In the euphotic zone above, by far the largest contribution to the aquatic food chain comes from the phytoplankton, the microscopic plant life that drifts suspended in the upper waters of the loch. None of the more abundant species of phytoplankton are restricted to any one part of the loch, although population densities vary considerably between the north and south basins. As would be expected in a situation where there are significant differences in nutrient concentrations, the total biomass of these plants is far greater in the mesotrophic and locally eutrophic waters of the southern basin than in the oligotrophic waters further north. During the warm and lengthening daylight hours of spring and early summer, there may be up to 65,000 individuals to every litre of water before, in the northern basin at least, the barrier of thermal stratification deprives them of stored nutrients stirred up from the deeper waters below. Under favourable conditions of prolonged sunshine and warmth the phytoplankton in the southern basin multiply rapidly to well in excess of the above figures, creating an algal 'bloom' visible to the eye. The filamentous green alga *Oedogonium* in the eutrophic waters around the mouth of the River Endrick can accumulate to such an extent that it has a detrimental smothering effect on the rich community of ephemeral mud plants concentrated in the more sheltered parts of this corner of the loch. In algal bloom years, another readily noticed is the blue-green alga *Coelosphaerium*, in particular where it collects by wind drift along the shore, coating the surface of the water with what resembles green paint. These algal blooms, together with the recent appearance and rapid spread in the loch of the naturalised Canadian pondweed (*Elodea canadensis*), which in turn is steadily being replaced by another North American species, Nuttall's pondweed (*E. nuttallii*), points to increased nutrient loading of the southern basin, despite Loch Lomond's resilience to water pollution through its large size. An expansion of the breeding population of mute swans (*Cygnus olor*) in the southern half of the loch, which has built up from a fairly static three to five nesting pairs in the early 1980s to 16 nesting pairs by 1996, is undoubtedly a response to the additional food resource now available from the two foreign pondweeds.

The next tier in the food chain is made up of the zooplankton, the smallest of aquatic animal life, including microscopic rotifers (*Rotifera*) and small crustaceans such as waterfleas (*Daphnia*) which are just visible to the naked eye. These feed on the phytoplankton, or in some cases, on other zooplankton. Occurring in much lower numbers than the phytoplankton, the populations of both herbivorous and carnivorous zooplankton fluctuate as the loch's seasonal phytoplankton crop waxes and wanes.

Included within the euphotic zone is the littoral zone, a term used here in a topographical sense to describe the loch bed from the water's edge to the lowest limit of light penetration. Although well represented in the southern half of the loch, the littoral zone is restricted to a very narrow band in the steepsided northern portion. At a casual glance there appears to be little in the way of plant growth at the water's edge around Loch Lomond's predominantly stony fringe, a hostile environment subject to scouring waves at high water fol-

Fig. 9.3 As the loch level falls, a dark band of lacustrine lichens is exposed on Torrinch.

lowed by desiccation when the loch level is low. Closer examination reveals a patchy growth of mosses and liverworts, amongst them *Cinclidotus fontinaloides, Grimmia retracta, Rhacomitrium aquaticum* and *Marsupella emarginata* var. *aquatica*, all typical of periodically inundated lakeside rocks. Even less obvious to the unpractised eye is an assemblage of lacustrine lichens that appear as a dark band on the exposed rocks when the water level drops in summer (Fig. 9.3). Several uncommon or rare species – *Dermatocarpon meiophyllizum, Placynthium flabellosum, P. pannariellum, Porocyphus kenmorensis* and *Verrucaria praetermissa* – are known to be represented. With its varied underlying geology, Loch Lomond could well prove nationally important for this little-studied community of specialised lichens, their water-line habitat evolved over millennia having been lost in a number of other large lochs in Scotland through substantial rises in water levels for the generation of hydro-electric power.

Throughout the greater part of the loch, the underwater macrophyte flora is fairly constant in its succession as the littoral zone falls away from the water's edge. Most characteristic of wave-cut terraces of cobbles of loose stones intermixed with coarse sand is a patchy lawn of shoreweed (*Littorella uniflora*) dotted, except in the enriched waters of the southern basin, with the rosettes of water lobelia (*Lobelia dortmanna*). This part of the loch bed above the low water mark can be exposed for many weeks at a time during the driest summers. As the water deepens, the loch bed slowly changes to ever finer particled sands, silts and muds. With depth the shoreweed is replaced by common quillwort, often associated with a sparse growth of alternate-flowered water-milfoil (*Myriophyllum alterniflorum*) and a stonewort, *Nitella flexilis*, one of a group of large green algae that superficially resemble higher flowering plants. At the deepest point of light penetration only the quillwort persists. Because of its submerged mode of life, the presence of this aquatic relative of the terrestrial ferns is only obvious through its naturally shed 'quills' amongst the gathered wrack along the shore. Away from the mainland and island shores, much the same community of littoral zone plants can be found on some of the loch's reefs and shoals. The cobbled bed of Rossdhu Bank, to the southwest of Inchmoan, exhibits at low water a fine mosaic of quillwort and the aquatic moss *Fontinalis antipyretica* growing between the tightly packed stones. At a deeper level, the McDougal Bank between Inchmurrin and the west mainland shore has sufficient accumulated silty mud and organic matter to support a lush tangle of alternate-flowered water-milfoil and perfoliate pondweed (*Potamogeton perfoliatus*), both growing exceptionally tall as they reach upwards towards the light.

Even with the enrichment of the waters around the southeast corner of Loch Lomond, the diversity of littoral plants present on the gently shelving Endrick Bank does not substantially increase because of the churning action by frequent wind-driven waves on this very exposed site. Where the sandy substrate is sufficiently compact, however, shoreweed and needle spike-rush (*Eleocharis acicularis*) carpet the loch bed between the high and low water marks (Fig. 9.4). Shielded from the force of the waves by the sand bar encircling the river mouth, the composition of the loch's aquatic flora undergoes a noticeable change. Weak growing mud plants, which barely have a toehold on the exposed western side of the bar, greatly increase in number; and given further protection behind Crom Mhin Point, emergent and floating-leaved species appear for the first time. Within the shelter of Crom Mhin Bay, a mixed bed of amphibious bistort (*Persicaria amphibia*) and yellow water-lily (*Nuphar lutea*) covers a large area of the water surface, with uncommon species such as lesser water-plantain (*Baldellia ranunculoides*), small water-pepper (*Persicaria minor*)

Fig. 9.4 Shoreweed carpets the exposed sandy bed of the loch along the edge of the Ring Point.

and awlwort (*Subularia aquatica*) found sparingly around the cattle-trampled muddy edge. It is only as the water level falls that a rich assemblage of small ephemeral plants is revealed, including water-purslane (*Lythrum portula*), and the nationally scarce six-stamened waterwort (*Elatine hexandra*) and eight-stamened waterwort (*E. hydropiper*), exposure stimulating them into flowering.

To see the best selection of aquatic plants around the loch's shoreline requires a visit to the Balmaha Marshes (Plate 1), once a lochside meadow worked for marsh hay by the cotters (sub-tenants) of nearby Auchengyle. Since broken up by storm-force waves into a patchwork of small islands and pools, the former meadow exhibits a colourful profusion of aquatic and marsh plants, including purple loosestrife (*Lythrum salicaria*), yellow loosestrife (*Lysimachia vulgaris*), tufted loosestrife *(L. thyrsiflora)* (see p. 130) and bogbean (*Menyanthes trifoliata*). Unfortunately, some of this diversity seems destined to be lost, as a vigorous growth of bulrush (*Schoenoplectus lacustris*) expands year by year, possibly in response to the water enrichment now experienced in the southeast corner of the loch. The occurrence in the Balmaha Marshes of the nationally rare Loch Lomond dock (*Rumex aquaticus*) (see p. 129) is of particular note, for as its English name suggests, in Britain this northern water docken is found only on Loch Lomondside. Despite attracting attention to itself by occasionally growing up to 2 m in height, the Loch Lomond dock was not added to the British flora until 1935, when it was first found by Glasgow botanist R. MacKechnie. Also present is the slender rush (*Juncus filiformis*), here at one of its few stations outwith the English Lake District, growing sparingly in alluvial grassland just above the water's edge. With the raising of the loch level for the Loch Lomond Water Scheme, however, this uncommon species is in danger of being lost through accelerated shore erosion. Just north of this productive spot lies Balmaha Bay, its water surface once described as 'powdered white' with the flowers of water crowfoot (*Ranunculus aquatilis*). The propeller blades of countless recreational boats have long since taken their toll on this idyllic scene, but in summer the botanist should still have little trouble identifying up to three dozen other aquatic and marsh species around the bay and boatyard grounds.

The water's edge vegetation of stony shores also benefits when sheltered from wave action, this no more evident than on Clairinsh, which is partially shielded by the bulk of neighbouring Inchcailloch. Periodically inundated and enriched with silt, Clairinsh's northwestern shore (Fig. 9.5) supports a well-developed tall herb community, made up of common bistort (*Persicaria bistorta*), hemlock water-dropwort (*Oenanthe crocata*), angelica (*Angelica sylvestris*) and a fine show of globeflower (*Trollius europaeus*). Other flowering plants found around the southern loch that appear dependent on nutrient replenishment of the shore-zone by flood or spray-carried silt include wood goldilocks (*Ranunculus auricomus*), columbine (*Aquilegia vulgaris*), lesser skullcap (*Scutellaria minor*) and dog violet (*Viola canina*), all four rather scarce in the west of Scotland. As an occasional inhabitant of the Loch Lomond shore-zone, the royal fern (*Osmunda regalis*) (Plate 2) still occurs in a few places, despite rapacious fern dealers and collectors having brought this fine species to the verge of extinction. With the over-steepened gradient to the northern half of the loch, the periodically inundated pebble and boulder shore forms only a narrow, nutrient-poor strip between the open water and the woodland edge. Given some protection from the erosive waves, however, a tussocky flora of bog-myrtle (*Myrica gale*), purple moor-grass (*Molinia caerulea*) and common sedge

Fig. 9.5 Globeflower and other wetland plants thrive in the periodically inundated stony shore-zone of Clairinsh.

(*Carex nigra*) may be found. Where the stones on the lochside shore are well compacted is the most likely spot to come across the very localised small-fruited yellow sedge (*Carex serotina*). The extremely rare creeping spearwort (*Ranunculus reptans*) may have once occurred on Loch Lomond's shores, the presence of the hybrid ((*R. x levenensis*)) between it and the closely related but widespread lesser spearwort (*R. flammula*) having recently been confirmed.

Completing the range of mainland and island lochside habitats are the headlands or points, which by their very existence are almost certain to be the hardest rocks in the vicinity. At the end of July some of these rocky headlands can be exceptionally colourful, with goldenrod (*Solidago virgaurea*), common knapweed (*Centaurea nigra*), devil's bit scabious (*Succisa pratensis*), harebell (*Campanula rotundifolia*) and several leafy-stemmed hawkweeds (*Hieracium* spp.) amongst the most frequent species encountered.

Compared to most other large lochs in Scotland, Lomond with its relatively shallow and enriched waters in the southern basin has an abundant and diverse benthic (bottom-dwelling) invertebrate fauna. The succession of stony, sandy and muddy substrates of the littoral zone supports the larval or nymph stages of a large number of flying insects – may-fly (Ephemeroptera), stone-fly (Plecoptera), caddis-fly (Trichoptera), crane-fly (Tipulidae) and dancing midges. Many other small animals such as the freshwater shrimp (*Gammarus pulex*) and the water slater (*Asellus aquaticus*) find food and shelter amongst the vegetation and stones. Of the truly limnic freshwater species of snails and limpets (Gastropoda) which occur, only half are to be found in the northern half of the loch, indicative of the low calcium content in the Highland waters. This north–south distribution of univalves is paralleled amongst the bivalve molluscs present. New species of mollusc are recorded in Loch Lomond from time to time. Little more than 40 years ago, the presence of Jenkin's spire snail (*Potamopyrgus jenkinsi*) was confined to the saline muds of the tidal reaches of the River Leven. Then in 1959 it was found for the first time in a stony stretch of the River Endrick, and in the following year along the southeastern corner of the loch itself. The species' discontinuous distribution at this early stage of the colonisation of Loch Lomond and its feeder rivers suggests dispersal by chance, possibly through the movement of water birds. A more recent and quite unexpected appearance in the southern basin of the loch was of an allied species, *Bithynia leachii*, which has few known localities in the northern half of Britain. It is suspected that this small water snail was inadvertently introduced alongside several translocated southern coarse fish species (see below).

Overall, the littoral zone in the southern loch sustains mean densities of 6,000 benthic animals per m^2, rising to 11,000 where protected from unstabilising waves. With the rich feeding of the Endrick Bank acting as a magnet to wading birds on spring and autumn migration, this corner of Loch Lomond is a favourite haunt of the rarity-seeking birdwatcher. The tally of different waders alone which have been recorded at the water's edge on one or more occasions stands at 35, including several North American species. Happily, these long-distance vagrants are no longer greeted with a hail of gunshot, as was the case in the Victorian collecting era.

Matching the abundance of planktonic and invertebrate life in Loch Lomond is the widest variety of indigenous and introduced fish found in any freshwater body in Scotland. The 15 native species are: sea lamprey (*Petromyzon marinus*) – Loch Lomond is the only site in Britain where the adult sea lamprey is known to feed in fresh water – river lamprey (see p. 130), brook lamprey (*Lampetra planeri*), Atlantic salmon, sea/brown trout, powan (Fig. 9.6, see also p. 130), pike, minnow (*Phoxinus phoxinus*), roach, stone loach *(Noemacheilus barbatulus)*, European eel, three-spined stickleback (*Gasterosteus aculeatus*), nine/ten-spined stickleback (*Pungitius pungitius*), perch and flounder (*Platichthys flesus*), with the occasional appearance of thick-lipped mullet (*Chelon labrosus*) which can enter the loch from the Clyde Estuary via the River Leven on a high spring tide. The absence of Arctic charr (*Salvelinus alpinus*) has engendered much discussion, especially as it is known from Highland lochs to the north, east and west of Loch Lomond, with the nearest charr water

Fig. 9.6 A relict species, the powan is found in very few British fresh waters (Peter Maitland).

only just outwith the catchment. A published account of one claimed to have
been caught in 1891 was discounted as a North American brook charr (*S. fontinalis*). Possible confusion with this allied species, then only recently introduced into Scotland, cannot explain away the inclusion of Arctic charr in a list
of Loch Lomond fishes prepared at the end of the eighteenth century by a
local minister, the Reverend John Stuart. Not only was Stuart an exceptionally
observant naturalist, he had spent the best part of 30 years living beside the
charr-inhabited Loch Tay and would undoubtedly have been familiar with the
species at first hand. It has been further suggested that the name of a small
island off Rowardennan – Eilean nan Deargannan – is derived from the Gaelic
name for Arctic charr (tarrdheargan), meaning little red-bellied fish. Whether
or not a small population of this relict species existed in Loch Lomond to within comparatively modern times is a question that may never be answered.

The North American brook charr was not the only introduction of a non-
indigenous sporting fish to Loch Lomond, although no game species has ever
become naturalised. A few rainbow trout (*Oncorhynchus mykiss*) are taken from
the loch most angling seasons, but this is not unexpected considering the number of smaller waters in the catchment that are regularly stocked with this popular North American fish. Translocation of coarse fish from southern Britain –
principally through the discarding of surplus live bait – has led to several viable
populations becoming established. Of these, the gudgeon (*Gobio gobio*) is confined to the shallow waters around the Endrick Mouth, but dace (*Leuciscus leuciscus*) have spread throughout the southern half of the loch. The most prolific
of all the introductions has been the ruffe (*Gymnocephalus cernua*), which from
the first few recorded in 1982 may now have caught up with the native powan
as the most abundant fish in the loch. This has had a significant effect on the
ecological balance between predator and prey in the loch's food chain through
altering the diets of most fish-eaters. Unconfirmed rumours of other new releases circulate from time to time, so the list of permanent additions to the loch's
coarse fish community is probably not yet closed.

Otters regularly frequent the loch and island shores, and examination of
their food remains confirms that they have increasingly turned to ruffe as part
of their diet. Sharing the upper position in the food chain are a number of
water birds: cormorant (*Phalacrocorax carbo*), great crested grebe (*Podiceps
cristatus*), grey heron, osprey (see p. 132) and several species of fish-eating wildfowl. During the summer months Loch Lomond supports small but regionally
important numbers of both fish-eating and bottom-feeding duck, such as red-
breasted merganser, goosander, shelduck (*Tadorna tadorna*), tufted duck
(*Aythya fuligula*) and, until only a few years ago, common scoter (*Melanitta
nigra*) (see p. 131). Apart from the goosander, the loch's populations of all
other species of duck have fallen sharply in recent years. The decline is attributable to the ever-increasing numbers of recreational power craft utilising the
breeding birds' feeding and nursery areas, coupled with the appearance on
the loch of North American mink (*Mustela vison*) (Fig. 9.7). Mink were first
farmed for their pelts in Scotland in the late 1930s, but it was to be the post-
war years before the industry really expanded. Two mink fur farms were established in the Loch Lomond area, one of them at Fintry beside the River
Endrick. By the mid-1960s it had become clear that a feral population originating from escaped animals was well entrenched in the middle reaches of the
river. Spreading yet further downstream, mink went on to colonise the loch.

Fig. 9.7 North American mink are well established throughout Loch Lomondside (Don MacCaskill).

Importantly, prior to the mink's invasion of Loch Lomond, the islands on which many waterfowl nested had virtually no mammalian predators, so the mink's impact on the resident breeding birds was all the greater. There can be little doubt that this unwelcome addition to the Loch Lomondside fauna is here to stay, local control measures effecting little more than a temporary reduction to numbers.

Considering some of the summering wildfowl in a little more detail, the shelduck was first confirmed breeding on Loch Lomond in 1877, when inland nesting of this estuarine species was still a rare event. Regular monitoring of the shelduck population in the shallow waters around the southeast corner of the loch during the 1970s showed the breeding population to be stable at around 18 pairs producing good numbers of young. Up to 70 non-territorial immature birds were also regularly present. Within just a few years of the mink's arrival the number of breeding shelduck was reduced by two-thirds, the immature flock having dwindled away completely through lack of recruitment. Numbers of red-breasted mergansers also fell significantly. The one-time assembled creches of almost 100 young mergansers are no longer seen. The goosander was first recorded nesting near the head of Loch Lomond in 1922, but was very slow to colonise right down to the southern basin. Probably because most pairs spend the early stages of their breeding cycle on running water away from the disturbance problems of the loch, they now appear to have overtaken the merganser as the most numerous diving duck. The last few years has seen late spring gatherings of 100 or more goosanders prior to their summer moult. Immature and post-breeding females undergo moult on the loch itself, but the males take themselves off to moult elsewhere, possibly as far north as the Norwegian fjords. Although the evidence is only circumstantial at present, it seems likely that the compelling attraction of Loch Lomond to goosanders is the presence of massive shoals of ruffe. The advent of the invasive ruffe has also significantly changed the diets of the loch's cormorants and grey herons, food analysis studies confirming that both species are taking full advantage of the seasonal abundance of this easily caught fish. Counts of cormorants indicate that the usual population on the loch is between 40 and 50 non breeding birds, although double that number is on record. Local recoveries of cormorants that had been ringed as young birds in the nest suggest that most originate from an inland freshwater colony at Mochrum and Castle Lochs in southern Scotland. Long-term monitoring of grey herons around Loch Lomond has demonstrated that the breeding population is subject to periodic fluctuations in its numbers. The highest count was achieved in 1975, with 60 nesting pairs in residence; the lowest count of only six breeding pairs in 1963 resulted from heavy mortality during the preceding very severe winter. The largest individual colony to date – up to 40 pairs in the 1970s – is situated beside the rich feeding grounds of the Endrick Marshes. Their choice of deciduous trees for nesting is not often seen in Scotland, where most grey herons show preference for conifers.

Hinterland wetland habitats

At times of prolonged heavy rainfall the loch's incoming rivers can become very swollen, causing them to back up and overtop their banks. The water spreads rapidly, the flood plain of the River Endrick, for example, sometimes forming a continuous sheet of water with the loch itself. Looking down at the Endrick's lower reaches from a high vantage point near Drymen, a seventeenth-century traveller described the area as 'besieged with bogs'. Several hundred years of agricultural drainage later, such hinterland wetlands are no longer in a pristine state, but neglected and half-forgotten spots that are rich in plant and animal life are still to be found.

Turning initially to the head of the loch, a popular locus for visiting botanists in the mid-nineteenth century was a series of low-level valley bogs running alongside the lower reaches of the River Falloch. The rarer species that they came specifically to see – pale butterwort (*Pinguicula lusitanica*), bog orchid (*Hammarbya paludosa*) and marsh clubmoss (*Lycopodiella inundata*) – have all apparently disappeared from this particular locality, victims of a combination of over-collecting and land drainage. A last remnant of these valley bogs can be found bordering the northern end of the Geal Loch near the Falloch Mouth. Consisting mainly of purple moor-grass/bog myrtle mire, the system does receive some mineral flushing along its eastern edge from base-rich schists on the hill slopes above. Characteristic plants still retaining a presence in this valley bog are the great sundew (*Drosera longifolia*) – one of a small group of insectivorous plants – cranberry (*Vaccinium oxycoccos*), white-beaked sedge (*Rhynchospora alba*) and few-flowered sedge (*Carex pauciflora*). A walk across the bog on a damp but warm summer's evening will quickly confirm that this type of habitat is a breeding ground *par excellence* for the scourge of Scotland, the biting midge, especially the ferocious Highland midge (*Culicoides impunctatus*).
, Unlike the almost vanished valley bogs, comparison with old photographs shows that the Geal Loch (Fig. 9.8) has changed little with time. Aquatic plants fringing its clear oligotrophic water include bogbean, bottle sedge (*Carex rostrata*), slender sedge (*C. lasiocarpa*) and common reed (*Phragmites australis*),

Fig. 9.8 The Geal Loch and a remnant of valley bog in lower Glen Falloch.

with water lobelia, bog pondweed (*Potamogeton polygonifolius*) and patches of white water-lily (*Nymphaea alba*) appearing as the loch progressively deepens. Just to the south of the Geal Loch, the edges of an overgrown pool that partially dries out in summer has mats of floating club-rush (*Eleogiton fluitans*). Most interesting of all is the elusive and nationally scarce pillwort (*Pilularia globulifera*), a mud-growing fern-ally susceptible to drainage schemes and declining throughout much of its range in Britain.

Wards Low Ground or Ponds lies just inland from the southeastern corner of Loch Lomond. Underlain by drainage-impeding clay, this eutrophic water body is noted for its beds of sedges (Fig. 9.9), principally bladder sedge (*Carex vesicaria*) and northern water sedge (*C. aquatilis*). A conspicuous stand of the uncommon hybrid *C.* x *hibernica (C. aquatilis* x *nigra*) attracts the sedge specialist's attention, while the presence of the horned pondweed (*Zannichellia palustris*) confirms the enriched nature of the ponds' shallow waters. Kept free of sedge growth only by the trampling of cattle, which are grazed there in late summer, the exposed margins to the drying-out ponds have a similar but less diverse community of small ephemeral plants as already described for the lochside edge around the Endrick Mouth. Water levels would appear to have to be just right, for two of the pond's specialities – the mudwort (*Limosella aquatica*) and the moss *Physcomitrium sphaericum* – are not seen every year. Mud samples collected in July from just above and below the water line produced an average density of over 4,000 invertebrates per m², providing an alternative feeding ground for summer resident and autumn migrant waders when higher than usual loch levels submerge the entire Endrick Bank. One noteworthy aquatic invertebrate recorded is the very local water beetle *Helophorus strigifrons*, which is found amongst the sedge litter around the seasonal pools. Duck mussels (*Anodonta anatina*) living in the rich mud of Wards Ponds have,

Fig. 9.9 Drained for the growing of crops in the nineteenth century, Wards Low Ground has reverted to open water with extensive sedge beds.

because of their exceptional growth, been mistaken in the past for the closely related but larger swan mussel (*A. cygnea*). Water rails (*Rallus aquaticus*) are well established in the sedge beds, but along with migrant spotted crakes (*Porzana porzana*) which turn up with some regularity in spring, their distinctive calls are more likely to be heard than birds actually observed out in the open. Because of the spotted crake's skulking behaviour, positive proof that they actually breed in the Endrick Marshes has yet to be obtained. At the end of the season almost all of the site is flooded as a sanctuary for wintering wildfowl. Such is the all-the-year-round wildlife interest of Wards Low Ground, it is hard to imagine that this was once cultivated land growing crops of turnips and potatoes.

Just a short distance from Wards lies the Aber Bogs (Plate 3), the largest remaining tract of flood plain fen on Loch Lomondside. The land-use history of the bogs is fragmentary, but the absence of any underlying peat points to the fen having developed over worked-out diggings for turf. Until the mid-1930s, this 24 ha former sedge-dominated meadow was cropped annually for marsh hay. Neglected apart from winter wildfowling from then on, the unharvested vegetation gradually built up a thick litter layer above the water table, the drying out surface receptive to an invasion of reed canary-grass (*Phalaris arundinacea*) followed by willow. The quality of water feeding into this low-lying site had deteriorated over the years, a result of domestic and agricultural pollutants finding their way into the old drainage channels. Subsequent management aimed at arresting the decay of the site and further loss of diversity in the fen flora has involved diverting the most polluted water sources, clearing away much of the colonising willow and raising the internal water level within constructed embankments. Initial results have been encouraging, with early signs of a recovery by the former mixed sedge and herb rich vegetation. Cowbane (*Cicuta virosa*) and tufted loosestrife are to be found in some abundance, the latter species in particular representative of northern fens. In contrast, the presence of the blunt-fruited water-starwort (*Callitriche obtusangula*) adds a southern element to the flora.

With the wet and cool climate, the Aber Bogs are not generally noted for butterflies, but in the sheltered south-facing sun traps where the herb-rich purple moor-grass fen at the drier northern edge of the bogs merges with woodland, the small pearl-bordered fritillary (*Boloria selene*), green-veined white (*Pieris napi*) and orange tip (*Anthocharis cardamines*) all fly in their appointed seasons. The additional presence of fenland moths such as the valerian pug (*Eupithecia valerianata*), marsh pug (*E. pygmaeata*), fen square-spot (*Diarsia florida*) and bulrush wainscot (*Nonagria typhae*) add considerably to the Aber Bogs' entomological status. Of several species of common damselfly and dragonfly recorded, the azure damselfly (*Coenagrion puella*) is by far the most abundant. Documentation of the other invertebrate life is still at an early stage, but the discovery of the nationally scarce money spider (*Maro sublestus*), at the time known only from Wicken and Woodwalton Fens in East Anglia, is an indication of what may await further study. Eels and pike have probably always been denizens of the bogs' man-made watercourses, but how and when the non-native crucian carp (*Carassius carassius*) first colonised is anybody's guess.

For birds, the open fen surrounded by a fringe of osiers (*Salix viminalis*) and other willows forms an ideal habitat for sedge warbler (*Acrocephalus schoenobaenus*) and reed bunting (*Emberiza schoeniclus*); and a visit at dusk-fall on a fine evening in mid-May can be a revelation as to the high numbers of grasshopper warblers (*Locustella naevia*) proclaiming territory occupation with their reeling song. The population of water rails noticeably increased after the internal water level was raised. Spotted crakes and even bitterns (*Botaurus stellaris*) have been known to occur. The odd marsh harrier (*Circus aeruginosus*) appears on spring passage most years, but hen harriers regularly hunt over the reed beds outwith the breeding season. One unexpected summer resident of the Aber Bogs is the whooper swan (*Cygnus cygnus*) (see p. 131), descended from captive Icelandic birds that gained their freedom when a local wildfowl collection was closed down. Roe deer (*Capreolus capreolus*) are perfectly at home in this rather swampy habitat; and compared to those which live in the less nutrient-rich conifer plantations, show superb antler growth. Although rarely seen, the water shrew (*Neomys fodiens*) – Britain's smallest aquatic mammal – is seemingly not uncommon in the bogs, for on several occasions the species' skeletal remains have been found in regurgitated food pellets of barn owl (*Tyto alba*) collected from a nearby roost.

Attention has already been drawn to the loch's southeastern shore as a regionally important stopping-off point for migrant waders, but together with the Endrick's lower flood plain the area is well known for its breeding species too. At a time when breeding populations of waders of agricultural land elsewhere on Loch Lomondside have been in serious decline, the loch shore and hinterland grazing marshes (Fig. 9.10) still attract the oystercatcher (*Haematopus ostralegus*), lapwing (*Vanellus vanellus*), ringed plover (*Charadrius hiaticula*), curlew (*Numenius arquata*), redshank (*Tringa totanus*), common sandpiper (*Actitis hypoleucos*) and common snipe, albeit in reduced numbers. Almost every spring dunlin (*Calidris alpina*) can be seen displaying, and not that many years ago up to three pairs stayed on to nest. Other passage waders have shown a promising interest in the area; wood sandpiper (*Tringa glareola*),

Fig. 9.10 The mouth of the River Endrick and its surrounding marshes.

black-tailed godwit (*Limosa limosa*) and jack snipe (*Lymnocryptes minimus*) have all been observed undergoing courtship display in spring. But even the most optimistic were taken aback when Temminck's stint (*Calidris temminckii*) was discovered nesting on the Ring Point in 1979. The grass-lined nest containing four eggs was concealed in low vegetation amongst widely spaced tussocks of soft rush (*Juncus effusus*), on a ridge of wind-blown sand some 9 m from the water's edge. Although only a one-off occurrence it was the ornithological event of the decade, the male's 'butterfly' display flight and trilling song transporting the observer for a moment to distant lands in the far north of Europe.

All the common species of dabbling and diving duck summer in the Endrick Marshes, including several pairs of shoveler (*Anas clypeata*), a species dependent on shallow enriched water. Amongst the less familiar ducks, pintail (*A. acuta*) and gadwall (*A. strepera*) regularly appear in April and May, but to date evidence of their breeding is lacking. Garganey (*A. querquedula*), on the other hand, have almost certainly nested on one or more occasions. Equally of note was a female scaup (*Aythya marila*) seen with a brood of ducklings in three successive seasons 1987–89. Wildfowl around the Endrick Mouth really come into their own as winter approaches, when migrants from as far away as the Arctic Circle take up seasonal residence. And when the smaller lochs and reservoirs in the north Clyde area begin to ice over as the temperature drops below zero, Loch Lomond can temporarily draw in hundreds of additional wildfowl to its slow to freeze waters. Regular counts undertaken over 40 years show that at some point during the winter months the combined presence of ducks – mainly wigeon (*Anas penelope*), mallard (*A. platyrhynchos*) and teal (*A. crecca*) – geese and swans in and around the Endrick Marshes can total 2–3,000 birds, rising to 4,000+ if the number of greylag geese (*Anser anser*) foraging the fields in the Endrick Valley happens to be particularly high. The size of the greylag popu-

lation is initially dependent on the availability of cereal stubble in the surrounding area, but as winter progresses, the number of geese present increases as they turn their less than welcome attention to the spring flush of sown
grass. Large skeins of migratory pink-footed geese (*A. brachyrhynchus*) pass
right through the area in autumn, but some of the birds do temporarily reap-
pear on Loch Lomondside if the winter weather in the east of Scotland is
severe. Until 1972, small numbers of the rare bean goose (*A. fabilis*) wintered
in the Endrick Marshes, their place now taken by a flock of Greenland white-
fronted geese (*A. albifrons*) (see p. 131).

Comparatively little attention has been paid to the numbers of gulls that pass
over the Endrick Marshes to roost overnight on the open waters of the loch,
but counts of 5,000 herring gulls (*Larus argentatus*), 2,000 common gulls
(*L. canus*) and 500 lesser black-backed gulls (*L. fuscus*) have been obtained.

A contrast of rivers

The River Endrick, or Anneric (meaning given to spates) as it was once known,
is the major inflow into the southern half of Loch Lomond. As the crow flies,
the Endrick is little more than 25 km from start to finish, yet because of its wan-
derings it covers almost twice that distance to complete its journey. A singular
feature of the river is that its final stretch suddenly turns north towards the
mountains, instead of continuing on a westward bearing towards the sea.
Rising at an altitude of 475 m as Mary Glyn's Burn in the Fintry–Gargunnock
Hills, it links up with several other headwater streams before taking the name
Endrick below Burnfoot Farm (Fig. 9.11). The Endrick is joined by additional
tributaries right up to within 1.6 km from where it discharges into the loch, the
most important of these being the River Blane which issues from the southern
Campsie Hills. Once clear of the slow to wear down Carboniferous Lavas, the

Fig. 9.11 The upper reaches of the River Endrick at Burnfoot.

Endrick winds its way through successive bands of much softer Calciferous, Upper and Lower Old Red Sandstones, becoming wider and deeper in stages the further west it flows. The nature of its substrate changes too, as both gradient and current slacken, beginning with a bed of bare rock strewn with large stones and moss-covered boulders, followed in succession by shingle, coarse sand and silt. In an average year the Endrick carries an estimated 13,870 tonnes of fine material in suspension to add to the silt and sand bar fanning out into the loch at the river mouth.

The old river terraces and oxbow ponds provide a visual record of past shifts in the Endrick's course. Nowhere can this be seen to better effect than its convoluted progress across the flat flood plain below Drymen bridge. Measurements taken from past Ordnance Survey maps of this stretch of the river show that, until about 1970, the looped meanders were moving position at an average annual rate of just under 0.5 m. Since then the rate of river bank erosion has significantly quickened, the cumulative effect of higher winter rainfall and a more rapid response in peak river flow resulting from an increase in agricultural and forestry drainage schemes throughout the Endrick catchment. In October 1983 a powerful surge of water cut through some 5.5 m of bank at the narrowest point of one of the loops, creating yet another alteration in the course of the river. Further upstream a more spectacular shift in the course of the Endrick will eventually take place where a crook in the river encircles the Haughs of Gartness. The stone-built revetment having broken down, the fast-moving water is slowly but surely eating into the south bank, so that at some point in distant time the Endrick will break through the morainic ridge that impedes its progress to form a new confluence with the River Blane, leaving the present Pot of Gartness section high and dry.

With such instability of the river's sandy banks, the natural development of water's edge vegetation along the Endrick is possible only where the current slows down as it approaches the loch. In the lower reaches between Woodend bridge and the river mouth there is a patchy growth of emergent and floating-leaved aquatic plants such as nodding bur-marigold (*Bidens cernua*), branched bur-reed (*Sparganium erectum*), amphibious bistort, yellow water-lily and the occasional clump of Loch Lomond dock. Almost all the adjoining fields are hard grazed, so that any water's edge plants spreading onto the river bank are soon eaten back by farm stock. To see the potential of the Endrick's riverside flora means a visit to a popular walk downstream from Balfron bridge (Plate 4). Formerly protected by a stock-proof thorn hedge, the river bank within this section was strengthened with stonework in the late eighteenth century to safeguard the Endrickfield printworks and bleach fields against floods. Mixed in with the riverside plants, which include marsh-marigold (*Caltha palustris*), water avens (*Geum rivale*), meadowsweet (*Filipendula ulmaria*) and yellow iris (*Iris pseudacorus*) is a surprising number of woodland species, remnants perhaps of the Endrick Valley's long-vanished forest cover. Fortunately, this varied assemblage of plants has not yet been completely overshadowed by a dense leafy cover of butterbur (*Petasites hybridus*), a fate which has befallen some other stretches of the river bank vegetation in the Endrick's middle reaches. It does, however, have its fair share of naturalised non-native species, including monkeyflower (*Mimulus guttatus*), pink purslane (*Claytonia sibirica*), and both lilac- and white-flowered forms of dame's-violet (*Hesperis matronalis*) among other garden escapes. The introduced Pyrenean valerian (*Valeriana pyrenaica*) appears confined to the river banks at Drumtean and Gartness, but a much more invasive alien – the giant hogweed (*Heracleum mantegazzianum*) – has become firmly entrenched in a number of places, especially below the golf courses either side of Drymen bridge. On the River Blane just downstream of Duntreath, the giant hogweed is accompanied by the Indian balsam (*Impatiens glandulifera*).

Following centuries of forest clearance, agricultural improvement and flood protection measures, the last vestiges of low-lying riverside woodlands that are seasonally inundated are one of the most fragmented and precarious wildlife habitats in Britain today. With a history of wood pasture followed by the growing of basket willows, the mixed woodland around the lower Mar Burn in the flood plain of the River Endrick is Loch Lomondside's best example of its type. Overshadowed by derelict coppice willows, their tangle of branches covered in the commoner epiphytes such as the lichens *Bryoria fuscescens* and *Usnea subfloridana*, the ground flora of these almost perpetually wet alluvial soils includes Loch Lomond dock, summer snowflake (*Leucojum aestivum*) (Fig. 9.12) – which may not be native to Scotland – and elongated sedge (*Carex elongata*) (see p. 130). A recent colonist here and in some of the lochside flood woodlands is the naturalised skunk cabbage (*Lysichiton americanus*). Little information is available on the site's invertebrates, but one species that warrants a mention is the solitary wasp *Trypoxylon attenuatum*, here found at the northernmost edge of its British range. In these flood woodlands this spider-hunting wasp's life cycle has been shown to be associated with the Loch Lomond dock, the wasp dividing the plant's hollow stems into larval/pupal cells by cross-partitions of mud. Of other animals present in the Mar Burn woods, the resident moles (*Talpa europaea*) have adapted surprisingly well to their watery environment; one huge mound or 'fortress' raised above the water table was measured at over 1 m in height. Grey herons begin nesting here as early as February and March, when the trees are still standing in winter flood water and the wood is raked with the last of the winter gales. If strong winds persist, some nests may be built little more than 2–3 m from the ground.

Well oxygenated and rich in invertebrate life, the productive waters of the Endrick are ideal for a wide variety of fish, and all but the upper stretch of the river is well frequented by anglers. The largest number of fish species is to be found only in the slow-flowing lower reaches, two waterfalls acting as barriers to free movement throughout the whole of the river system. Full grown

Fig. 9.12 Probably an inadvertent introduction, the summer snowflake is very much at home in flood woodlands beside the River Endrick.

Atlantic salmon and sea trout migrating upstream to their gravelly spawning
beds have the ability to leap or swim up the autumn spate water tumbling down
into the Pot of Gartness, but they are unable to surmount the much higher
Loup of Fintry further upstream. The Loup or 'Leap' can be bypassed only by
the eel, which, under the cover of darkness, will temporarily take to the land.
Stocking the Endrick Valley's man-made mill dams and other small waters with
non native fish dates back many years, but this activity has been stepped up in
recent times. Non-indigenous species present within the river catchment, but
not previously mentioned in connection with Loch Lomond – common carp
(*Cyprinus carpio*), rudd (*Scardinius erythropthalmus*) and tench (*Tinca tinca*) –
have all been introduced either as sporting or ornamental fish. The releasing
of unwanted live bait into the lower Endrick almost certainly accounts for the
recent establishment of bream (*Abramis brama*) and chub (*Leuciscus cephalus*).

Thanks to the vigilance of officers from the Scottish Environment Protection
Agency (formerly the Clyde River Purification Board in the Loch Lomond
area) and the Angling Association bailiffs, pollution of watercourses within the
Endrick catchment has been kept to a minimum, although there have been
several individual serious incidents. With generally good water quality throughout, the otter population on the river has continued to thrive at a time when
the species was in decline in many parts of lowland Britain. The number of
otter territories on the Endrick is less determined by food availability than by
the presence or absence of riverside vegetation unaffected by stock grazing or
bank erosion. Otters require well-developed river bank cover where they can
lie up during the day, safe and undisturbed. Trees at the water's edge with partially exposed roots are particularly favoured for otters' breeding dens or holts,
studies showing that it is the females that hold the individual territories, the
males ranging over two or three. Compared to the satisfactory status of the
otter, the water vole (*Arvicola amphibius*) (Fig. 9.13) has fared badly. The once-
thriving population of water voles on the Endrick, which had proved resilient
to the colonisation of the river banks by the predacious brown rat (*Rattus
norvegicus*), unwittingly introduced to Loch Lomondside by commercial boat
traffic in the nineteenth century, has been unable to absorb the additional
losses from mink.

Fig. 9.13 The
native water
vole faces local
extinction since
the establishment
of North
American mink
(Norman Tait).

Most visual of all the riverine creatures on the Endrick are the birds. Dipper and grey wagtail (*Motacilla cinerea*) are found along almost the entire length of the river from Burnfoot to the last stony shallows that were once the Drymen ford. Having a catchment area underlain with fairly base-rich rocks, the river is well buffered from the effects of acid precipitation which could lead to the depletion of these birds' freshwater invertebrate food. Both dipper and grey wagtail are to be found using bridges and rocky gorges for nesting, safe from rising water levels after heavy rain. Sand martin (*Riparia riparia*) nest holes in the river banks are all too often washed out by flash floods, leaving those birds that have prudently burrowed into nearby sandy morainic mounds unaffected. The kingfisher (*Alcedo atthis*) was temporarily lost as a breeding bird on the Endrick after the severe winter of 1962–63, but has since recolonised its former haunts in the 'pool and riffle' stretches between Fintry and the confluence with the River Blane. The Endrick Valley has just witnessed a colonisation by shelduck, the parent birds seeking out the still waters of flooded riverside fields when they have small young. Another comparative newcomer to the bird community is the oystercatcher, for in the first half of the twentieth century it was still being described as only an occasional shoreline nesting species on some of the Loch Lomond islands. Today, few of the Endrick's larger shingle banks are without their demonstrative pair in spring. Most of these shifting shingle banks have a very sparse flora and fauna, one exception being where the course of the river divides for a short distance upstream of Fintry bridge. On this more stable shingle island a willow-dominated shrub cover has developed, which in April and May comes alive with woodland bird song, the willow warbler (*Phylloscopus trochilus*) just for once living up to its English name.

The major inflow into the northern half of Loch Lomond is the River Falloch, which begins its short life at just over 800 m on Beinn a' Chroin. Some 17 km long, almost two-thirds of the river is inaccessible to migratory salmonids because of the impassable Falls of Falloch. Although the mountainous catchment area of the Falloch is relatively small, the exceptionally high rainfall draining from hard impervious rock ensures that the flow is often fast and furious, with most of the gravel beds continually on the move. Compared to the Endrick, the water of the Falloch has a low mineral content, which is a further limiting factor on the diversity and density of the invertebrate life of the river bed. Anglers maintain that in the spring and summer months, the fish in the lower stretch of the river are to some extent dependent on the many woodland invertebrates that drop into the water from the overhanging trees. Untypical of the mollusc family as a whole, one species that favours the calcium-poor conditions of the Falloch is the freshwater pearl mussel (*Margaritifera margaritifera*). Once much sought-after by the makers of top class jewellery, some of the finest freshwater pearls ever found in the country adorn the Scottish crown. In years past, itinerant pearl fishermen have been observed working the River Falloch's sandy gravel beds, but this now legally protected animal's continuing presence there requires confirmation.

The River Leven, which carries Loch Lomond's overflow waters to the Clyde Estuary, shares little in common with the Rivers Endrick and Falloch. Barely 11 km long from source to mouth, the Leven has a natural fall of only 7.5 m from the loch's outlet to mean sea level, the river becoming tidal below Dalquhurn Point. Since 1971, when the Central Scotland Water Board's barrage at Dalvait came into operation, the rate of river flow through its gates has been subject to control. There are no other physical obstacles such as waterfalls to impede the movement of migrating fish. Unlike the Endrick Valley, which bears few signs of its former riverside textile works, the banks of the Leven still retain much of their industrial past even after a number of landscaping projects.

Aside from patches of river water-crowfoot (*Ranunculus penicillatus*) clinging tenaciously to the Leven's gravelly shoals, there is little to catch the botanist's eye as the river threads its way through the Vale's commercial heartland. Once this is left behind, however, the diversity of water's-edge vegetation downstream considerably improves, only to disappear almost completely again under urban and industrial development once Dumbarton is reached. But upstream of Dumbarton bridge there are several good stands of riverside marsh where there is an increase in siltation at the interface between the outgoing freshwater and the incoming tidal waters. One of the most extensive marshes on the west bank lies below Mains of Cardross (Fig. 9.14). With its head-high beds of greater reed-mace (*Typha latifolia*) and reed canary-grass, dotted here and there with crack willow (*Salix fragilis*), such a wild spot is all the more unexpected after following the old towpath with its crumbling industrial frontage for any length of time. Readily identified even at a distance by its distinctive colour, the grey club-rush (*Schoenoplectus tabernaemontani*) in the marsh's muddy creeks is a clear indication of increasing salinity as river and estuary waters intermix. The characteristic plants of brackish water can also be seen on the Leven's east bank, where marshy ground was cut off when Dumbarton's Broadmeadow was embanked in 1859 as a high tide flood prevention measure. As well as the grey club-rush, the sea club-rush (*Bolboschoenus maritimus*), sea arrowgrass (*Triglochin maritima*), common scurvy-grass (*Cochlearia officinalis*) and sea aster (*Aster tripolium*) are all to be found in these saltings. In 1705 it was at this spot that a Dumbarton minister recorded a bittern 'booming' in the reeds, remarking: 'those that first

Fig. 9.14 Brackish marshes fringe the River Leven below Mains of Cardross.

1. The diversity of the lochside aquatic flora in the Balmaha Marshes is a reflection of the site's sheltered position.

2. The magnificent royal fern was brought to the brink of local extinction through over-collecting.

3. Floristically rich fens such as the Aber Bogs are found in few parts of Scotland.

4. The River Endrick below Balfron bridge has a well-developed river bank flora.

5. An eye-catching plant, the Loch Lomond dock is found nowhere else in Britain.

6. Tussocks of elongated sedge in periodically flooded woodland.

7. Undisturbed by the plough, the grassland fringing Dumbrock Loch is particularly rich in orchid species.

8. The tufted loosestrife is a characteristic member of the Endrick flood meadow community.

9. Short-eared owls are attracted by the high number of voles found in young conifer plantations (John Knowler).

10. A male capercaillie at his courtship display area in spring (John Knowler).

11. A hen capercaillie incubates her eggs at the foot of an aspen tree in deciduous woodland.

12. Cloudberry is abundant on the slopes of Hart Hill in the Campsies.

13. Red campion and mossy saxifrage grow in profusion on a basalt cliff in the Campsie Fells.

14. A red carpet of nationally scarce waterworts on the exposed bed of Kilmannan reservoir.

15. A red-throated diver nests beside a lonely high-level lochan (John Knowler).

16. The mountain ringlet is Britain's only alpine butterfly (Norman Tait).

heard the fowl make this noise were mightily afraid; whereupon they concluded it to be no less than the devil'.

As the final tidal stretch of the Leven flows through Dumbarton, one cannot
fail to notice in summer the congregation of 150 or more mute swans, such an
unusually high number leading to the conclusion that here, as in the southern
basin of the loch, their food of subaqueous vegetation is being enhanced by
some form of nutrient enrichment. Up to the mid-1950s at least, the town's
quayside area was the district's last retreat for the black or ship rat (*Rattus rattus*); the fleas of this animal are now known to have been responsible for outbreaks of bubonic plague or 'black death' in the old medieval town. With the
merchant ship warehouses and other old buildings swept away under redevel-
opment, this inadvertently introduced but now rare rodent would appear to be
locally extinct.

After passing through the town, the river widens considerably where it discharges in the Clyde Estuary. At low tide in autumn and winter the exposed
mud flats can hold up to 500 redshanks, together with smaller numbers of
other waders. These gatherings of feeding birds are well worth checking
through for the possibility of a rare vagrant, such as the terek sandpiper (*Xenus
cinereus*) which drew ornithologists from far and wide in late September 1996.
Going back to the eighteenth century, when salmon were far more numerous
in the then unpolluted Clyde, common porpoises (*Phocaena phocaena*) regularly followed the fish into the Leven as they headed upstream to spawn.
Whales too are not completely unknown about the mouth of the Leven. After
becoming stranded on a sandbank at ebb tide, a minke whale (*Balaenoptera
acutorostrata*) was killed at the river mouth in June 1905. Ninety years later in
February 1995, cetacean watchers had the opportunity of observing a hump-
back whale (*Megaptera novaeangliae*) feeding on large shoals of small fish in the
main navigation channel below Dumbarton Castle, an unprecedented event in
modern times and one which must give satisfaction to those responsible for
cleaning the River Clyde of industrial pollution. Cleaner water means that the
pleasures of sea angling in the tidal reaches of the River Leven are being redis-
covered. Several estuarine species are now caught regularly, in particular the
thick-lipped mullet and pollack (*Pollachius pollachius*), but the days of large
shoals of herring (*Clupea harengus*) making their way upriver as far as
Dumbarton quay are long past.

Some notable aquatic and water's-edge species

The river jelly lichen *Collema dichotomum* grows only on permanently immersed
rocks, unseen except by botanists prepared to risk a soaking. Extremely sensitive to water pollution and in consequence declining throughout most of
Europe, the continuing presence of this now rare species in the middle stretch
of the Endrick reflects the cleanness of the river.

The Loch Lomond dock (Plate 5) is most frequently found alongside watercourses and in swampy clearings within wet woods, but is capable of successfully colonising even abandoned cultivated land where the drainage system has
completely broken down. For such a robust-looking species, the Loch Lomond
dock has a surprising number of Achilles heels. It is, as might be expected, very
susceptible to any lowering of the water table; one large woodland colony of
some 250 plants had virtually disappeared within ten years of a single drainage
ditch being excavated through the middle of the site. Foraging cattle, which

more often than not ignore the ubiquitous broad-leaved dock *(R. obtusifolius)*, will eat the fresh growth of Loch Lomond dock with apparent relish. Similarly, it appears more prone to defoliation by the dock-leaf beetle (*Gastrophysa viridula*) than any other species of *Rumex* found in the area. The most serious threat of all to the Loch Lomond dock's survival is its readiness to cross with the broad-leaved dock; some pure stands of just a few years ago have been entirely replaced by hybrids.

The tufted loosestrife is at its most abundant in Britain in the Forth–Clyde Valleys, although it is often overlooked on account of its being very shy at flowering. A perennial rhizomatous species, the tufted loosestrife appears to have been unaffected by the annual cutting of the former wet meadows.

Nationally scarce, the elongated sedge was once thought to have been lost to Scotland. In 1967, however, a small but thriving colony was discovered on Loch Lomondside in alder carr fringing the loch shore below Boturich Castle. Subsequent searching revealed two larger populations in wet woodland, one beside the lower reaches of the River Endrick and the other in Rossdhu Park near the loch shore, where shallow lagoons (Plate 6) have formed behind a raised storm beach of sand and gravel. The bright green tussocks appear early in spring, showing preference for sites that are flooded for prolonged periods in winter, and which only partially dry out in summer. A characteristic feature of the elongated sedge's lifestyle is its habit of occasionally growing in an epiphitic manner on decaying fallen trees, the roots finding sufficient moisture in the thick growth of mosses covering the rotting wood.

A dwarf form of river lamprey which spawns in the River Endrick and its tributaries is the only population in Britain known to mature in a freshwater lake instead of migrating to the open sea. In Loch Lomond the lampreys almost exclusively feed on live powan, attaching themselves to their prey with sucker-like mouths. This dependence of river lampreys on powan is found in few other regions of Europe.

The powan or whitefish was first mentioned as occurring in Loch Lomond by George Buchanan (tutor to the young King James VI) in his *History of Scotland* published in 1582. A relict cold water species, in Britain the powan is confined to just a few mountain lakes and tarns. Powan feed mainly on zooplankton, spawning in Loch Lomond's gravelly shallows, where it is believed that the introduced ruffe has become a significant predator of their eggs. The powan has long been recognised as an important link in the loch's food chain. Describing this in 1911, local fisherman/naturalist Henry Lamond wrote: 'the powan forms the daily food of a vast number of aquatic and semi-aquatic creatures. Black-headed gulls, common gulls and terns pick them up in thousands. Every rocky islet where the gulls have a permanent retreat shows a kitchen midden of mouldering bones. Eels and pike regard it as their staple diet.' Powan in Loch Lomond show a high incidence of fresh and healed lamprey-inflicted scarring, with up to 25 wounds recorded on a single fish. Another dependent predator of the Loch Lomond powan appears to be the elusive 'ferox' or ferocious trout, a deep water form of brown trout which has turned away from its normal invertebrate diet to feed voraciously on other fish, with a resultant large increase in size. Because of the powan's vulnerability to 'baldspot' disease and secondary fungal infection, which is capable of causing mortality on a massive scale – thousands were washed up on the shore in June 1968 – reserve stocks of this now legally protected fish have been successfully introduced to neighbouring Loch Sloy and the Carron Reservoir.

The common scoter is misleadingly named, for the entire Scottish breeding population is probably less than 100 pairs. The few scoter nests found on Loch Lomond have all been on the islands, the eggs concealed beneath ling heather (*Calluna vulgaris*), bramble (*Rubus fruticosus*) or dead bracken. Spring counts of territory-holding scoters in the island strewn Luss–Strathcashell basin showed that the population peaked at nine pairs in 1977. Attempts at censusing females with young after the males had returned to the sea met with only limited success. Numbers of birds fell away from 1978, with only sporadic sightings after 1987. The buildup of powerboat activity in the feeding/nursery areas and the impact of predatory mink on vulnerable incubating females undoubtedly played their parts, but another contributory factor in the scoter's decline may have been the effect on duckling survival of overwhelming competition for food from large shoals of the introduced ruffe which, like the scoter, feed exclusively on bottom-dwelling invertebrates.

A comparative newcomer to Loch Lomondside is the Greenland white-fronted goose, the first small flocks of this legally protected species wintering regularly in the Endrick Marshes from 1960. After a slow but steady increase, the late winter population has levelled out at a maximum of 350 birds.

Between 1979 and 1995, one or two pairs of whooper swans nested almost annually in the Endrick Marshes (Fig. 9.15). Originally pinioned captives that escaped or were released from a local wildfowl collection, these were gradually replaced by free-flying descendants. For those cygnets that survived the critical first few days of life, predation by marauding foxes (*Vulpes vulpes*) is believed to be the principal cause of losses at the juvenile stage. Usually the surviving full grown young dispersed from their natal area in the following spring; perhaps coincidentally, but often at the same time as migrating whooper swans

Fig. 9.15 Whooper swans nested regularly in the Endrick Marshes for a number of years.

were passing through the Endrick Marshes en route to their breeding grounds in the far north.

Of all the fish-eating birds associated with the Loch Lomond area, the one which most attracts the public's attention is undoubtedly the osprey. Once lost to Britain as a breeding species through being harried by gamekeepers and collectors, the osprey began recolonising the Scottish Highlands from about 1954. For local ornithologists it took another 36 years of patient waiting before a pair reared young on Loch Lomondside in 1990, the first for certain since 1829 when a pair that nested annually on top of Inchgalbraith Castle was destroyed. After two successful breeding seasons, disaster struck in 1992, when the ospreys were robbed of their eggs, and only the male returned to the site in 1993. Fortunately, a second pair successfully reared three young in a more secluded locality in that year, choosing an old stag-headed oak tree to build their large wind-proof nest instead of the more usual Scots pine. Yet another pair nested for the first time in 1996. Loch Lomond is bountiful enough to support additional pairs of ospreys and, given freedom from disturbance and deliberate persecution, numbers are likely to increase in future as the fledged young that have survived the hazardous period of inexperience reach sexual maturity at around three to four years old. From many observations made on ospreys hunting over the loch and nearby waters, the most frequent prey item is the pike. As the level of the loch falls in late summer, the bottom-living flounder is occasionally taken around the sandy mouth of the River Endrick.

10

The Lowland Fringe

'To the visitor with an interest in natural history, the first impression
of the Lowlands of Scotland is of a tidy, well farmed scene ... In the
broad valleys and foothills the naturalist must be selective, and seek
out those relatively wild places which have been ignored by agriculturists and foresters, or which, due to the efforts of the old estates, have
been preserved down the ages specially for amenity and sport.
What he will find is a surprising diversity of flora and fauna within a
small compass.'

'The Lowlands' (James McCarthy) in
Wildlife of Scotland (Holliday, 1979)

Occupying roughly a quarter of Loch Lomondside's land surface, most of the
area under consideration as Lowland fringe lies below the old head dykes and,
with the exception of the low-lying ground between Arden and Luss, south of
the Highland Line. Ever since the first Neolithic settlers first cleared the forest
and cut into the predominantly sandy soils with their primitive ploughs, the
principal use made of the Lowland fringe has been mixed farming, although
with the gradual increase in animal husbandry over the last 50 years, little
more than five per cent of the cultivatable ground is currently given over to
cereals and other crops. The present emphasis in agricultural practice is firmly placed on improved grassland, with a high stocking rate of cattle and sheep.

Despite the long history of farming on southern Loch Lomondside, the
familiar patchwork of individual fields dates back no further than the eighteenth century, when the open ground was enclosed by planting thorn hedges
and building dry stone dykes (Fig. 10.1), altering the former open landscape
beyond recognition. In recent years the practice of enclosure has gone into
reverse, with some internal hedges grubbed-up to create the field size required
by the larger farm machinery. The remaining hedges and stone dykes are
being steadily replaced by more easily maintained fences of posts and wire.
Throughout the Lowland fringe, the last few decades have witnessed an accelerated loss of some of the most productive farmland to both housing development and new road construction, this encroachment at its most noticeable in
the Vale of Leven.

Plant and animal life of the Lowland agricultural land

Herb-rich pasture on Loch Lomondside was well in retreat even before the
outbreak of the Second World War in 1939. With the interruption of essential
food imports from abroad due to enemy blockade, County and District
Agricultural Committees were formed to enforce the ploughing-up of permanent grassland for cereals and other crops in a drive for national self-suffi-

Fig. 10.1 The pattern of field enclosure in the Lowland fringe was not laid out until the eighteenth century.

ciency. Only those pastures with very shallow soils or which were particularly difficult to drain were exempt. Today, the same fields which have also escaped modern selective herbicides and grass fertilizers are just about all that remains of a bygone low input/low output agricultural age. These grasslands' continuity with the past is evident from the variety of flowering plants found in their undisturbed turf. Typical representatives are bird's-foot trefoil (*Lotus corniculatus*), purging flax (*Linum catharticum*), yellow rattle (*Rhinanthus minor*), lady's bedstraw (*Galium verum*), mouse-ear hawkweed (*Pilosella officinarum*) and flea sedge (*Carex pulicaris*). One of the best remaining examples of ancient pasture is to be found beside Dumbrock Loch near Mugdock (Plate 7). Dumbrock Muir's relict grasslands owe their survival to the underlying basaltic lavas lying so close to the surface that ploughing the land was impracticable. Several uncommon species are to be found growing on the drier and in places moderately alkaline soils, including moonwort (*Botrychium lunaria*), burnet-saxifrage (*Pimpinella saxifraga*), field gentian (*Gentianella campestris*), mountain everlasting (*Antennaria dioica*) and fragrant orchid (*Gymnadenia conopsea*). A recent decline in the hitherto strong colony of frog orchids (*Coeloglossum viride*) has been attributed to the cessation of winter cattle grazing, which kept the coarser vegetation under control. Open grassland butterflies such as the common blue (*Polyommatus icarus*), small copper (*Lycaena phlaeas*) and small heath (*Coenonympha pamphilus*), together with the six-spot burnet moth (*Zygaena filipendulae*), favour the warm, south-facing slopes that lead down to the loch. A contrasting type of old pasture can be found in a drainage-impeded hollow near the southeast corner of Loch Lomond. Known as the Whin Park, this overgrown field is all that remains of the communal grazings of the former farm township of Aber, the soil just too wet and peaty for worthwhile agricul-

Fig. 10.2 The Twenty Acres Meadow; a flood meadow once regularly harvested for marsh hay.

tural improvement. Although dominated by purple moor-grass and sharp-flow-ered rush (*Juncus acutiflorus*), the sward is considered exceptional for its abun-dant gypsywort (*Lycopus europaeus*), bog asphodel (*Narthecium ossifragum*) and whorled caraway (*Carum verticillatum*), with occasional tawny sedge (*Carex hos-tiana*) in the water seepage areas. Well sheltered from the boisterous westerly winds by the adjoining woodland and heathy scrub, the Whin Park has also been identified as a key site for grassland moths, including the nationally scarce pyralid moth *Crambus uliginosellus*.

Traditional floristically-rich hay meadows on the better drained land have completely disappeared, replaced by artificially fertilized monocultures of cul-tivated grasses intended primarily for the production of silage. A few former bog (marsh) hay meadows enriched by river or stream-borne silt linger on, although the days of harvesting the lush vegetation for animal fodder and bedding is just a distant memory. Only one such meadow is still regularly cut – the Twenty Acres (Fig. 10.2) in the lower flood plain of the River Endrick. Very little of this damp field appears ever to have been ploughed, and its flora is made up of well over a hundred different meadow and marshland plants. An abundance of tufted loosestrife (Plate 8) is one of the meadow's many delights. The continuing presence of the Loch Lomond dock in the wetter parts of the field calls for explanation, as the field is usually mown at the beginning of August, well before this late-flowering species reaches the stage of ripe seed. Persistent rain followed by flooding will delay the cutting for a month or more in only about one year in ten, but this would appear sufficient to maintain at least small populations of this rare water dock and other late-seeding perenni-al species. All of the other remaining bog hay meadows on Loch Lomondside are in a derelict and overgrown condition, used now only for rough grazing.

Of these, one especially worth preserving is the Bog of Ballat, a high profile site beside the junction of the A81 and the A881 on the extreme eastern edge of the region. Last cut by scythe in the late 1940s, the central compartment of Ballat meadow has a very uncommon sward of brown sedge (*Carex disticha*), with globeflower in the adjoining compartment to the south.

The population of breeding birds found on Loch Lomondside's lowland farmland can fluctuate year by year through weather-related causes alone, but more permanent decreases in numbers of some species have been attributed to recent changes in agricultural management practices. With the trend towards improved grassland and a reduction in cereal growing, the virtual elimination of many arable weeds and the unavailability of autumn stubble has been matched by significant population declines in the small seed-eating birds. One species, the corn bunting (*Miliaria calandra*), has vanished from the area altogether. Gone too is the corncrake (*Crex crex*), its eggs and small young all too readily destroyed by the early cropping of grass for silage, which has replaced the cutting of hay in late summer. Other farmland birds have been affected by the gradual loss or deterioration of the once substantial stock-proof hedges and accompanying hedgerow trees. No longer carefully maintained by hand, farm hedges today are mechanically trimmed with cutter-bars or flails, in the process decapitating the young saplings which would have become the next generation of hedgerow trees. These skimpy hedgerows can also be subjected to pesticides, either indirectly by wind-drift or, on occasions, deliberately targeted for harbouring agricultural weeds and invertebrate pests. The end result is that most hedgerows on Loch Lomondside provide little in the way of protective cover, nest sites or food for small birds.

A breeding bird survey carried out on a 133.5 ha mixed agricultural plot in mid Strathendrick for ten nesting seasons from 1975 showed that the overall population (less uncensused wood pigeons, starlings and carrion crows) averaged almost 300 pairs per km², between three to four times the density of birds occupying the most intensively farmed arable land on the east side of Scotland. The top ten passerine species (in descending order) were chaffinch (*Fringilla coelebs*), willow warbler, skylark (*Alauda arvensis*), blackbird (*Turdus merula*), yellowhammer (*Emberiza citrinella*), blue tit (*Parus caeruleus*), wren, robin (*Erithacus rubecula*), great tit (*P. major*) and song thrush (*T. philomelos*), the high percentage of woodland birds represented being a reflection on the large number of small woods and plantations scattered throughout the Lowland agricultural zone (Fig. 10.3). Changes noted during and immediately after the survey period included a significant reduction in the populations of skylarks, yellowhammers, grey partridges (*Perdix perdix*) and lapwings. The sharp fall in skylark numbers was attributed to an increase in silage making, as the early cut destroys their nests. Yellowhammers were affected not only by the severe pruning of hedges, but the clearing away of patches of gorse as part of a general 'tidying-up' which took place in the study area. The virtual disappearance of the grey partridge from the area appeared connected to the practice of ploughing right up to the hedgerows for increased yield, in the process removing the field margins where formerly the partridges and their young found much of their invertebrate food. As a breeding species the lapwing was well established (up to 29 pairs) in the Strathendrick study plot, but has since fared badly not only there, but throughout southern Loch Lomondside. Until recently, two of the largest concentrations of lapwing were to be found along

Fig. 10.3 Small woods and plantations are a feature of the agricultural land in mid-Strathendrick.

the flatlands of Strathblane and Glen Fruin; both originally the beds of pro-glacial lakes as described in Chapter 3. Several factors involved in the lapwing's decline have been identified, not least land drainage which makes possible the conversion of rush-infested grazings to improved grassland. Following drain-ing and re-seeding, much higher numbers of cattle and sheep can be kept, increasing the risk of ground nests being trampled underfoot. Incubating lap-wings are also more conspicuous on grasslands that are closely cropped, adding to the chances of nest predation by crows. The local populations of red-shank and common snipe have been similarly affected by the upgrading of damp pasture into improved grassland.

It has not been all doom and gloom for the region's farmland birds. At one point it seemed likely that the barn owl might be lost, but the timely provision of specially constructed nest boxes to replace the rapidly disappearing lofted outbuildings to farms formerly used as breeding sites, has initiated a promising recovery in barn owl numbers; this despite an overall reduction in the avail-ability of small animal prey on the best land due to the attrition of hedges and field margins. Most barn owls in the area are very dependent on the short-tailed voles (*Microtus agrestis*) they can still find in the longer grass of the peripheral rough grazings and newly established forestry plantations. When vole numbers are high, as in 1997, the eight pairs of barn owls monitored that year success-fully reared an average of over three young each. Another species that has made a comeback on the lowland agricultural ground is the common buzzard (*Buteo buteo*). Once banished from the Lowland fringe by game preservers, it is now the most widespread bird of prey. Farmland interspersed with numerous small woods is the species' favoured habitat, with densities of up to 25 occupied ter-ritories per 10-kilometre square where there is a healthy population of rabbits

(*Oryctolagus cuniculus*) and persecution in defiance of the law has completely ceased. The buzzard is very much an opportunist hunter and scavenger; mole, salmon, powan, slow-worm (*Anguis fragilis*) and even common frog (*Rana temporaria*) are among the less usual items that have been identified at local nests. Raptor enthusiasts look forward to the day not too distant when the soaring buzzard in the Lomondside sky is joined by the red kite, following a successful release programme of young kites in central Scotland. Before the species was ruthlessly extirpated by nineteenth-century game preservers, the resident minister for Campsie observed 'so common is the glade [red kite] with us that its various modes of flight are considered an almanac for the weather'.

No resident bird on Loch Lomondside's lowland farms has attracted ornithologists' attention more than the rook (*Corvus frugilegus*), with periodic nest counts at breeding colonies dating back to 1945–46. In the immediate post-war years almost all the rookeries were to be found in the grounds of country houses, one long-established colony totalling over 600 nests. With the gradual fragmentation of many of the larger estates and felling of mature trees, the larger rookeries dispersed, in the process trebling the number of separate but smaller colonies. Oak and Scots pine share equal first place in the rooks' choice of nesting tree. Recent census figures have showed that, under a predominantly grassland regime, the overall number of nesting pairs increases or decreases with the rise or fall in the comparatively small amount of land under cultivation. The present population of rooks on the 16,835 ha of Loch Lomondside's improved low ground is around 2,700 nesting pairs, a high density for northwestern Britain and one reflecting the wide range of feeding opportunities available to the birds. One potentially lean period for rooks is the occasional sustained dry spell in late spring, when the birds desert the hard-crusted fields to feed on the superabundance of defoliating caterpillars in the neighbouring oak woods. If the drought persists, they move on to the still damp high ground of the surrounding hills. Winter too can be a difficult time for rooks, especially after a heavy fall of snow. At such times they concentrate where cattle and sheep are feeding in the fields. Not only do the foraging beasts scrape through the snow to expose potential food sources for the rooks in the ground below, the birds are quick to take advantage of anything they can find edible amongst the supplementary fodder put out for the stock. A welcome bonanza of invertebrates is also provided with the winter spreading of byre manure over the frost-stiffened fields.

Best known of all the mammals that inhabit the lowland agricultural ground are the mole, rabbit and brown hare (*Lepus capensis*). Although the mole is seldom seen above ground, its conspicuous strings of mounds in the cultivated grasslands attract both the casual observer's attention and the farmer's wrath (Fig. 10.4). A recent upsurge in their damaging activities has been attributed to the virtual disappearance of the professional mole-catcher. Rabbits were unknown on Loch Lomondside until the 1820s, when the newly improved agricultural land proved so congenial to the early colonists that they rapidly increased to pest proportions. By the end of the nineteenth century the Montrose Estate gamekeepers alone were killing nearly 5,000 rabbits each year in an effort to limit damage to pasture and crops. The first real check on the rabbit population came with an outbreak of the virus disease myxomatosis in 1955, followed by a more severe reoccurrence two years later. One of the consequences of the rabbit coming close to local extinction was a dramatic reduc-

Fig. 10.4 Fresh molehills thrown up through the snow show that the animal is active all year round.

tion in the numbers of the animal's predators, such as the stoat (*Mustela erminea*) and weasel (*M. nivalis*). From an agricultural point of view it was an opportunity missed not to have mopped up the last few rabbits, for the survivors' descendants have developed a partial immunity to the disease, leading to the population increasing again year by year, together with reports once again of damage to crops. Estimated losses to agriculture throughout Scotland have once again risen to several million pounds per annum. Like the rabbit, the brown hare population on Loch Lomondside has had its ups and downs. Numbers rose in line with agricultural development, but then decreased significantly following a change in the law in 1880 which gave tenants equal rights with landowners to kill and take ground game. This in turn led to the *Hares Preservation Act 1892*, which afforded the hares a measure of protection during their breeding season, March–July. Although relatively common throughout the southern agricultural zone, the brown hare's presence is not always easy to detect because of its habit of lying up in its concealed 'form' during the day and feeding by night.

The older faunal works covering the Loch Lomond area distinguish only three species of bat – pipistrelle (*Pipistrellus pipistrellus*), brown long-eared (*Plecotus auritus*) and Daubenton's (*Myotis daubentonii*). Thanks to an upsurge in interest in these small nocturnal mammals, breeding colonies of natterer's (*M. nattereri*), whiskered (*M. mystacinus*) and the recently described soprano bat (*Pipistrellus pygmaeus*) – the last so named because it echolocates using a higher frequency than the closely related pipistrelle – have all been found in the district. This extended list is probably still incomplete, as improved identification techniques have shown Nathusius' pipistrelle (*P. nathusii*) to be present in the neighbouring Forth Valley.

Roadside verges

At the end of the eighteenth century, the naturalist Thomas Garnett, touring Scotland, wrote in his journal:

> 'Both sides of the road from Dumbarton to Luss are interesting to the botanist. The *Digitalis purpurea*, or foxglove, enlivens the hedgerows the whole way with its purple spikes: opposite Cameron, are amazing quantities of the *Spiraea ulmaria*, or meadow-sweet, and *Valeriana officinalis*, or great wild valerian, the largest I ever saw. Near Ross Lodge, on the opposite side of the road, the *Narthecium officinalis*, or bog asphodel, grows in abundance. In many parts of the road between Rossdhu and Luss, the *Erica tetralix*, or cross-leaved heath, beautifies the banks with its elegant purple flowers.'

A contemporary travel guide writer on the same highway where it passed through the Vale of Leven added: 'beautiful hedges bound the road, which in the season of summer, are finely interwoven with the wild rose, honeysuckle and other sweet smelling plants'. One thing is certain – neither would recognise this much changed main thoroughfare today.

Left undisturbed, grassy verges fringing the sides of the country roads can offer a refuge for flowering plants and ferns that have been unable to withstand modern farming practices on the other side of the fence. Roadside verges also act as a means of plant and animal dispersal through areas of intensive farming, the recent east to west spread of the ringlet butterfly (*Aphantopus hyperantus*) in southern Loch Lomondside being a case in point. Yet it is a wildlife habitat that is all too often taken for granted; one that is all to easily destroyed under the current programme of road widening and straightening necessitated by the continuing increase in vehicular traffic. One individual casualty already has been spignel (*Meum athamanticum*), this locally rare umbellifer now lost from its only known roadside site. Less obvious, but affecting the botanical quality of the verges none the less, is the disappearance of the old-style parish roadman or 'lengthsman', his often selective scything around the more herbaceous stretches replaced with a uniform trim by machine and (thankfully not a regular occurrence) spraying the verges with a chemical herbicide.

Although most of the local verges have very limited floras, a few stretches can produce a pleasing diversity of species before the tall grasses take over in mid summer and the local authority mechanised cutters appear on the scene. Usually the earliest spring flower of the wayside to be noticed, even from a moving car, is the appropriately named jack-by-the-hedge (*Alliaria petiolata*), immediately followed by cow parsley (*Anthriscus sylvestris*), occasionally in such profusion as to turn entire roadsides snow-white. The observant pedestrian will quickly discover that the most productive spots for wayside flowers and ferns are to be found where the older, scarcely modernised back roads wend their way through undulating glacial topography, giving the verges to these partially sunken byways a three-dimensional profile, the upper half of the bank out of reach of the damaging effects of combustion engine fumes and road de-icing salt. A good example can be seen near the Park of Drumquhassle on the brow of the Gartness road, where in May its seasonal splash of colour includes a patriotic display of red campion (*Silene dioica*), the

Fig. 10.5 Ancient roadside verges can be rich in wild flowers and ferns.

white flowers of earthnut (*Conopodium majus*) and bluebell (*Hyacinthoides non-scripta*) (Fig. 10.5). The richness of the verge flora there is not by chance, for this part of the road is the last surviving stretch of a very old and long-since abandoned direct route from Drymen to Killearn. By way of contrast to Drumquhassle, a heathy flora can be found on the south-facing raised verge close by the Loup of Fintry on the Carron Valley road. Amongst the plant assemblage on these less fertile hill soils are ling heather, blaeberry or bilberry (*Vaccinium myrtillus*), mountain pansy (*Viola lutea*) and bitter-vetch (*Lathyrus linifolius* var. *montanus*), along with the shuttle-cock shaped tufts of the golden-scaled male fern (*Dryopteris affinis*). Different again are the verges near the radio mast at the summit of the Muirpark, where the soft peaty ground regularly catches out unwary motorists as they attempt to pass one another on this single track road. Characteristic of these rather wet acidic soils are bog asphodel, heath spotted orchid (*Dactylorhiza maculata* ssp. *ericetorum*), common butterwort (*Pinguicula vulgaris*) and an eyebright with a north-westerly distribution, *Euphrasia arctica* ssp. *borealis.*

Apart from spignel already mentioned, a few other locally uncommon plant species have been reported from the Lomondside roadside verges. The broad-leaved helleborine (*Epipactis helleborine*) grows alongside a now bypassed wooded section of the Strathblane road immediately south of Blane Smithy. Another – the great horsetail (*Equisetum telmateia*) – has conspicuously colonised a verge in Glen Fruin, just a short distance east of the dismantled old bridge at Dumfin. A single patch of melancholy thistle (*Cirsium heterophyllum*) manages to survive beside the northern approach to the Queen's View, despite the almost annual decapitation of the flowers by the grass cutter before they have a chance to set seed. A few stretches of roadside hedgerow contain species that are virtually unknown elsewhere in the area, such as hop (*Humulus lupulus*) and field rose (*Rosa arvensis*), both either deliberate or accidental introductions. Also worth looking for are some fine clumps of the extremely local rustyback fern (*Ceterach officinarum*) growing on a roadside wall bordering the Edenkiln road from Mugdock to Strathblane.

Non-indigenous plants springing from thoughtlessly discarded garden refuse are a fairly frequent sight in the roadside verge, although few species can survive the competition from the vigorously growing grasses for more than a season or two. One that has proved persistent is *Pilosella aurantiaca* from Central Europe, this vivid orange coloured hawkweed going under several English names, the devil's paint brush being one which describes the flower particularly well. There are also several instances of native species taken into cultivation for use as ornamental garden plants, only to make their escape back into the wild by spilling out on to the adjoining roadside verge; lords and ladies (*Arum maculatum*), orpine (*Sedum telephium*) and pendulous sedge (*Carex pendula*) are three Loch Lomondside examples that come to mind.

An unusual mix of plants has been recorded springing up on the landscaped verges to the region's new roadworks. Unlikely bedfellows such as cowslip (*Primula veris*) and northern marsh orchid (*Dactylorhiza purpurella*) grow almost side by side. Apart from the seeded grasses, most of the introduced species decline and often disappear after only a few seasons. One of the exceptions is the oxeye daisy (*Leucanthemum vulgare*), which occurs in some abundance alongside the upper route through Glen Fruin. Another survivor is likely to be the dwarf gorse (*Ulex minor*), planted as a soil stabiliser beside the same road. Hybrid lupins (*Lupinus* x *regalis*) and massed daffodils (*Narcissus* spp.) have been used to create seasonal swathes of colour along the bypass to the Vale of Leven.

Kirkyards and castles

Botanists delight in old edifices that are in a picturesque state of decay, for the nooks and crannies where the crumbling mortar has fallen away offer sanctuary to rock plants, some of which appear to flourish better on this artificial substrate than in their natural habitat; that is until the decision is taken to tidy the buildings up. Local historian John Guthrie Smith wrote that the walls of Duntreath Castle in Strathblane were covered in wild flowers and ferns before renovation work was carried out in the mid-nineteenth century.

Today, grass cutting in kirkyards throughout the Loch Lomond area is undertaken with such Calvinistic zeal that even those wild flowers that formerly escaped the scythe or mower by growing close to a memorial stone or wall, are now efficiently dispatched with the ubiquitous strimmer. It would not be too far from the truth to say that the botanical interest of most of these kirkyards is now confined to the lichen-covered gravestones and the occasional unpointed boundary wall. The early headstones are of local sandstone and

Fig. 10.6 An early nineteenth-century gravestone in Drymen kirkyard with a well-developed lichen flora.

usually very plain in design, so that their appearance can be enhanced by an encrustation of lichens (Fig. 10.6). But as one visitor to the island burial ground on Inchcailloch observed, they render their engraved wording increasingly difficult to read:

'I trace the old inscriptions dear,
Fast fading now from mortal ken,
And through the silvered lichens peer,
To read MacAlpine's [MacGregor's] name again'.

Those with a special interest in this group of small flowerless plants will almost certainly wish to visit Luss kirkyard to see the memorial stone to the Reverend John Stuart D.D. (1743–1821), amongst other things an early lichenologist of note. Apart from lichens, there is not a great deal growing on the well-maintained churches themselves. An exception is the now roofless Old Kirk of Killearn, its time-worn stonework adorned with a variety of species including the rustyback fern. Flowering plants and ferns most likely to be found on the kirkyard perimeter walls are ivy-leaved toadflax (*Cymbalaria muralis*), wall-rue (*A. ruta-muraria*), maidenhair spleenwort (*A. trichomanes*), hart's-tongue (*Phyllitis scolopendrium*) and the common polypody (*Polypodium vulgare*). In late spring, the internal face of the east wall to Strathblane kirkyard is enlivened by an impressive show of the naturalised fairy foxglove (*Erinus alpinus*). Almost every Loch Lomondside kirkyard has its evergreen symbol of immortality – the yew tree – usually the cultivated Irish variety which is readily distinguished from the common form by its upswept limbs.

Turning to four ruinous old castles in the district, Rossdhu Castle is Loch Lomondside's only known site for pellitory-of-the-wall (*Parietaria judaica*), a herbal remedy once prescribed for a variety of common complaints. Crevices in the walls of Kilmaronock Castle have been colonised by the naturalised mossy sandwort (*Arenaria balearica*) and Siberian wallflower (*Erysimum* x *marshallii*), while Bannachra Castle in Glen Fruin is covered with garden flowers in profusion. In the late eighteenth and early nineteenth centuries, a sightseeing visit to the pair of ospreys nesting on top of Inchgalbraith Castle in the loch formed part of the Scottish 'grand tour'. Amongst those who took a boat out to this island castle to see the nest was the celebrated Dr Johnson and his companion James Boswell in 1773. Today, it is common gulls that find sanctuary on the castle ruins.

For all-round natural history interest, Dumbarton Castle, perched on its twin-topped volcanic plug, is in a class on its own. Formerly surrounded by the sea at high tide, Dumbarton Rock's 'island' character was lost during the late eighteenth century when the extent of the intertidal area was reduced through the dredging of a deep navigation channel in the estuary of the River Clyde. This allowed the saltmarshes on the north side of the castle to be reclaimed and developed for industrial use. The Rock itself, with its cloak of spring flowers, has for many years been a special favourite with botanical excursionists, not least to search for the naturalised culinary and medicinal herbs formerly grown in the castle's kitchen and physic gardens. Heading the list of both native and introduced species that are eagerly sought after because of their very restricted distributions in the west of Scotland are greater celandine (*Chelidonium majus*), musk mallow (*Malva moschata*), common mallow (*Malva sylvestris*), wallflower (*Erysimum cheiri*), spring vetch (*Vicia lathyroides*), Alexanders (*Smyrnium olusatrum*) (Fig. 10.7) and hemlock (*Conium maculatum*). The early botanists also recorded Our Lady's thistle (*Silybum marianum*) – a plant with early religious connections and one of the contenders for the title of the true Scottish thistle – woolly thistle (*Cirsium eriophorum*) and that malodorous flower, the henbane (*Hyoscyamus niger*). All three now seem to have disappeared. In times past, Dumbarton Rock was justly famous for two associated birds. The first – the peregrine (*Falco peregrinus*) – had from time immemorial nested on one of the more precipitous cliffs. King Robert I employed three professional falconers at his Levenside manor house just a short distance away, so that it is conceivable that Dumbarton Rock was one of their sources of young peregrines selected for training. They were almost certainly taken by falconers in the service of the sporting 11th Earl of Eglinton, who was governor of the castle from1764–82. The occupied peregrine eyrie on the Rock was examined on one occasion by the late eighteenth–early nineteenth-century ornithologist Colonel George Montagu, who noted that both red and black grouse (*Tetrao tetrix*) were brought to the nest as food for the young. If peregrines ever return to this once favoured site, it is unlikely they will get the opportunity to dine very often on such rich fare again. The second bird of historical interest is the barnacle goose (*Branta*

Fig. 10.7 Alexanders was probably introduced as a potherb to Dumbarton Castle's kitchen gardens.

leucopsis); as early as 1597 annual wintering flocks were described as feeding on the mud flats and salt marshes around the Rock. Loss of estuarine habitat and continual disturbance by boatloads of shooters eventually caused the geese to move elsewhere. Ravens looking for an opportunist meal still occasionally haunt the castle walls, just as their ancestors must have done from man's earliest occupation of the site.

Parkland

Many of the private parklands that once provided the picturesque settings to Loch Lomondside's oldest country mansions have been put to other uses, such as golf courses, housing and industrial estates. For a number of years the one surrounding Cameron House was run as a safari-style wildlife park, leading to a string of exotic escapes from skunks to brown bears. Other proprietors of parks have been responsible for the introduction of ornamental wildfowl, the most successful being the Canada goose (*Branta canadensis*). From the first escaped pair discovered nesting on Loch Lomondside in 1968, feral flocks established in the area together exceed 250 birds.

The largest of the remaining parks is the 81 ha Balloch Castle Park situated beside the loch's southwestern shore. Although it has a history dating back to the motte and bailey castle of the early Earls of Lennox, the planted woodlands and great sweeps of open grassland around the present castellated building were not laid out until the nineteenth century. Subsequently purchased by the far-sighted Corporation of Glasgow as an open air 'lung' for its smoke-weary citizens, the estate was formally designated as a country park in 1980. Despite the popularity of Balloch Country Park with recreation seekers, the grounds are by no means devoid of wildlife interest, the combination of land and water-side habitats ensuring a wide range of breeding birds. Woodland species pre-dominate, with the novice ornithologist given ample opportunity in spring to learn to distinguish between the similar songs of the garden warbler (*Sylvia borin*) and the closely related blackcap (*S. atricapilla*) coming from the well-established clumps of rhododendron. A favourite pastime amongst visitors to the park is feeding the remarkably tame squirrels. Originally these were all red squirrels (*Sciurus vulgaris*), but today this native animal has been entirely usurped by the North American grey (*Neosciurus carolinensis*). First introduced into the west of Scotland in 1892, the grey squirrel had spread to Loch Lomondside by 1903, colonising the entire area within 40 years. Other mid-summer attractions of Balloch Country Park to the naturalist include a variety of the more common butterflies drawn to the sun-lit flowering shrubs in the vicinity of the visitor centre, the many hundreds of greater butterfly orchids (*Plantanthera chlorantha*) that appear in the uncut grassland, and bats flitting around the castle turrets at dusk.

Parkland elms throughout southern Loch Lomondside are very much at risk of Dutch elm disease which has swept much of Britain, having apparently been introduced into the country with imported timber. The unwitting carrier of the deadly fungus *Ophiostoma nova-ulmi* is the elm bark beetle (*Scolytus scolytus*). Since diseased trees were first reported in the west of Scotland in 1975, elms within the grounds of Culcreuch and Balloch Castles have been particularly badly affected.

The legacy of mineral exploitation

Opening up the ground for minerals can permanently disfigure the landscape, so it is fortunate that the majority of Loch Lomondside's quarries and pits in the Lowland fringe and southern foothills have been on a relatively small scale. The most prominent eyesore of the nineteenth century was the Camstradden slate quarry near Luss, but even there woodland regeneration is well on its way to healing over the scar. Despite their initial unsightly appearance, there is no question that old mineral workings can provide a refuge for certain plants and animals whose natural habitats the quarry resembles. All too frequently, how-ever, large holes in the ground are seized upon as convenient places for the dumping of domestic refuse and other waste material, euphemistically described as land-fill or land-restoration sites.

The worked faces of disused red sandstone quarries, particularly those in some dark and damp recess, are eminently suited to a luxuriant growth of ferns. Although most of these are ubiquitous species, Dalreoch and Bonhill sandstone quarries can both lay claim to the royal fern, although it is possible the first colonists originated from garden stock rather than from the wild.

Associated exclusively with Upper Old Red Sandstone are beds of calcium carbonate rich rocks known as cornstones. Valued as an agricultural fertilizer up to the mid-nineteenth century, former cornstone workings can be traced in the district from Carman Muir in the west to Kippen Muir in the east. The heaps of discarded spoil are almost always closely grazed by sheep, but the wet flushes that drain from them can be rich in calcicole (lime-loving) plants, such as the lesser clubmoss (*Selaginella selaginoides*), broad-leaved cottongrass (*Eriophorum latifolium*), few-flowered spike-rush (*Eleocharis quinqueflora*), dioecious sedge (*Carex dioica*) and long-stalked yellow sedge (*C. viridula* ssp. *brachyrrhyncha*). On Loch Lomondside, the delicate bog pimpernel (*Anagallis tenella*) appears confined to the cornstone flush habitat.

Carbonated serpentinite, which outcrops in the Highland Boundary Fault zone, was also used as an agricultural fertilizer. It is to be regretted that most of the calcium-rich serpentinite exposures and flushes on Ben Bowie overlooking the west side of the loch have been largely covered over by a recently established conifer plantation, but at Creag Mhor on the opposite side of the loch, the dry spoil heaps from the quarry have abundant stone bramble (*Rubus saxatilis*) and false brome grass (*Brachypodium sylvaticum*). The plant assemblage in the seepage zone below the worked serpentinite on Conic Hill is very similar to that found in the cornstone flushes, but with the addition of the black bog-rush (*Schoenus nigricans*), a species generally confined to the coast in the west of Scotland. Of interest to the fern specialist is a serpentinite form of the black spleenwort (*Asplenium adiantum-nigrum*). Distinguished by its less rigid and more broadly triangulate fronds (Fig. 10.8), it is now recognised as an ecotype rather than a distinct species. Higher up the hillside, serpentinite-influenced boggy vegetation with marsh violet (*Viola palustris*) and marsh thistle (*Cirsium palustre*) is a favoured habitat of the dark green fritillary (*Argynnis aglaja*), this fast-flying butterfly on the wing from mid-July.

Fig. 10.8 The serpentinite form of the black spleenwort fern.

Glacial sands and gravels have been extensively worked in southern Loch
Lomondside. When freshly excavated the disturbed ground temporarily acts as
a refuge for once common arable weeds, which have become very restricted in
their distribution with so few fields now under the plough. Amongst several
locally uncommon species that occur in these abandoned pits are yellow bartsia (*Parentucellia viscosa*), great mullein (*Verbascum thapsus*) and weld (*Reseda
luteola*), the latter formerly cultivated as a yellow colouring agent used by the
then thriving textile industries in the Vale of Leven. Infill material of unknown
origin dumped in the worked-out sand and gravel pits in the Vale is probably
responsible for the unexpected appearance of several species of mainly southern distribution in Britain; the smooth tare (*Vicia tetrasperma*) and spiked sedge
(*Carex spicata*) at Dillichip and the grass vetchling (*Lathyrus nissolia*) at
Dalmonach are three which have attracted the botanical recorder's eye. Such
casuals usually disappear when the workings become overgrown or the site is
redeveloped. Now nearing the end of its working life, Drumbeg pit near
Drymen has for many years boasted the largest sand martin colony in the
Glasgow area, at peak over 600 pairs strong. On the west side of the loch, the
Midross quarry is sited beside the lower reaches of the Fruin, an area of old
river meanders noted for its wetland birds even before sand and gravel extraction created the first artificial lagoons. Excavations began in 1947, each
worked-out and then water-filled pit being left to the natural process of ecological succession. Shingle-nesting species such as the ringed plover, oystercatcher and common tern (*Sterna hirundo*) have now all but given way before
the encroachment of willow, alder, birch and broom (*Cytisus scoparious*), their
place taken by a community of scrubland birds, with sedge warbler, garden
warbler and lesser redpoll (*Carduelis flammea*) amongst the earliest colonists.
Shelduck prospecting for nesting holes have on occasions been attracted by
rabbit burrows in the sandy banks. Elsewhere, the partially water-filled
Muirhouse Muir quarry near Blanefield attracted over 300 nesting pairs of
black-headed gulls (*Larus ridibundus*) within a few years of gravel extraction
coming to an end. The totally flooded workings adjoining Drumkinnon Bay
were much frequented by coarse anglers before work began on the site for a
major tourist development, with crucian carp and tench known to have been
introduced. Even the smallest area of standing water in the sand and gravel pits
can quickly attract several species of dragonflies and damselflies, including the
common and Highland darters (*Sympetrum striolatum* and *S. nigrescens*), both
recent additions to Loch Lomondside's invertebrate fauna.
    The zoological interest of other abandoned mineral workings has attracted
little attention. Until a rock fall destroyed the chosen ledge, a pair of peregrines nested on a worked face of Camstradden slate quarry; and before the
quarry was infilled, the mounds of discarded slate dross formed a shady hide-
away for the slow-worm. A curious find was a small population of almost colour-
less common frogs living in the semi-darkness of a partially flooded barytes
mine near Kilmannan Reservoir. The only obvious sources of food for these
underground mine-living frogs are hibernating herald moths (*Scoliopteryx liba-
trix*) and flies (*Diptera*) on the passage walls.

Lochs and reservoirs

Standing waters of natural origin are not a prominent feature of the lowland
agricultural zone. Of the two largest, Loch Ardinning south of Blanefield is a

Fig. 10.9 Caldarvan Loch is affected by water enrichment through its close proximity to agricultural land.

glacially excavated rock basin lochan, whereas Caldarvan Loch in Kilmaronock nestles amongst mounds of glacially deposited material. Both have a long history of maturation and are rich in wildlife interest.

Loch Ardinning, whose size has been increased by damming, is one of a number of natural and artificial water bodies which once served the former corn mill and textile industries in Strathblane. Protected from the prevailing wind by a wood along the loch's western perimeter, Ardinning's emergent aquatic vegetation is well developed, including a fair-sized stand of common reed. The little grebe (*Tachybaptus ruficollis*) is very much at home in this reed bed habitat. What is fairly unusual for a lowland loch is the well-established presence of water lobelia, which flowers profusely if the surface level is drawn down in summer. Loch Ardinning drains into the Mill Dam just a short distance away, a small but attractive water body noted for greater spearwort (*Ranunculus lingua*) and round-leaved crowfoot (*R. omiophyllus*), both uncommon plants in the region.

Caldarvan Loch (Fig. 10.9), on the Blaeu map of the Province of Lennox (1654) shown as Loch Breac – the loch of the trout – suffers from the problem of over-enrichment as a consequence of fertilizers finding their way in to the loch from the surrounding agricultural land. During warm weather in summer, a thick algal growth covers large areas of the water surface, stifling underwater plant and animal life alike. The coot (*Fulica atra*), which is one water bird that can thrive in such a nutrient-rich environment, occurs in good numbers. Caldarvan's botanical interest lies in the lush plant growth that has spread over the water surface at its western end. Common aquatics such as bogbean and water horsetail (*Equisetum fluviatile*) make up the bulk of the floating mat of vegetation, but more localised species such as tufted loosestrife and lesser tussock sedge (*Carex diandra*) are also well represented. Set within this quaking greenery are several tree-covered islets, which rise sufficiently above the influence of the loch's eutrophic waters for the woodland floor to be dominated by bog mosses, here and there carpeted with cranberry and accompanied by occasional spikes of lesser twayblade (*Listera cordata*).

In contrast to the natural water bodies described above, the 3.9 km² Carron Reservoir is not only entirely man-made, its construction is comparatively recent. Nevertheless, when the Carron Valley was gradually flooded in the late 1930s it still possessed one of the last worked water meadows in Scotland, so there was already some diversity of marshland plants in place to adapt as a marginal community at the water's edge wherever conditions proved suitable. The reservoir's wildlife potential underwent a significant change from the late 1980s, when the water level was raised to a new height. In the summer months what was formerly a sandy delta around the mouth of the incoming River Carron has become a mosaic of reed canary-grass and northern water sedge, with scattered 'rafts' of amphibious bistort. The ringed plover's loss of habitat has proved to be a gain for the great crested grebe, for up to five pairs now nest in this sheltered spot. Concealed in the reeds little grebes make themselves heard and even the rare Slavonian grebe (*Podiceps auritus*) is not unknown. With the reservoir well stocked with fish, the osprey is a frequent summer visitor. The Carron Reservoir is also one of the few places in Scotland where a flock of bean geese still occasionally appears in winter.

Raised bogs

The fragments of low level peat bog that still survive in the parish of Kilmaronock to the south of Loch Lomond are the Lowland fringe's last remnants of the ancient landscape that existed before the beginnings of agricultural improvement and reclamation of the 'wastes'. Unlike the valley bogs of Glen Falloch and the fens of the Aber Bogs mentioned in the previous chapter, both of which are enriched to varying degrees by minerals carried by water draining from higher ground, the only source of nutrients for these isolated bogs are the meagre dissolved salts deposited by rain. In such a mineral-deficient environment the bog mosses flourish, even though the rainfall is less and evaporation greater in Kilmaronock than in the mountainous Highlands to the north. Providing a hydrological balance is maintained, bog moss growth will exceed decay in the anaerobic waterlogged conditions, so that over the course of centuries the gradual accumulation of plant material is such that the increasingly dome-shaped profile of the bog surface stands well above the surrounding land. These are known as raised bogs. In an actively growing raised bog, the surface is a mosaic of bog moss hummocks, the hollows between them saturated with water. The most common higher plants are ling heather, cross-leaved heath and hare's-tail cottongrass (*Eriophorum vaginatum*), with locally frequent bog asphodel, round-leaved sundew (*Drosera rotundifolia*) and occasional white-beaked sedge.

As a result of peat cutting for domestic fuel in the past, none of the Kilmaronock raised bogs are still intact, the least modified example being the birch-fringed Blairbeich Moss (Fig. 10.10), whose development probably began as a marsh in a glacial morainic hollow. The site is best known as a locality where the bog-rosemary (*Andromeda polifolia*) can still be found, a species generally declining in Britain with loss of suitable habitat through drainage,

Fig. 10.10 Blairbeich Moss is the most intact of Loch Lomondside's raised bogs.

peat extraction and afforestation. The zoological interest of Blairbeich and other raised bogs in the immediate area centres on their invertebrate fauna normally associated with moorland at higher altitude. Day-flying moths found on these lowland raised bogs, and whose larvae feed on heather, include the common heath (*Ematurga atomaria*), northern eggar (*Lasiocampa quercus* ssp. *callunae*) and the eye-catching emperor moth (*Pavonia pavonia*). Periodically, the larvae of the fox moth (*Macrothylacia rubi*) occur in such huge numbers as to severely defoliate the heather. Especially noteworthy at Blairbeich is an isolated colony of the large heath butterfly (*Coenonympha tullia*), its larvae feeding on cottongrass and the adults turning to cross-leaved heath as a favourite source of nectar. The Paisley lepidopterist A.M. Stewart in a little book entitled *British Butterflies* (1912) recommended to his readers that the most comfortable way he found to pursue the large heath over such squelchy ground was 'with bare feet and legs, and the trousers well tucked up', advice that is best disregarded in what is adder (*Vipera berus*) country. The open and sunlit birchwood on the moss's southern flank is ideal for the green hairstreak butterfly (*Callophrys rubi*), the food plant of its larvae confined to blaeberry in raised bog vegetation.

A keenly anticipated excursion amongst west of Scotland naturalists of yesteryear was a boat trip to the raised bog on Inchmoan, but today this Loch Lomond island is largely tree-covered (see Chapter 11) and its character totally changed. The Peat Isle, as it was alternatively named, formerly held both red and black grouse. Lapwing, curlew and common snipe also once regularly bred. What particularly intrigued visiting botanists was the presence of cloudberry (*Rubus chamaemorus*), an upland plant growing on Inchmoan's bog surface at little above sea level.

11

Deciduous and Coniferous Woodlands

'Coppice woodland ... we have only to glance at it as it decks the
shores of many of our most beautiful Scottish lakes, or contemplate it
as it clothes the rugged slopes of some romantic mountain or deep
glen, to realise how peculiarly appropriate it is, and how well adapted
to contribute to the wild grandeur and natural scenery of these
Highland situations.'

Oak Coppice in Scotland
Andrew Gilchrist (1874)

The deciduous woodlands

With their carpets of bluebells or wild hyacinths in spring and the tapestry of
changing leaf colours in autumn, the deciduous woodlands on Loch
Lomondside are amongst the most admired glories of Scotland. As the loch is
almost entirely surrounded by continuous tree cover, here at least it is easy to
forget for a moment that woodlands such as these (Fig. 11.1) are to be found
over an incredibly small percentage of the country's land surface. Despite continuous use and modification since the arrival of man thousands of years ago,
the region can still claim to have one of the most diverse broad-leaved woodland flora and faunas to be found in northern Britain. Oak predominates, followed by birch and alder, with much smaller amounts of hazel, holly and ash.
Weeding-out of the less commercial species during the oak coppicing era has
left the managed woodland stands with only a scattering of mature rowan,
wych elm, aspen, hawthorn (*Crataegus monogyna*), crab apple (*Malus sylvestris*),
grey willow (*Salix cinerea*), bird cherry and gean (*Prunus avium*).

Very little information has been passed down in local naturalists' accounts on
how the woodland flora and fauna would change after each periodic cut when
oak coppicing was at its peak. It can be assumed, however, that a greater diversity and abundance of light-demanding flowering plants would appear on the
re-illuminated woodland floor. It follows too that sun-loving woodland butterflies were far better represented than is the case today. In the almost total
absence of old-growth trees with naturally formed holes, nineteenth-century
ornithologists knew redstarts (*Phoenicurus phoenicurus*) exclusively as nesters in
cavities of dry-stone walls. The great spotted woodpecker (*Dendrocopus major*),
which depends for its food on the larvae of wood-boring invertebrates found
only in mature trees, was unknown on Loch Lomondside until coppice management had all but ceased. Taking the now thickly wooded Inchcailloch as a
specific example, it is difficult to visualise that this island once supported open
habitat species such as black grouse and brown hare, but the Montrose Estate's
game books for the end of the nineteenth century confirm that this was so. As
the value of oak bark declined, enclosure fences and walls ceased to be regu-

Fig. 11.1 The former oak coppice woodlands on the islands have been less subject to stock grazing than those on the mainland.

larly maintained, and most of the mainland woodlands and those on the larger islands were turned over to year-round foraging by domestic stock. A uniform ground vegetation and a lack of any woody regeneration is a clear indication of prolonged use as wood pasture and winter shelter by cattle and sheep. Where long-term grazing within these woodlands has been brought to an end, the ground flora can become dominated by a thick growth of greater woodrush (*Luzula sylvatica*), often to the exclusion of almost all other flowering plants.

For convenience, most studies of Loch Lomondside's deciduous woodland habitats have been classified by the dominant tree, even though there can be considerable overlap in both plant and animal life whichever broad-leaved species makes up the most common tree in the canopy. Significant differences do appear with the different soil types and when grazed and ungrazed woodlands are compared.

The former oak coppice woodlands

Most of the trees that form the present oak-dominated canopy are of no great size, concealing the fact that many of these once intensively managed coppice stands may have persisted on the very same spots for centuries, the ground flora at least having some continuity with the wildwood of the past. The diversity of ground flora types reflects Loch Lomondside's varied geological formations from hard grits and slates to calcareous schists, serpentinites and even occasional limestones, which in turn has produced a wide range of acidic, through neutral to alkaline woodland soils. Beneath the trees on the woodland floor, fallen leaves and dead wood are continuously being broken down by small organisms and incorporated into the soil, the tree's roots picking up the soluble nutrients only for them to be returned as decaying material in a continuous soil-building cycle. Even where the tree cover has vanished, the presence and depth of forest brown earths can often be deduced from the vigorous growth of bracken.

Commonly encountered indicator species of the oak-dominated woodlands with fertile brown earths are bramble, dog's mercury (*Mercurialis perennis*) and primrose (*Primula vulgaris*), with ramsons (*Allium ursinum*), opposite-leaved golden saxifrage (*Chrysosplenium oppositifolium*) and bugle (*Ajuga reptans*) where the ground is less freely drained. Far less frequent, but equally telling of humus-rich soils, are wood sanicle (*Sanicula europaea*), wood stitchwort (*Stellaria nemorum*), sweet woodruff (*Galium odoratum*), wood speedwell (*Veronica montana*), moschatel (*Adoxa moschatellina*) and wood sedge (*Carex sylvaticus*). Creinch, right in the centre of the loch's southern basin, deserves a special mention for its magnesium and calcium-rich soils with an exceptionally lush ground flora. The reason for this is the underlying geology, which in the northern half of the island comprises serpentinite with small pockets of limestone. Several locally uncommon plants are to be found here, such as wood goldilocks and soft shield-fern (*Polystichum setiferum*). Very rare as a Scottish species is the toothwort (*Lathraea squamaria*), which on Creinch is parasitic upon the roots of wych elm (Fig. 11.2). The presence of moonwort is quite unexpected in the island's assemblage of flowering plants and ferns, for it is normally never found under a shade-casting woodland canopy. Creinch's exposed rock faces are rich in bryophytes, a number of which are essentially southern in their distribution. These include the lime-loving liverworts *Cololejeunea rossettiana* and *Marchesinia mackaii*, together with the moss *Tortella nitida*, protected by the surrounding expanse of water that ameliorates the damaging effects of all but the severest frosts.

Fig. 11.2 Not needing to photosynthesise for itself, the parasitic toothwort has dispensed with green coloration.

Podsolic soils, which are formed where rainwater combines with organic acids from decaying vegetation and largely removes the soluble salts necessary for plant growth, support a much poorer species diversity. Blaeberry, ling heather, foxglove, common cow-wheat (*Melampyrum pratense*), hard fern (*Blechnum spicant*) and the silvery-green cushions of white fork moss (*Leucobryum glaucum*) are amongst the most frequently encountered representatives of the plant community. Locally rare and very elusive, the wood cow-wheat (*M. sylvaticum*) has been reported in the past from acidic soil woodlands at Rowardennan, Inversnaid and Tarbet, perhaps persisting in all of its old haunts and just waiting to be re-found. Hummocks of common hair moss (*Polytrichum commune*) and bog mosses can dominate on gleyed soils, which is where the ground is waterlogged and oxidisation of the soil is greatly reduced.

A feature of the Loch Lomondside woodlands in summer and autumn is the abundance of ferns, in particular the broad buckler fern (*Dryopteris dilatata*), male fern (*D. filix-mas*) and lady fern (*Athyrium filix-femina*), but the most widespread of them all is bracken. An invasive species, bracken appears forever on the increase at the expense of less competitive vegetation, although a redeeming feature is that it substitutes as cover for ground-nesting birds in hard grazed woods and often acts as a support for a delicate tracery of climbing corydalis (*Ceratocapnos claviculata*). When visiting Loch Lomondside in August 1803, the poet Samuel Taylor Coleridge enthused over the profusion of corydalis flowers he observed adorning the bracken-thatched cottages at Luss. Recent taxonomic advances point to several kinds of bracken in Britain. One is ssp. *atlanticum*, which is generally confined to the country's western seaboard. Recognisable by its unfurled croziers covered in a mass of white, silky hairs, specimens answering to this description have been reported from wood pasture on Inchmurrin. One of Lomondside's most interesting fern records from the late nineteenth century is the hybrid *Dryopteris* x *remota* (scaly male fern x northern buckler fern *D. expansa*). Collected from a rocky woodland somewhere between Tarbet and Ardlui, the precise site of this rare hybrid has been lost. It should perhaps be added that the finder – W. B. Boyd – had an eye for the unusual, and in fact was famous in botanical circles as the discoverer of a montane pearlwort (*Sagina boydii*), which has never again been seen in the wild. A quite unique 'lattice-work' fronded variety of lady fern, which was found by chance at Buchanan in 1861 and named *Victoriae* in honour of the reigning monarch, is happily still maintained in cultivation.

The larger fungi of the Lomondside oak woodlands are not well documented except for around the southeastern corner of the loch. Here on the mainland and several of the islands about 400 of the British macro-species have been recorded, a significant number of them reflecting the southwestern element of the British fungi flora. Representatives of this group include *Lactarius chrysorrheus*, *Tricholoma acerbum*, *Boletus pulverulentus* and the death cap (*Amanita phalloides*), the most poisonous of all the British toadstools.

Loch Lomondside's ageing coppice woodlands are especially rich in moths, many cryptically coloured, which renders them almost invisible against the oaks' rough bark and covering of bryophytes and lichens. A few of the species that have been recorded are either nationally scarce or very local in Scotland, such as the saxon (*Hyppa rectilinea*), dotted carpet (*Alcis jubata*), silvery arches (*Polia hepatica*) and brindled white-spot (*Paradarisa extersaria*). In some years, whole stretches of oak woodland can be almost totally defoliated in late spring

Fig. 11.3 Scottish wood ants congregating on the sunny side of their large nest on a chilly day in May.

by the caterpillars of moths present in incredible numbers. The principal culprits would appear to be the winter moth (*Operophtera brumata*) and the mottled umber (*Erannis defoliaria*). Opportunistic insectivorous birds rear large broods of young with the temporary glut of invertebrate food. A defoliated oak has the ability to produce a second flush of leaves within a few weeks, but the drain on its energy reserves seriously diminishes the tree's rate of growth for that year. In stark contrast to the diverse moth fauna, there is only one entirely woodland dependant butterfly – the purple hairstreak (*Quercusia quercus*) (see p. 171). A partial explanation for this paucity of butterfly species is Loch Lomond basin's atypical north–south alignment, with hardly any of the hillside woodlands facing due south, directly into the all-important warming influence of the sun.

On the mainland and at least one of the islands, Scottish wood ants (*Formica aquilonia*) just about reach the southern limit of the species' known distribution in Britain. The outer layer of their large domed nests (Fig. 11.3) is thatched, which is essential to prevent the structures becoming saturated in the frequent rain.

No mention of Loch Lomondside's woodland invertebrates would be complete without inclusion of at least some of the many beetles associated with broad-leaved forest, especially where over-mature and decaying trees have not been felled and removed. Amongst those present with an ancient forest lifestyle, which inevitably limits their distribution in Britain, are the four-spotted carrion beetle (*Dendroxena quadripunctata*), which despite its English name hunts caterpillars high in the woodland canopy; the distinctive wasp beetle (*Clytus arietis*), whose larvae burrow into the tree; and the fungus beetles *Phloiophilus edwardsi* and *Scaphidium quadrimaculatum*. Perhaps most restricted

Fig. 11.4 Partly sheltered from the wind by the surrounding trees, the Dubh Lochan is noted for dragonflies and damselflies.

of all is *Eutheia linearis*, a member of the chequered beetle family that feeds on microscopic mites found on dead and dying oaks.

Unlike the neighbouring Trossachs area, there is a dearth of standing waters in the region's woodlands. However, the Dubh Lochan (Fig. 11.4) at Sallochy is a particularly fine example, having a well-developed fringe of common reed, water horsetail, bottle sedge and bog-myrtle, with both white and yellow water-lilies dotted over the water surface. The tree-sheltered lochan with its peaty waters is the district's premier site for dragonflies and damselflies, with ten confirmed breeding species. Most of these are common and widespread, but the list does include the downy emerald (*Cordulia aenea*) and the beautiful demoiselle (*Calopteryx virgo*), both of which are extremely rare in central Scotland. A potential eleventh species – the recently colonised Highland darter – was recorded in the vicinity of the Dubh Lochan for the first time in 1999.

The summer bird communities of the Loch Lomondside oak woodlands were comprehensively investigated between 1972 and 1980 using the common bird census mapping method throughout. This involves a set number of visits, the observer entering the position of every bird heard or seen onto a site map. Comparability between individual woodland stands was further enhanced through all but one of the surveys conducted after an exceptionally long run of relatively mild winters. Not only was the effect of long-term stock grazing on some woods' ornithological potential clearly demonstrated, but the survey results also brought out the influence on woodland bird communities of island isolation. In the chain of islands stretching across the wide southern portion of the loch, it was found that both species diversity and density decreased with distance from the mainland shore. In descending numerical order within the deciduous woodland community, the census showed that chaffinch, wren, willow warbler and robin made up over half the total number of birds present, the willow warbler as a summer migrant likely to take second position in seasons preceded by even a moderately severe winter which could reduce the numbers of the resident wrens.

With leaf-eating moth caterpillars and other invertebrates present in their millions during the spring and early summer, small insectivorous birds can achieve remarkably high numbers. The highest density of deciduous woodland birds in the region was found on Inchcailloch, this ungrazed, oak-dominated island close in to the mainland shore having a population calculated at over 1,500 pairs per km^2, a figure that compares favourably with the finest oak woodlands in southern England, albeit with fewer species represented. On Loch Lomondside no bird is more characteristic of the best structured woodlands with a reasonably developed shrub layer than the garden warbler. In one plot on Inchcailloch the species reached 76 pairs per km^2 – a high density unmatched by garden warblers in any other censused oak wood in northern Britain. Birds typical of more open situations – redstart, tree pipit (*Anthus trivialis*), pied flycatcher (*Ficedula hypoleuca*) (see p. 173) and wood warbler (*Phylloscopus sibilatrix*) – were shown to make up over a fifth of the total number of birds recorded in the sessile oak woods of Glen Falloch (Fig. 11.5). Loch Lomondside figures obtained for wood warblers, most markedly in the Glen Douglas grazed oak wood plot at 60 pairs per km^2, are amongst the highest of any obtained in Scotland. The most common bird of prey within the oak woodland community is the tawny owl (*Strix aluco*), but because the species breeds very early in the year it hardly ever figured in the late May–June census results. A dearth of suitable large holes in the former coppice trees means that it is not unusual for the tawny owl to nest on the ground. In both the grazed and ungrazed oak woodlands, it is anticipated that the generally low populations of hole-nesting birds (except where sufficient nest boxes have been provided) will expand in line with the nesting opportunities available as these former coppice stands gradually mature into semi-natural high forest.

Thirty-five species of native and established foreign mammals currently inhabit the region, and all but the most montane or water-dependent are regularly found in broad-leaved woodland. Unlike the summer woodland birds which advertise their whereabouts by song during the hours of daylight, the woodland mammals are at their most active at night, so that the casual visitor would probably not be aware of more than one or two different species present during the course of a morning's stroll. However, once the observer's eyes and ears become attuned to the presence of forest creatures – a black smear below a hole in a tree that shows it is a regularly used bat roost, the freshly thrashed honeysuckle (*Lonicera periclymenum*) territorial announcement of a fallow deer buck, or the telltale shuffling of a vole or shrew in the undergrowth – then the number will steadily rise. Like the woodlands they inhabit, the fortunes of Loch Lomondside's mammals have ebbed and flowed in line with man's activities, and some of their stories are well worth recounting here.

The badger (*Meles meles*) is Britain's largest remaining native carnivore. It was a sorry day for the badger in Scotland when Queen Victoria's consort Prince Albert popularised the fashion of wearing Highland dress, for from the mid-nineteenth century badger hair became much in demand for making the finest sporrans. Fortunately, it would seem that the landed proprietors on

Fig. 11.5 The widely spaced sessile oaks in Glen Falloch are ideally suited to birds that prefer an open woodland habitat.

Loch Lomondside did not encourage the exploitation of the animal and little inroad was made on the local population. Badger dens or setts assume their highest density along the wooded slopes on the east side of the loch, well away from the centres of human population. Because of the badger's ancient lineage, it is not unexpected that several Lomondside place names still in use originate from its older name of brock, such as Dumbrock, Craigbrock and Tom nam Broc.

As already described in Chapter 7, during the nineteenth century the wildcat – together with the pine marten (see p. 173) and polecat – was banished from the area by gamekeepers intent on destroying any predator that posed a potential threat to the lairds' pheasants and red grouse. In the 1920s, however, the wildcat reappeared in the district, assisted like several other recolonists by a respite from 'keepering during the First World War and the cover provided by extensive conifer planting in the post-war years. Yet even after all this time, the size of the population of this usually solitary animal is difficult to assess, but it is known to have spread as far south as the wooded glens in the Kilpatrick Hills. The most serious threat to the continuing survival of the true Scottish wildcat today is the ever-present risk of interbreeding with the much smaller domestic cat, first introduced to this country at the time of the Roman occupation. We may never see the like again of the magnificent creature reputedly weighing nearly 24 lb (10.9 kg) which was killed in 1832 near Rob Roy's cave north of Inversnaid. Like the badger, there are a few rocky outcrops on Loch Lomondside that continue to bear its name – Cat Craig, Creag Cait, Craighat (Creag a' Chait) and Sgorr a' Chait.

Any suggestion of keeping the number of feral goats (*Capra* spp.) within reasonable bounds is guaranteed to raise a few hackles. Those in favour of reducing the population on Loch Lomondside's east bank point to the indisputable evidence of their harmful effect on woodland regeneration, through browsing the leading shoots and stripping the bark of young trees. Opponents to control claim that protection in perpetuity for the goats was decreed as far back as the time of Robert I – a good story, but one supported only by constant repetition rather than historical proof. The lineage of the present stock of 'wild' goats almost certainly dates no further back than the late eighteenth-early nineteenth centuries, from animals abandoned as Highland steadings fell empty one by one. But even if the goats' supposed historical pedigree back to Robert the Bruce does not stand up to scrutiny, at least their cultural connection with pre-improvement farming in the area does; and there can be little doubt that many visitors to the area would consider a chance encounter with feral goats (Fig. 11.6) one of the highlights of their day out. The problem of tree damage became more acute following a relaxation of active goat control by the Forestry Commission in the 1970s, the goats' numbers eventually rising three-fold to something in the order of 300 animals, a level which could not be sustained without severe consequences for the woodlands they inhabit. A combination of selective culling and translocation of some of the goats by one con-

Fig. 11.6 'Wild' goats browsing in the Inversnaid woodlands (Mike Trubridge).

servation body was considered the only practical way to protect the native broad-leaved woodlands and new plantings in their charge. Tree damage aside, even the goats' severest critics admit to a sneaking admiration for these sure-footed animals as they move effortlessly from ledge to ledge on a precipitous cliff. Still tied to the timing of the breeding cycle of their Mediterranean ancestors, the young are born in February, which in Scotland can bring the severest weather of the year. In the coldest winters, only the strongest goat kids survive. Local topographical features associated with goats include Allt a' Mhinn, Cnoc na Goibhre (Gobhar) and Buck Craig.

Through the combined efforts of several conservation organisations, the future of many of Loch Lomondside's former coppice woodlands is now more secure from indiscriminate felling and the attentions of farm stock and other browsing animals than at any time since they ceased to be actively managed for coppice in the early twentieth century. However, their continuation as oak-dominated woodlands in the long term is far less certain. Any discussion on what the composition of these woodlands is likely to be in the future invariably turns to Clairinsh, a small (6 ha) island that at one time was regarded as the last more or less untouched broad-leaved stand in the area. It is now thought that intensive coppicing merely ceased much earlier on Clairinsh than any other woodland on the Montrose Estate. With a closed canopy overhead and browsing deer not a particular problem on such a small island, an understorey of shade-tolerant woody species such as holly and rowan has sprung up, but next to no light-demanding young oak. It seems inevitable, therefore, that despite the species' longevity, the oak's predominant position amongst the island's tree community will eventually be challenged.

Mixed species woodlands less influenced by the intensive coppicing regime

To judge from the diversity of tree species present, including ash and wych elm where mineral-rich soils occur, there are surviving pockets of woodland in the Highland zone that have been little modified by coppice management in the past. These are usually to be found in steep-sided glens and ravines which are difficult to access and in some cases, dangerously unstable. Shaded from direct sunlight by the topography and permanent tree cover, such sites, with their tumbling streams and spray-wreathed waterfalls, are characterised by high humidity and luxuriant plant growth. Hay-scented buckler fern (*Dryopteris aemula*), Tunbridge filmy fern (*Hymenophyllum tunbrigense*), Wilson's filmy fern (*H. wilsonii*) and many bryophytes unable to tolerate desiccation have a chance to thrive in the permanently damp conditions. Not always recognised for what they are, Loch Lomondside woodlands with an almost perpetually wet micro-climate represent relicts of a largely disappeared temperate rainforest on Europe's Atlantic edge.

More survey work is needed on the western bryophyte community of these rock-strewn damp woodlands, but amongst the Atlantic species recorded to date are the liverworts *Adelanthus decipiens, Tritomaria exsecta, Leptoscyphus cuneifolius, Lophocolea fragrans, Radula voluta, Frullania microphylla, Plagiochila killarniensis* and *Jubula hutchinsiae,* together with the moss *Sematophyllum micans.*

In the southern half of Loch Lomondside, the wooded glens of Ballagan, Finnich, Gallangad, Gartness and Mar are amongst the most botanically rewarding for higher plants. The majority of the flowers and ferns that thickly carpet or drape the more vegetated lowland ravines are fairly ubiquitous woodland species, but worth searching for are specialities such as the giant bell-flower (*Campanula latifolia*), wood vetch (*Vicia sylvatica*), alternate-leaved golden saxifrage (*Chrysosplenium alternifolium*), pendulous sedge, wood fescue (*Festuca altissima*), wood millet (*Milium effusum*), mountain melic (*Melica nutans*) and green spleenwort (*Asplenium viride*), almost all of which have very localised distributions in the district.

Upland pasture birch woodlands

The maximum height reached by the postglacial tree line on the Scottish mountains has attracted much speculation. On one point all would agree; the upper tree limit must have advanced and retreated more than once during different postglacial climatic periods long before it ever felt the first influence of man and his domestic animals. Today, oak trees at Craigrostan on the eastern slopes above the loch show clear evidence of stunting well before the 300 m contour is reached. Several climatic factors are involved in these trees' poor growth: high rainfall and the resultant wetness of the soil, direct exposure to the prevailing southwesterly winds, but probably the most important is the region's rapid temperature fall with increasing altitude which significantly shortens the growing season on even moderately high ground.

The highest birch woodlands on Loch Lomondside at present are not necessarily in places best suited to tree growth, but probably those least suited to the grazing of stock. It is with some justification that much of the blame for the shrinking tree cover on the high ground is laid at the door of the incoming eighteenth-century flockmasters, but the damage caused by domesticated grazing animals to upland woodland was by then nothing new. Lamenting the lack of replacement seedlings and saplings under the preceding shieling system, one parish minister noted that when cattle were taken up to the summer pastures: 'this precious crop, the hope of future forests, is for ever destroyed'.

Well into the 1920s, the moribund remains of a once extensive birch forest could still be found up to 500 m on the northern slopes of Beinn a' Chroin at the head of Glen Falloch. These trees have since completely disappeared. Today, the largest high-level stand of woodland in the area ascends to about 450 m alongside the head-waters of the Stuckindroin Burn (Fig. 11.7) on the northeast face of Ben Vorlich. Above the influence of forestry activities, this birch-dominated woodland almost certainly has a lineage that goes back to the original wildwood, although intensive sheep grazing and deer browsing have ensured the absence of a shrub layer. The ground flora between the widely spaced trees gradually changes from a bracken-infested grassy sward to a more heathy assemblage of blaeberry, cowberry (*Vaccinium vitis-idaea*) and crowberry ssp. *hermaphroditum* at the wood's diffuse upper edge. The additional presence of common montane plants such as alpine lady's mantle (*Alchemilla alpina*) reflects the wood's elevation.

Ornithological census figures for Loch Lomondside's upland birch woodlands are only available for Coire na h-Eanachan, high above Glen Douglas in the Luss Hills. During the summer months the willow warbler was found to be the most numerous species, the tree pipit taking second place over the chaffinch. Cuckoos (*Cuculus canorus*) are very much in evidence in these open woodlands in May.

High up on the wooded slopes of Beinn Bhreac in the northern Luss Hills is a birch-fringed tarn known as the Fairy Lochan. Even after the fanciful stories

Fig. 11.7 A relict stand of high-level birch woodland on Ben Vorlich.

of little people are set aside, this small water body is not without interest. The drainage area around the Fairy Lochan is in fact a known site for one of Loch Lomondside's rarest freshwater invertebrates – the predatory alpine flatworm *Crenobia alpina*, a relict species found only in perpetually cold springs and caves.

The coniferous woodlands

The pine woods

The full extent to which the ancient Caledonian pine forest spread into Highland Loch Lomondside may never be known for certain, for much of it had disappeared long before written records were kept. Oral sources, not transcribed until the nineteenth century, tell of a destructive pine forest fire around 1640 that began near the head of Loch Sloy and swept northwards to Glen Falloch. One local historian's description of shepherds making 'fir-candles' from the charred but still resinous pine stumps well over 200 years after the disastrous event adds substance to the traditional story.

By the early 1980s, the last remnant of Loch Lomondside's pine forest consisted of less than 130 mature and semi-mature trees scattered over 121 ha of exposed hillside on the east side of the River Falloch (Fig. 11.8). A few of the 'granny' pines recently examined proved to be about 400 years old, which means they were already present at a time when what remained of Loch Lomondside's original forest cover was still home to the much-feared wolf. Very little of the characteristic flora and fauna of a pine wood community has survived, the ground vegetation having been heavily grazed by sheep and browsed by red deer over a long period. Placed in a high 'at-risk' category, the first trial enclosure around some of the pines was erected in 1982, with almost all of the remaining trees fenced off from sheep and deer by 1993. Apart from

Fig. 11.8 Remnants of the ancient Caledonian pine forest in Glen Falloch.

natural regeneration within the security of the enclosure, restoration of the Glen Falloch pine wood is being assisted by the planting of young trees grown from locally gathered seed.

The ability of Scots pine to regenerate freely following the removal of grazing pressure is convincingly shown on Inchmoan, the only large island in Loch Lomond that was not well clothed in woodland within living memory. Colonisation of the island's raised bog surface by pine and birch began during the agricultural depression years of the 1930s and the resultant cessation of regular grazing. The source of the Scots pine was just a few trees of unknown provenance planted around an uncompleted folly in the western corner of the island, yet so rapid has the encroachment of woodland been, that, despite several fires, few areas of open ground on the island remain. A summer bird survey conducted amongst the mixed pine and birch showed an extremely high density of breeding birds – almost 1,700 pairs per km^2 – although the diversity of species was only half that of Loch Lomondside's best oak woods. Compared to other ungrazed woodlands censused in the area, much higher values were achieved for willow warbler, robin, tree pipit and coal tit (*Parus ater*). The addition of siskin (*Carduelis spinus*) to the community reflects the presence of pine. Inchmoan has attracted visiting ornithologists for well over a century, not least for the offchance of observing capercaillie (*Tetrao urogallus*) (see p. 172), the largest and most spectacular member of the grouse family in the world.

According to the nineteenth-century Stirlingshire naturalist John A. Harvie Brown, the last red kites resident in the woods at the foot of Ben Lomond built their nests in Scots pine, confirming an observation made by John Colquhoun that kites nested in pine on the wooded slopes of the Luss Hills. Today, an old planting of Scots pine in Glen Fruin is the site of Loch Lomondside's only pair of tree-nesting ravens. If the tree-nesting habit was to catch on with their descendants, it could pave the way for the raven to recolonise Lowland and even urban areas from where it was driven out many years ago.

The yew tree island

'A slender crosslet form'd with care
A cubit's lenth in measure due
The shafts and limbs were rods of yew
Whose parents in Inch-Cailloch wave
Their shadows o'er Clan Alpine's grave.'

These well-quoted lines from Sir Walter Scott's *Lady of the Lake*, which tell of the fiery cross used to summon armed clansmen in times of war, would lead the reader to believe that the material used for the crosslet was cut on the MacGregors' burial island of Inchcailloch. If the story has any truth in it at all, it is far more likely that the island source of the yew would have been Inchlonaig, which the sixteenth-century map-maker Timothy Pont said was 'adorned with an aboundance of Ew trees, which it alone hath among the rest'.

Said to number several thousand trees in 1794, the yew wood on Inchlonaig sustained both a major fell and a destructive fire in the early part of the nineteenth century. Some replanting followed, so that approximately 800 well-grown yews are still to be found on the island in small groves (Fig. 11.9) or as scattered individuals, the proportion of male and female trees shown to be roughly equal. Despite the reduction in the number of trees through felling and fire, this is still the most important assemblage of yews in Scotland.

Fig. 11.9 The ancestors of the yew trees on Inchlonaig are reputed to date back to the reign of King Robert I.

Repeating a popular folk tale that has been passed down through the years, the yews were planted on Inchlonaig on the orders of Robert the Bruce to provide bows for the Scottish army; and two venerable but long since vanished trees of large girth measured by the Reverend John Walker in 1770 probably dated back to the fourteenth century and the birth of the legend. Some of the surviving yews are also very old, their gnarled roots penetrating deep into crevices and grasping the exposed bedrock in a vice-like embrace.

A curious feature of the island's yew woodlands is the frequency of 'dual' specimens amongst the older trees. This is where a woody epiphyte on the yew – birch, holly and rowan in Inchlonaig's case – has become enveloped by the host, the two continuing to grow as one. Crab apple partnered with rowan, and rowan with birch have also been reported as dual trees on the island. Equally of interest is the presence of the rare bracket fungus *Ganoderma valesiacum*, a Central European species associated with high altitude stands of larch (*Larix decidua*), but which in Britain is found almost exclusively on yew. Also worth drawing attention to is the presence of the southern lichen (*Rinodina roboris*), which occurs in some abundance on well-lit yews along the south shore of the island.

Still with open, bracken-covered areas, Inchlonaig appears to be the last remaining island in the loch where the adder still thrives. At the height of oak coppicing in the mid-nineteenth century, when none of the woodlands had a dense shade-casting continuous canopy, this poisonous reptile was well known on a number of the larger islands. Inchtavannach and Inchconnachan were said to be 'much infested with them'. Naturalists' correspondence of the time mentions that, in the summer of 1877, Montrose Estate gamekeepers killed 130 adders on Inchmurrin alone. A word of caution at this point would not be out of place. Some adders on Loch Lomondside are poorly marked, the usually diagnostic dark zig-zag along the back barely visible. This makes it possible for the unwary to mistake them for the harmless grass snake (*Natrix natrix*), a species that does not occur in the area.

Compared to that found in most other types of conifer woodland in the region, the summer bird population of Inchlonaig's yew groves is unexpectedly high – 925 pairs per km^2 – although made up of few species. Goldcrests (*Regulus regulus*) and wrens are the two most numerous birds, followed by chaffinch and robin. Another well-represented member of the avian community is the redstart, the constant flicking of its orangey-red tail conspicuous against the dark foliage of the yew. The redstart is apparently unknown as a nesting species in yew woodland anywhere else in Britain and Ireland. The replacement of the willow warbler by the chiff-chaff (*Phylloscopus collybita*) is unusual for a Lomondside wood. Although no longer managed as an island deer park, Inchlonaig does still have a small population of fallow deer, one of the few mammals able to browse on the poisonous foliage of the yew without ill effect. It has been observed that the deer rarely, if ever, browse on alder, which has selectively favoured this particular tree's dominance over some parts of the island. Similarly, an exceptionally large alder wood in the centuries-old deer park on Inchmurrin would appear to be another legacy of the tree's unpalatability to fallow deer. Brown, black and white (often mistaken for albinos) colour forms of the deer occur on Inchlonaig as elsewhere in the area, only the fawns having the characteristic dappled coat typical of parkland fallow.

Modern conifer plantations

The modern conifer plantations differ from those established in the nineteenth century in the high density of trees and by being taken up to much higher ground. These plantings, laid out on a scale never previously undertaken, mainly comprise non-native species. On commercial maturity, the straight-edged, tightly packed blocks lack the beauty and diverse wildlife of the original pine forest and older conifer plantations, which were both characterised by their widely spaced trees, a mixture of other species – most commonly birch and rowan – and a ground flora made up of a variety of ericaceous plants and ferns.

After the initial planting, a few of the open habitat birds – such as the meadow pipit (*Anthus pratensis*) – linger on for a while, but these are gradually replaced by species representative of scrubby heathland. Whinchat (*Saxicola rubetra*) (Fig. 11.10) and stonechat (*S. torquata*) are often the most conspicuous of the new colonists through their habit of often perching right at the very top of the young trees. Heard more often than seen, the grasshopper warbler is also a member of this transient community. Where existing birches are ring-barked and left standing, rather than removed completely as a competitor to the young conifers, fair numbers of lesser redpolls may be attracted, remaining long after the other heathland birds had abandoned the plantation as the trees thickened out.

The post-Second World War boom in conifer plantings on former sheep-walks initially provided heady days for ornithologists with a special interest in upland raptors, for exceptionally high numbers of hawks and owls were attracted by the temporary increase in small mammals and birds. Deep amongst the luxuriant flush of vegetation protected from sheep grazing by forestry fencing, short-tailed voles multiplied rapidly. In the fertile Carron Valley these small rodents reached plague proportions. At the western end of the valley, which was planted out in 1948–50, the tussocky grass became totally undermined by

Fig. 11.10 The whinchat is just one of several heathland species that readily colonise young conifer plantations (John Knowler).

the voles' relentless tunnelling, with serious damage caused to the new plantation by their gnawing the bark of the young trees. By the spring of 1954, an
investigation showed that 16 pairs of short-eared owls (*Asio flammeus*) (Plate 9)
had taken up residence on Gartcarron Hill alone; on average each pair's hunting range was about 16 ha in extent. Then, as inevitably happens after peaks of
excessive abundance, the vole population collapsed. Only two pairs of owls persevered, but both were forced to extend their hunting range by about eight
times. After such a promising start to the breeding season, only one pair managed to fledge young, but even they were unable to find a sufficient number of
voles for their full brood to survive. The numerical relationship between predator and prey is never more in evidence than when glut is followed by famine.

The main thrust of colonisation by the hen harrier centred on the young
plantations of the Kilpatrick Hills, where planting of the hill ground began in
1967. Although the first two or three pairs regularly hunted for small birds
amongst the young trees, they nested on heathery moorland outwith the
forestry enclosures. This was on land still actively 'keepered as grouse moors,
with the result that the first broods of young were illegally destroyed. The
spread of new forestry continued on the Kilpatrick Hills at a rapid pace, and
by the mid-1970s up to six pairs of hen harriers were nesting in or just outside
the afforested areas. As the plantations matured they became progressively
unsuitable for harriers, so that only the odd pair lingers on at the present time.

A game bird to benefit temporarily from the change in land use was the
black grouse, which had experienced a significant fall in numbers through the
loss of its natural habitat of open birch and willow woodland as the result of
overgrazing. But like the other early colonists of the newly planted ground,
black grouse numbers fell back again as the conifers closed in. At this, the plantation's thicket stage, the branches of the closely planted trees interweave with
one another. Brashing (removal of the lower branches up to a height of
approximately 2 m) to give forestry workers access to the plantation and
reduce the size of knots in the wood product, regrettably now seems a thing of
the past. With the light blocked out by an impenetrable mass of dead and
dying branches, the ground flora beneath is suppressed and most of it dies.

Ornithological interest returns when the plantations reach semi-maturity at
around 40 years old, ironically, usually the most economic stage for the trees
to be clear-felled. Unlike Loch Lomondside's native broad-leaved woodlands,
no survey work using the common bird census mapping method has been carried out in the older conifer plantations, not least because of the difficulty in
walking through the unbrashed trees. Line transect counts during the breeding season have been undertaken along some of the forestry roads and fire-
breaks, but these can over-emphasise the semi-open habitat species using the
plantation edge. Within the solid blocks of conifers proper, the most frequently encountered birds are goldcrest, chaffinch, wren, coal tit and robin,
although numerically not always in that order. What really draws the birdwatcher back to the conifer plantations in their latter stages is the siskin and
the common crossbill (*Loxia curvirostra*) in the years which enjoy a prolific
cone crop, especially Sitka spruce. The plumage of the male crossbill can be
either yellow or red, but the bird is readily identifiable by its crossed mandibles
with which it can prise open the cone scales to extract the seeds. This ability to
exploit the yet-to-ripen cones ahead of all the other seed-eating forest birds
allows the crossbill to nest very early in the year, sometimes when the branch-

es are still laden with snow. The top avian predator at the moment in these semi-mature plantations is the sparrowhawk (*Accipiter nisus*), with larch (*Larix* spp.) a favourite nesting tree. However, following a successful reintroduction, the larger goshawk (*A. gentilis*) is making a comeback in Scotland after being driven to extinction by game preservers. The goshawk has already re-established itself as a breeding species in a neighbouring central Scotland forest, with colonisation of Loch Lomondside only a matter of time.

None of the mammals resident on Loch Lomondside are exclusive to the conifer plantations. The red squirrel, which evolved in the boreal forests of Europe, comes the closest. De-afforestation and a prolonged period of cold winters both played their parts in the disappearance of the red squirrel from much of Scotland by the eighteenth century, but the creature recolonised the region from about 1830, following an introduction of Scandinavian animals into the country towards the end of the eighteenth century. So numerous did they become that hundreds were trapped or shot because of the damage they caused to the then newly established larch plantations on Luss Estate. The first half of the twentieth century not only saw a second retraction of the red squirrel's range on Loch Lomondside, but the species' gradual replacement by the introduced North American grey squirrel. Greys have a competitive edge over the reds with their greater ability to exploit deciduous woodland as well. Today, the red squirrel's presence on Loch Lomondside appears dependent on immigration along conifer corridor links with the adjoining Loch Ard and Ardgarten Forests in Perthshire and Argyll.

The extensive forestry plantations have not only been responsible for a substantial increase in the numbers of roe deer in the area, but also a southwards spread of red deer from the Highlands into the Carron Valley and on to the Kilpatrick Hills (Fig. 11.11). Japanese sika deer (*Sika nippon*) are well estab-

Fig. 11.11 The shelter provided by conifer plantations has encouraged red deer to spread throughout the region (Don MacCaskill).

lished in the neighbouring Argyll plantation forests and have already begun to move east. In the event of a major colonisation of Loch Lomondside, this will not be just one more species added to the already long list of non-native animals, but a very real threat to the bloodline of the native red deer with which sika readily interbreed. Introgressive hybridisation with this smaller interloper would be a sad end to Britain's largest surviving land mammal.

Specimen trees

Most of Loch Lomondside's ancestral houses are set within their own parkland. To enhance the landscape further, the planting of ornamental deciduous and conifer trees dates back at least to the seventeenth century. When planted on fertile soil and in spots well sheltered from the wind, some introduced North American species such as Douglas fir (*Pseudotsuga menziesii*) grow well in the cool, moist summers with long daylight hours experienced in the west of Scotland. Measuring and photographing the most noteworthy trees may not be as popular as it once was with the late Victorians, but enthusiasts still occasionally publish their findings. These would seem to suggest that the most productive country house grounds on Loch Lomondside for specimen trees are Culcreuch Castle, Balloch Castle and Stuckgowan House. In 1982, a giant sequoia (*Sequoiadendron giganteum*) at Stuckgowan measured 50 m in height. Unfortunately for what is believed to be Loch Lomondside's tallest tree, its leading shoot suffered dieback during the prolonged drought of 1984.

Less attention has been paid to specimen trees with substantial girths, but a pollarded pedunculate oak in Strathleven Park that measures nearly 9 m at chest height must be one of the largest in the area. To continue to thrive, this fire-hollowed old tree needs to be slowly released from the dense shade created by the conifers unthinkingly planted around it. Robert the Bruce's yew at Stuc an t-Iobairt between Inverbeg and Tarbet has a girth of almost 6 m. As an assumed living link with history, it is one of very few individual trees in Scotland to be named on an Ordnance Survey map. Popular tradition has it that in 1306 while on the run from his enemies, the newly crowned king and a few followers rested for a while under the shelter of its branches. Disappointingly, the pruned central stem was recently aged by a count of its annual rings, showing the tree to be little more than 350 years old. There still remains the possibility that the name Robert the Bruce's yew was transferred from a more ancient but long-gone tree which grew close by. In 1811, it was recorded that this much older yew had a massive girth of 8.5 m (28 ft) with a crown in proportion, but by then was in a state of advanced decay.

What could prove to be a pair of record trees was stumbled upon by chance in a remote glen in the Luss Hills. Examined in 1999, the girth of one fused-stem alder (Fig. 11.12) measured almost 5.72 m. Just a short distance away is a rowan with an exceptional girth for the species of 2.85 m.

Venerable broad-leaved trees are more than just pleasing to the eye, for they provide a habitat for a whole range of woodland invertebrates and epiphytic plants. Many slow-growing corticolous (bark-growing) lichens, which are very sensitive to disturbance, are dependent for their survival on the longer-lived trees such as those that stud the late seventeenth-century parkland around the old castle at Rossdhu. Fortuitously, the northern half of the park was laid out around a stand of ancient woodland that had survived intact into historical

Fig. 11.12 Venerable
trees such as this massive
alder offer refuge to
some of Britain's rarest
invertebrates and lichens.

times, and for landscaping purposes the most picturesque trees were spared the
woodsman's axe. This contrasted with the fate of old woodlands outside of the
park walls, which were regularly cut-over after being drawn into the coppice
management regime. By the time of publication of the first *Statistical Account* for
Luss in 1796, the only trees of large size left in the parish were within the
grounds of Rossdhu House. On the unshaded boles of the well-spaced park
trees over 200 different species of epiphytic lichens have been recorded, some
of them considered indicative of unbroken continuity between their present
hosts and the wildwood of a past age. These include *Arthonia vinosa, Catillaria
atropurpurea, Nephroma laevigatum, Pachyphiale carneola, Schismatomma quercicola,
Thelopsis rubella* and all four members of the *Lobaria* genus occurring in Britain
– *L. amplissima, L. pulmonaria, L. scrobiculata* and *L. virens.* Perhaps not quite in
the same league as one or two outstanding sites in the pollution-free atmosphere of the west coast, Rossdhu Park is nevertheless still classed as one of the
richest localities for lichens of ancient woodland in Scotland.

Some notable woodland species

The purple hairstreak is by far the commonest species of butterfly in the Loch
Lomondside woodlands, but because most of its adult life is spent in the

Fig. 11.13 The purple hairstreak population in Scotland is centred on the Loch Lomondside/Trossachs oak woodlands.

canopy of the trees, making only short fluttering flights from branch to branch, it is rarely noticed from below. The secret of locating this small butterfly during its flight period of mid-July to August is to find a spot where oaks grow at the foot of a small cliff, with the crowns of the trees appearing alongside the observer's vantage point on top of the outcrop (Fig. 11.13). The iridescent coloration of the upper side of the purple hairstreak's wings is only visible from certain angles as it basks open-winged in the sun.

According to an unverifiable report, the ornithologist George Montagu was present when the last of the indigenous race of capercaillie in the area was killed near the head of the loch in 1784, which is only one year before this woodland grouse is believed to have become extinct in Britain. Following a nineteenth-century reintroduction of Scandinavian birds into Scotland in the interests of sport, the 'cock of the woods' was breeding again on Loch Lomondside from 1878, slowly colonising the new conifer plantations over the next 20 years (Plate 10). Partly as the result of large-scale tree felling on the Lomondside estates during the two World Wars, the centre of population moved away from the mainland to the larger wooded islands in the Luss-Strathcashell basin of the loch. Organised counts in late winter have shown the densities of capercaillie recorded on the islands to be amongst the highest in Scotland. Numbers fluctuate from year to year, and reached their peak in 1992 when the mixed pine-birch wood of Inchmoan alone was holding up to 30 birds. One of the most interesting aspects to the Loch Lomond capercaillies is their regular use of woodland other than conifers. The birds are able to nest and rear young successfully in broad-leaved woodland (Plate 11) as long as there is a ground flora of ungrazed blaeberry providing an abundance of invertebrate food for the newly hatched chicks. Fortunately, there are next to no high deer fences on the islands, which have been responsible for a significant casualty rate in capercaillie populations elsewhere. Away from the islands, small numbers of capercaillies are present on the Ross Point at Sallochy and in one isolated large conifer plantation on the Kilpatrick Hills.

As part of a colonisation of Scotland, the pied flycatcher first began to be seen in the district from the early 1950s, although it was not until 1966 that breeding on Loch Lomondside was positively confirmed. Assisted by several nest box schemes, this attractive species has spread throughout most of the more open deciduous woodlands around the loch and on the islands. Particularly favoured by the flycatchers are the sessile oak woods of lower Glen Falloch, where even without the provision of nest boxes, a density of about 20 pairs per km² has been achieved.

After several years of unconfirmed rumours, the first definite sighting of a pine marten on Loch Lomondside for more than a century was made on the Muirpark in May 1984. Later that same year, a single animal was found hanging on a gamekeeper's gibbet at an estate bordering on the Campsie Hills. By 1989 martens were making their presence felt in the Inversnaid woodlands, by tearing off the lids of wooden nest boxes occupied by pied flycatchers and other hole-nesting birds in order to prey on the young (Fig. 11.14). This local problem was overcome by replacing the wooden boxes with marten-proof 'woodcrete' (mixture of sawdust and cement) boxes, already in use at the University Field Station to thwart the destructive attentions of great spotted woodpeckers. Although naturalists welcome the return of the marten, they are aware that these agile, tree-climbing predators could pose a threat to the district's few remaining red squirrels. As the pine marten continues to recolonise its old Lomondside haunts, casual observations suggest it is already making significant inroads into the well-established North American grey squirrel population. If this proves to be the case, it will be the first effective check in grey squirrel numbers since this species began to colonise the district almost 100 years ago.

It may seem a little odd to include an antipodean marsupial as a notable woodland species, but no other Loch Lomondside animal has attracted the

media's attention more than the feral population of red-necked wallabies (*Macropus rufogriseus*). Descended from two Whipsnade Zoo-bred pairs released on Inchconnachan about 1975, a census in 1999 produced a count of 43 individuals on the tree-covered island. Contrary to popular conception, the wallabies experience little difficulty in swimming over open water, an unknown number of them having dispersed onto the mainland over the years. A study of the Inchconnachan wallabies' feeding habits has showed their diet to consist mainly of blaeberry and heather, together with various grasses.

Fig. 11.14 Pine martens can easily predate conventional bird boxes (Don MacCaskill).

It would seem that freedom from disturbance and the relatively mild winter temperatures experienced in their water-surrounded woodland habitat have been key factors in the Inchconnachan colony's establishment. But this success may yet prove the animals' undoing, for at their present level of browsing the wallabies are considered a threat to the island's blaeberry-dominated ground vegetation and its dependent native fauna.

12

Muirs and Mountains

'The hill lands are one of Scotland's most precious features ... from all
over the world visitors come to see their magnificent scenery. The
wildlife is an important part of this richness. Imagine how bleak our
hills would be if no golden eagles swept over the ridges, no arctic-
alpine flowers shone like jewels on the dark rocks, and no heather
bloomed on the moors.'

'Wildlife on the Hill' (Adam Watson) in
Wildlife of Scotland (Holliday, 1979)

Completing Loch Lomondside's outstanding diversity of wildlife habitats is the
high country above the old head dykes. It is unfortunate that when compar-
isons are made with Scotland's most imposing massifs, such as Ben Nevis, the
Cairngorms and the Torridon range, the Lomondside hills and mountains
hardly ever receive their just recognition. Yet they have their own individual
appeal. This lies not only in the variety of topographical features, but in their
ready accessibility to Scotland's largest urban population.

Muir burning coupled with sheep grazing have together brought about dramatic changes to the vegetation cover of the Loch Lomondside uplands in the
last 250 years. Fire as a management tool has been used by stock graziers since
Neolithic times. Carried out in a judicious manner, burning is an effective
method of removing old plant growth to make way for a flush of palatable
young shoots, the soil becoming temporarily richer in minerals absorbed from
the ashes of the fire. But from the middle of the eighteenth century, when the
practice was followed by a high stocking density of sheep selectively feeding on
the new growth, loss of heather was inevitable. As one agricultural writer of the
period observed: 'Where the heath has been burned, there is always a powerful growth of grass ... the heath has by degrees disappeared, and the dusky
mountains become covered with a lively verdure'. This apparent satisfaction at
the change in appearance of the uplands was ill-founded, for on the rain-sodden and mineral-depleted soils of the west of Scotland the ling heather and
other heathland plants were being replaced by nutritionally poorer species
such as mat-grass (*Nardus stricta*), purple moor-grass, deergrass (*Trichophorum
cespitosum*), common cottongrass (*Eriophorum angustifolium*) and heath rush
(*Juncus squarrosus*). Bracken too was gaining a competitive advantage from the
practice of over-firing the heather, the dormant rhizomes of this aggressive
fern safely under the ground when the spring burning was carried out. As the
quality of the pasture gradually declined, the high numbers of sheep could no
longer be sustained, with the result that in recent years, large areas of the
upland grazings have been sold off for conifer afforestation.

For the purposes of this chapter, the Lomondside uplands have been divid-

Fig. 12.1 The Campsie Hills or Fells, the alternative name derived from the old Norse word *fjell*.

ed into four geographical areas: the southern foothills, the Luss Hills bordering the Highland Line, the northern plateaux and finally the mountains with their high-level crags and sub-arctic summits.

The southern foothills

Dissected by the movement of past glaciers, the southern foothills comprise three sections of the Clyde Lava Plateau – the Kilpatrick, Campsie (Fig. 12.1) and Fintry Hills. Each of the plateau's three distinct blocks differ in their main habitat types; the Campsie Hills' high-level blanket bogs and northern corries, the Fintry Hills' south facing and, in places, calcareous basaltic crags, the Kilpatrick Hills' reservoirs, extensive conifer plantations and remaining sweeps of heather moor, which descend to relatively low levels on the hills' north-western edge.

The most elevated land of the lava plateau is covered by blanket bog, a thick layer of compacted and partly decomposed plant remains that has developed directly on top of the waterlogged mineral soils. Like all of the Loch Lomondside uplands, the foothills have been subject to intensive sheep grazing and regular heath burning over a long period, and much of the former ling heather cover has been replaced by common bent (*Agrostis tenuis*), sheep's fescue (*Festuca ovina*) and mat-grass dominated grasslands. With their close proximity to the Clyde conurbation, the southern foothills also have a history of being affected by atmospheric pollution since the beginning of the coal and coke-fired Industrial Revolution. As far back as the 1870s, Glasgow cryptogamists had become aware that something was seriously amiss, recording that there was scarcely any species of lichen to be found in a state of fructification within a 10 mile (16 km) radius of the city. Few observations on dele-

terious changes to other plants of the city's surrounding countryside appear
to have been made, but moorland species such as the round-leaved sundew,
bog-myrtle, woolly fringe moss (*Rhacomitrium lanuginosum*) and, most importantly, the peat-forming bog mosses, have been shown in other parts of industrialised Britain to retreat in the face of soot-laden emissions from mill, factory and town. Providing the level of pollution is not too high, however, a few
upland plants such as cottongrass and blaeberry show no visible sign of deterioration; in fact with reduced competition they may even spread over a much
wider area.

With low cohesion within the accumulated peat, all blanket bogs are inherently unstable and susceptible to natural erosion by the weather elements. It is
believed, however, that on Loch Lomondside's southern foothills the pace of
this degenerative process has quickened over the last two hundred or so years,
the result of poor growth in the peat-forming sphagnum mosses. Apart from
atmospheric pollution, excessive muir burning can destroy the living top layer
of water-retentive sphagnum moss. Moor-gripping (the cutting of open drains
in the peat) is also implicated, accelerating the fragmentation of the bog surface. Hart Hill (522 m) in the Campsies is the least degraded example of blanket bog, but even here the surface has broken up into a network of peat haggs
bisected by deep gullies. Despite this deterioration, just to see the carpeting of
cloudberry (Plate 12) and cowberry is well worth the climb. Up to the mid-
1980s, a strong presence of golden plover (*Pluvialis apricaria*) was another of
Hart Hill's attractions. Some of the birds were 'northern' in type, in that the
black markings on the face continued in a narrow but unbroken strip to the
black underparts. There was even an accompanying pair or two of dunlin,
sometimes referred to as the 'plover's page'. Regrettably, the current depleted
numbers of upland waders holding territory on Hart Hill in spring is a story
repeated throughout the southern foothills. With a marked reduction in pest
control, unchecked increases in both fox and carrion crow (*Corvus corone*)
numbers have undoubtedly played their parts in the decline. The few breeding pairs of hen harriers present on the southern foothills are not confined to
heather moor or young forestry – the most common habitats for the species –
but will readily nest in a bed of rushes, a fact first noted over 200 years ago by
one of the local parish ministers.

Remains of old shooting butts, where sportsmen awaited the driven red
grouse, point to this game bird's former importance in the area. Red grouse
are unique to Britain, and as such have attracted sportsmen from all over the
world to pit their shooting skills against these fast-flying birds. The numbers of
grouse go through cyclic fluctuations on these rather wet heather moors. In
the autumn of 1988 – following one of the best breeding seasons in recent
years – a quite exceptional assemblage by today's standards of over 250 red
grouse gathered on Hart Hill for the berry crop. Another species present that
is subject to rises and falls in abundance is the blue hare. Curiously, none of
the early naturalists' accounts of Loch Lomondside's mammal fauna make any
mention of the blue hare below the Highland Line, which would seem to suggest that the isolated population on the southern foothills originates from
sporting introductions by the nineteenth-century proprietors of the moors.
The animal's numbers were at an exceptionally high peak when the Forestry
Commission established a 464 ha plantation on the northern Kilpatrick Hills
in 1967. In order to protect the seedling trees, several hundred blue hares

were shot within the enclosure in the two years following the completion of the encircling fence.

The successive layers of basaltic lavas exposed along the northern and western edges of the Campsie hills vary considerably in their mineral content and in consequence both calcicole and calcifuge plants can often be found growing in close proximity. One moderately rich basalt outcropping at Black Spout, a minor waterfall near the base of the north-facing scarp, is festooned with mossy saxifrage (*Saxifraga hypnoides*), wood crane's-bill (*Geranium sylvaticum*) and red campion (Plate 13), with sheets of opposite-leaved golden saxifrage where water continually trickles down the rock. Higher up the northern face, the vegetation becomes distinctly more montane in the twin Corries of Balglass, both carved out by small corrie glaciers at the time of the Loch Lomond Stadial glaciation. In addition to the basalts, a high-level exposure of Ballagan Cementstones in the Little Corrie of Balglass adds to the beneficial effect of mineral flushing on the flora. Upland species represented in the two corries include roseroot (*Sedum rosea*), pink stonecrop (*S. villosum*), northern bedstraw (*Galium boreale*), chickweed willowherb (*Epilobium alsinifolium*), yellow mountain saxifrage (*Saxifraga aizoides*) and fine tufts of the silky red moss *Orthothecium rufescens*. More typical of the acidic outcrops, parsley fern (*Cryptogramma crispa*) maintains a precarious footing in the unstable screes of loose stones below the frost-shattered cliffs. Even though the Campsies reach 578 m in height, these hills lack a surprising number of the commoner mountain flowers of Scotland, such as alpine lady's mantle, which is both widespread and abundant in the Highlands just to the north. The covering of forest on these hills during the climatic optimum could explain these flowers' local extinction, the Clyde Lava Plateau's isolated position ensuring that few montane species would recolonise after the tree cover disappeared.

Contrasting with the shady and usually damp northern corries of the Campsies are the dry, south-facing cliffs of the Fintry Hills on the other side of the Endrick Valley. One of these outcrops – Double Craigs (Fig. 12.2) – supports a very localised assemblage of calcicole plants, including limestone bedstraw (*Galium sterneri*), spring cinquefoil (*Potentilla neumanniana*), vernal sandwort (*Minuartia verna*), kidney vetch (*Anthyllis vulneraria*) and common rockrose (*Helianthemum nummularium*). Exposed to most of the available sunlight, these basalt crags are particularly rich in saxicolous (rock-growing) lichens. The drought-resistant grasses squirrel-tail fescue (*Vulpia bromoides*) and yellow oat-grass (*Trisetum flavescens*), which are present in the dry grassland below the Double Craigs, are an indication of the much lower average annual rainfall experienced in the extreme southeastern portion of an otherwise very wet region. Jumbles of fallen rocks below the cliffs offer a retreat for the hill fox; and despite the strenuous efforts of the foxcatchers every cubbing season, the local population continues to hold its own. One dog fox killed near Fintry in January 1998 was found to weigh 12.25 kg (27lb), a remarkable size for the species by any standard. Todholes and Balgair are two settlements in the Fintry area named after the fox.

Upland birds are generally well represented on the Clyde Plateau's terraced scarps or amongst the boulders and screes below; peregrine (see p. 192), kestrel (*Falco tinnunculus*), common buzzard, raven, ring ouzel (*Turdus torquatus*), wheatear (*Oenanthe oenanthe*) and twite (*Carduelis flavirostris*) all finding a nesting niche. Observations have shown that the kestrel population rises and

Fig. 12.2 On the southern flank of the Fintry Hills, the Double Craigs are noted for their community of calcicole plants.

falls with the periodic fluctuations in the numbers of short-tailed voles in the hill grazings. In years of high vole activity, up to three pairs of kestrels have been found nesting on a single cliff. Buzzards soar effortlessly on the scarp's updraughts, their keen eyes watching for the slightest movement betraying the presence of rabbits, or the corpse of an unfortunate sheep that had strayed too near the cliff edge. The ravens on the Kilpatrick–Campsie–Fintry Hills have been much persecuted since intensive sheep raising and grouse management began. Despite the suppression of their numbers, up to the 1960s at least four ancestral breeding sites were still occupied, but these fell vacant one by one until only a single tenacious pair remained. Circumstantial evidence relating to the latter stages of the raven's decline pointed to an upsurge in the illegal laying-out of poisoned baits to kill foxes and carrion/hooded crows instead of the more traditional methods of control. From the late 1980s onwards, the species made an almost unbelievable comeback with up to eight nesting pairs in residence, some in locations not known to hold ravens in living memory.

After a long winter, the far-carrying song of the first ring ouzel of the season is guaranteed to lift the spirit of anyone out and about on the hill in early April. Sad to say, however, in the last few years the numbers of ring ouzels have been steadily dropping, and favourite sites that could once be depended upon are now disappointingly silent. Usually the first bird to attract observer attention by its warning 'chacking' from a prominent position, the wheatear shows a strong preference for turf closely grazed by sheep and rabbits amongst the fallen boulders below the cliffs. The twite or mountain linnet on the other hand can be easily overlooked until one becomes familiar with the male's 'sweazy' song. On the Campsie and Fintry Hills the twite's favoured nesting habitat is a well-vegetated cliff out of reach of sheep, a good example being the steep east

Fig. 12.3 The Corrie of Balglass on the north face of the Campsies; a habitat for upland plants and birds in the Lowlands.

face of the Corrie of Balglass (Fig. 12.3) with its patchy covering of dark-leaved willow (*Salix myrsinifolia*) and eared willow (*S. aurita*). Differing markedly in their choice of habitat from the heather-moor nesting twite of the English Pennines, these low shrub-nesting birds of the southern foothills could well be direct descendants of those early colonists of the boreal scrub that covered these hills following the last glacial period.

Two hundred years ago the impressive amphitheatre of the Corrie of Balglass was home to the southern foothills' only nesting pair of golden eagles. Just the occasional eagle is seen on the Campsies these days, usually when the population of blue hares is at one of its periodic peaks. Another lost breeding bird of the area is the chough (*Pyrrhocorax pyrrhocorax*). Reported as already rare on these hills by the 1790s, the 'red-legged crow' vanished as an inland species throughout the Clyde area soon after. Naturalists of the day attributed its retreat to the west coast to an increase in the number of jackdaws (*Corvus monedula*) taking over the chough's nesting cliffs, although it is probable that another contributory cause was the run of severe winters that set in towards the end of the eighteenth century, seriously affecting food availability for this essentially insectivorous bird. Playing a part too must have been the move away from hill cattle in favour of sheep, depriving the chough of an invertebrate food source beneath the numerous cow-pats.

The Kilpatricks stand out from both the Campsie and Fintry Hills in the number of lochans and man-made reservoirs. In spring, Burncrooks Reservoir attracts several pairs of ringed plover and common sandpiper to nest around its wave-eroded stony edge. Some of the commoner species of waterfowl – including the occasional pair of feral greylag geese – and gull nest safely on its largest island. Close to Burncrooks is Kilmannan Reservoir, which has had a chequered history of use. Originally one of the very few natural water bodies in the Kilpatrick Hills, it was enlarged in the late eighteenth century to provide compensation water to the River Kelvin, which was being drawn upon to top up the newly opened Forth and Clyde Canal. The fact that the River Kelvin powered Glasgow's meal mills at Partick is the reason why Kilmannan Reservoir is also known as the Bakers' Loch. Ownership of Kilmannan by the British Waterways Board was relinquished in the late 1970s, when it was linked to Burncrooks and incorporated into the public water supply. Since then Kilmannan Reservoir has been subject to wide fluctuations in surface levels, adversely affecting the nesting success of its great crested grebes. The change in regime does appear to have favoured Kilmannan's population of tiny water-worts (*Elatine* spp.), for exceptionally large carpets of these infrequently seen plants, together with the rare moss *Bryum cyclophyllum*, appear on the drying-out bed of the reservoir in summers when the water level is drawn down (Plate 14). At 310 m, the wind-sheltered western edge of the Lily Loch below Duncolm has several patches of the rare hybrid water-lily *Nuphar* x *spenneriana*, although neither of the parent plants (yellow water-lily and least yellow water-lily *Nuphar pumila*) appear to be present today.

Only small scattered pockets of blanket bog remain on the Kilpatricks, with much of the upper ground either planted with conifers or moor-gripped and drying out. Draining has been least successful in a rock basin hollow just to the north of the Lily Loch, where the two bog sedges *Carex limosa* and *C. magellanica* still hang on. Despite recent forestry planting, there are still extensive stands of ling heather. This is the chosen habitat of the merlin (*Falco columbarius*), which preys almost exclusively on small birds like the meadow pipit. The larger day-flying moths will also be taken by this smallest of falcons. In such wide open country a merlin territory can be difficult to locate, the few records available suggesting that tree-nesting in an abandoned crow's nest is more frequent than a ground nest site on these moors. Golden plover and dunlin seem to have disappeared as nesting species on the northern Kilpatrick Hills, but curlew are still common along the moorland edge. On Pappert Muir, in the northwest corner of the Kilpatrick Hills, the heather merges with rough grazings partially covered with bracken and common gorse. In summer this heathland is ideal for nesting whinchat and stonechat, any black grouse present showing preference for areas with small clumps of trees.

The Luss Hills

Just over the Highland Line on the west side of the loch, the rounded tops of the Luss Hills (Fig. 12.4) contrast with the irregular relief of the mountains beyond them to the north. It is on the Luss Hills that the botanist first meets up with the Highland schists, although at the southern slaty edge of the formation, mountain flowers are initially rather sparse on these mineral-poor rocks. Careful searching of the upland flushes and rills will, however, reveal the presence of alpine bistort (*Persicaria vivipara*), alpine meadow-rue (*Thalictrum alpinum*) and three-flowered rush (*Juncus triglumis*), all three of these relatively common upland species apparently absent from the foothills of the Clyde Lava Plateau only a short distance away. The most southerly cliffs – Corrie Cuinne at the head of Glen Finlas – offer mountain male fern (*Dryopteris oreades*), holly fern (*Polystichum lonchitus*), purple saxifrage (*Saxifraga oppositifolia*) and an inland colony of sea campion (*Silene uniflora*). Although the sea campion is

Fig. 12.4 The Luss Hills on the southwestern fringe of the Grampian Highlands.

understandably considered a coastal plant, it too is as much a postglacial colonist as the other montane species, surviving in scattered upland localities where it has not been shaded out by woodland cover. Creag an Leinibh in Glen Luss adds alpine scurvy-grass (*Cochlearia pyrenaica* ssp. *alpina*), alpine saw-wort (*Saussurea alpina*) and the whortle-leaved willow (*Salix myrsinites*) to the list. Another upland plant, the northern buckler fern, finds shelter amongst the boulder scree below Beinn Eich on the opposite side of the glen. Doune Hill (734 m) above Glen Douglas has the most diverse montane flora of all the Luss Hills, with moss campion and Scottish asphodel (*Tofieldia pusilla*) reflecting the hill's outcrops of calcareous schist.

There are a few localised colonies of the scotch argus butterfly (*Erebia aethiops*) amongst the purple moor-grass in some of the glens, usually where the insect can gain a little shelter from the wind in a scattering of small trees. Upland birds tend to be rather thin on the ground, making it possible to walk over the closely grazed summits without seeing more than a distant glimpse of a wary hooded crow. On these hills the ornithologist must select the most profitable looking spots very carefully, such as choosing Creachan Hill with its eroding peat haggs as the best chance of picking up golden plover. Peregrine and raven are about, but tucked away in hidden ravines. Even the golden eagle has nested in one or two remote corners of the Luss Hills in years past and could well do so again.

The northern plateaux

The slow but continual breaking down of mica schist by weathering gives the southwest Grampian Mountains their characteristic moderately steep silhouettes. Slope erosion is much slower where there are outcrops of more resistant

Fig. 12.5 Studded with small lochans, the Caorann Plateau is Loch Lomondside's premier habitat for upland waders.

rock. A prime example is to be found on the southern flank of the Ben Lui–Ben Oss–Beinn Dubhchraig watershed ridge, where the gradient abruptly eases off into the high-level Caorann Plateau (Fig. 12.5). For the most part between 400 and 525 m, the plateau is underlain by a hard garnetiferous schist. Its mantle of blanket bog, dominated by ling heather, deergrass, cottongrass and purple moor-grass, is broken up by a mosaic of exposed knolls and ridges, in places covered by a dwarf-shrub heath of blaeberry, crowberry, cowberry and cloudberry. A feature of the area is the high number of lochans and pools – about 70 in all – scattered over the plateau. Although the vegetation in and around the peaty lochans and pools is generally rather sparse, the isolated Lochan a' Mhadaidh (the lochan of the wolf) is one of the exceptions, with an aquatic flora that includes awlwort and Nordic bladderwort (*Urticularia stygia*), but best of all a large patch of the very uncommon least yellow water-lily.

Both approach glens to the Caorann Plateau from the Glen Falloch road are not without interest in themselves. In early spring the call of the ring ouzel still rings out from amongst the rowans that cling to the cliffs. Especially noteworthy is the occurrence of the very local pale butterwort. On Loch Lomondside this markedly western species is confined to the warmer south-facing slopes where ground water draining from mineral-rich rocks above seeps out of exposed peat below.

Red deer are usually to be seen on the Caorann, except during the warmer summer months when they move up to the ridge tops to pick up a breeze to escape the persistent attention from flies, or to seek out a north-facing late snow patch to cool off in the midday sun. From late September through October, the return of the stags to the plateau and surrounding glens is proclaimed by their 'roaring' as they challenge for the hinds during the rut. Only in the face of

severe weather do they descend right down to the low ground to forage wherever they can. Of additional interest on the plateau to the visiting mammalogist
is a high-altitude population of water voles, which extends all the way up to
Loch Oss at 640 m. Despite the area's high rainfall, the steep slopes immediately below the plateau ensure a rapid runoff of excess water, so that the voles'
tunnels beside the lochans and burns are only infrequently washed out. This is
in marked contrast to their cousins along the Lowland river banks, where the
voles are forced to migrate to higher ground to avoid the seasonal flooding.
Mink have been observed following up the watercourses issuing from the
plateau, showing all too clearly the potential threat of this alien predator to
water vole colonies throughout their Loch Lomondside range.

In spring, the plaintive piping of golden plover and the trilling song of displaying dunlin captures the very spirit of the Caorann. Census figures confirm
that in a good year, there can be up to 16 territorial pairs of golden plover and
14 pairs of dunlin. These relatively high densities of the two species on the
plateau are quite atypical of Loch Lomondside as a whole. Snipe and common
sandpiper are also present in small numbers. For the upland ornithologist,
however, the blue riband wader is the occasional nesting pair of greenshank
(*Tringa nebularia*) (see p. 192), although just as exciting for the observer concerned was the chance discovery of a displaying wood sandpiper in June 1968.
But winter-like conditions are always waiting in the wings; and what would be
just a spring shower lower down in the glens can be a blizzard at these altitudes. Periodic monitoring undertaken over a number of years has shown that
the plateau's wader population is very vulnerable to any prolonged deterioration in the weather conditions in May and June. When this occurs, few birds
are able to rear young successfully.

Roughly 8 km to the southwest is another rewarding, yet seldom visited,
locality for upland waders as well as the occasional pair of nesting red-throated divers (*Gavia stellata*) (Plate 15). The Maol Meadhonach–Maol
Breac–Beinn Damhain Plateau is underlain by a complex of hard igneous
rocks, exhibiting a similar terrain to the Caorann of glacially scoured knolls
and gouged depressions occupied by shallow lochans. The flora of the plateau
has been little studied, but bearberry (*Arctostophylus uva-ursi*) and dwarf
juniper are both on record.

The mountains

The given summit heights of Loch Lomondside's higher hills and mountains
vary slightly according to which edition of the Ordnance Survey map is consulted. In the list below, the imperial measurements of the summit heights
are taken from the out of print but still much used *Loch Lomond and the
Trossachs Tourist Map* (1983), and are followed by the measurements from the
most recent metric maps, on which spot-heights are rounded off to the nearest metre.

'Munros' (summits over 3,000 ft / 914 m) within the Loch Lomond catchment are:

The Highland fringe
Ben Lomond 3,194 ft (974 m)
The Arrochar range (in ascending order)
Ben Vane 3,004 ft (915 m)

Beinn Narnain 3,040 ft (926 m)
Ben Vorlich 3,093 ft (943 m)
Beinn Ime 3,318 ft (1,011 m)
The Glen Falloch range eastern group (in ascending order)
Beinn Chabhair 3,053 ft (933 m)
Beinn a' Chroin 3,084 ft (940 m)
An Caisteal 3,265 ft (995 m)
Cruach Ardrain 3,428 ft (1,046 m)
The Glen Falloch range western group (in ascending order)
Beinn a' Chleibh 3,008 ft (916 m)
Beinn Dubhcraig 3,204 ft (978 m)
Ben Oss 3,374 ft (1,029 m)
Ben Lui 3,708 ft (1,130 m)

There are also seven mountain tops over 2,500 ft (726 m), but only two – Meall an Fhudair 764 m and Beinn a' Choin 770 m – are classed as 'Corbetts', which in order to qualify must have a drop of at least 500 ft (152 m) between the hill's summit and any adjacent higher peak. This ruling disqualifies such fine hills as A'Chrois at 848 m in the Arrochar range, as the drop between its summit and beginning the ascent of neighbouring Beinn Narnain is only 107 m. Observed from most angles, however, A'Chrois appears as a well-defined individual peak in its own right.

The altitudinal zonation of the region's mountain vegetation can be seen to advantage on the open ground above the forestry plantations on Ben Lomond, especially if viewed from the opposite side of the loch in late summer. At that time of the year the bracken on the lower slopes is just beginning to turn gold, succeeded up the hillside by the fading purple of the remaining ling heather. The heather gives way to the dark green of blaeberry where it is not hard grazed, followed in turn by the yellowing mat-grass merging into the partially vegetated thin soils and frost-shattered rock detritus at the very top. What is totally missing above today's abrupt upper tree line is a montane shrub zone, which, throughout the Lomondside uplands, has long since vanished in the face of relentless browsing by domestic stock, first cattle and goats and then sheep.

The story of the scientific exploration of Loch Lomondside's mountainous region begins on Ben Lomond – Scotland's most southerly and Stirlingshire's only Munro – with an ascent by the Reverend John Lightfoot on 13 June 1772, while gathering material for his *Flora Scotica* (1777). For the most part only the commoner mountain species were recorded by Lightfoot and his companion the Reverend John Stuart on that day, but it was enough to put Ben Lomond on the botanical map. Regrettably, the depredations of covetous collectors and nurserymen with an eye to profit which followed the book's publication was to lead to the extirpation of several of the Ben's rarer arctic-alpines. Such was the demand for trailing azalea (*Loiseleuria procumbens*) for example, that the asking price at the time was half a guinea per plant, more than a week's wage for most. The former presence of some of the species that have apparently disappeared from Ben Lomond can at least be confirmed from preserved dried specimens in botanical collections, such as the rare mountain bladder fern (*Cystopteris montana*). Most intriguing of all of Ben Lomond's 'lost' plants is a herbarium specimen of the Arctic bramble (*Rubus arcticus*), which has not been reported from the Scottish Highlands since the mid-nineteenth century. Although it is

Fig. 12.6 The east face of Ben Lomond rises steeply above the old steading of Comer – birthplace of Mary MacGregor, wife of Rob Roy.

unlikely that all of the following species would be seen during the course of a single visit, montane flowering plants that still occur sparingly on the Ben's higher slopes and rock ledges include alpine mouse-ear (*Cerastium alpinum*), downy willow (*Salix lapponum*), hoary whitlowgrass (*Draba incana*), alpine saxifrage (*Saxifraga nivalis*), alpine cinquefoil (*Potentilla crantzii*), sibbaldia (*Sibbaldia procumbens*), alpine willowherb (*Epilobium anagallidifolium*), spiked woodrush (*Luzula spicata*), black alpine sedge (*Carex atrata*), glaucous meadow-grass (*Poa glauca*) and the alpine meadow-grass (*P. alpina*), in addition to most of the upland plants already listed for Loch Lomondside's southern hills. Hardier species growing on the summit ridge, where the sub-alpine soils are poorly developed and the protective snow cover is frequently blown away by strong winds – dwarf willow, dwarf cudweed (*Gnaphalium supinum*), stiff sedge (*Carex bigelowii*), three-leaved rush (*Juncus trifidus*), alpine clubmoss (*Diphasiastrum alpinum*) and the woolly fringe moss – are adapted to withstand repeated freeze-thaw winter temperatures and exposure to wind by their prostrate, cushion or low tussock modes of growth. Of the high-level flowerless plants, the high northeastern corrie of Ben Lomond (Fig. 12.6) has at least three montane lichens at the southern edge of their British range – *Pertusaria dactylina*, *Stereocaulon tornense* and *Micarea subviolascens* – the last two associated with late snow patches, which in the corrie can persist until late June. The snow bed moss *Kiaeria starkei* is also present, along with meltwater-fed greyish carpets of the liverwort *Anthelia julacea*. These tiny lichens and bryophytes were almost certainly amongst Lomondside's earliest colonists in the wake of the final retreat of glacial ice, providing a foothold for a succession of other plants and the botanist with a link through time to a much colder age.

It was after his second tour of Scotland in 1772 that zoologist Thomas

Pennant became the first traveller to report that ptarmigan (*Lagopus mutus*) (see p. 193) were to be found on the upper slopes of Ben Lomond. The south-west ridge leading down from the summit appropriately bears the bird's name. Another visitor, a nineteenth-century excursionist who made it to the top, wrote of ravens waiting patiently about the summit to feed on the discarded scraps of his repast. There are a number of other early records of Ben Lomond birds scattered in the travel and ornithological literature, the most unusual a snowy owl (*Nyctea scandiaca*) which, according to Robert Gray in his *Birds of the West of Scotland* (1871), was regularly observed in the early winter of 1869. The owl made frequent descents to the low ground and appeared to be feeding almost entirely on grouse. Although forestry plantations have covered over most of the lower purple moor-grass slopes, the scotch argus butterfly can still be found locally immediately above Ardess. However, the main attraction to the butterfly enthusiast is the presence further up in the southwest corrie of the small mountain ringlet (*Erebia epiphron*) (see p. 191). The moths of the higher ground are very underworked despite Ben Lomond's accessibility, but to be fair the sheep-degraded state of the heather and blaeberry offers little incentive for visiting lepidopterists to devote their time. Amongst the upland species recorded to date are the grey mountain carpet (*Entephria caesiata*), the yellow-ringed carpet (*E. flavicinctata*) – the larvae apparently feeding exclusively on yellow mountain saxifrage on Ben Lomond – and a montane grassland pyralid moth *Udea uliginosalis*.

Beinn Ime, the highest of the Arrochar Hills, has a mountain flora much akin to Ben Lomond. Although two or three species already listed for Ben Lomond are apparently absent, the botanist ascending Beinn Ime on its northeastern side is compensated by some fine flushes of russet sedge (*Carex saxatilis*), alpine lady fern (*Athyrium distentifolium*) and the only known station in the district for the Arctic mouse-ear (*Cerastium arcticum*) (Fig. 12.7). The montane lady's mantles *Alchemilla glomerulans* and *A. wichurae* are also known from this hill. Chestnut rush (*Juncus castaneus*) was reliably reported in the past and, although there are no modern records, further careful searching and a little luck could well lead to this species' reinstatement. Before moving on, those of a nervous disposition should perhaps be warned that the summit has a reputation for being haunted. In *Highland Gathering* (1960), ornithologist Kenneth Richmond recalled how, when looking for ptarmigan on a winter's day, he met up with the Old Man of Beinn Ime who left no footprints in the snow, the reason he insisted he would never go back there again.

Easily reached even in the nineteenth century by making use of the steamer services on the loch, Ben Vorlich was a favourite haunt of that doyen amongst Scottish naturalists, John Hutton Balfour, Professor of Botany at the University of Edinburgh. Balfour's diaries for 1846–78 confirm that he often took his students there on summer field excursions. One montane plant regularly found and entered into his meticulously kept journal was the interrupted clubmoss (*Lycopodium annotinum*). Ben Vorlich is the most southerly extant site for the species in Scotland. Another good find of Balfour's on this hill was the spring quillwort (*Isoetes echinospora*), an aquatic plant of nutrient-poor mountain pools. Amongst several other famous names attracted to Dunbartonshire's highest mountain was the Reverend C.A. Johns, best known as author of *Flowers of the Field* which passed through numerous editions. In one of his other popular works, *Botanical Rambles* (1846), the umbrella-carrying cleric tells us that

Fig. 12.7 The Arctic mouse-ear – which occurs on Beinn Ime – is very uncommon in the southern Highlands.

on reaching the summit, he enlivened his sandwiches with the tart leaves of mountain sorrel (*Oxyria digyna*). A second distinguished man of the cloth, the Reverend E.S. Marshall, was to add mountain scurvy-grass (*Cochlearia micacea*) and a high-level form of yellow rattle (ssp. *borealis*) to Ben Vorlich's already extensive plant list.

Contrasting with the moderately calcareous rock outcrops, which occur here and there on the hills and mountains already mentioned, are the acidic schists and hard igneous intrusions of the Meall an Fhudair–Troisgeach ridge near the head of the loch. This is the best locality in the district to look for the trailing azalea, although it is a plant of rock crevices rather than a component of a stony ground community as on Scotland's granite hills further north. A generally uncommon species in the southwest Highlands, the dwarf cornel (*Cornus suecica*) grows in late snow lie hollows on Troisgeach's northern face. Troisgeach is also one of the few known sites in the area for the small and inconspicuous bog orchid. A few pairs of golden plover are thinly scattered over the summit ridge in summer, but with most of the ridge below 726 m, the other attraction is as one of the least exhausting to reach haunts of ptarmigan on Loch Lomondside.

Beyond the old inn at Inverarnan, where many of the early botanists regularly stayed, Glen Falloch offers a number of opportunities to familiarise oneself with the region's montane flora. It should be noted, however, that the really productive ground of some of these West Perthshire mountains lies on their northern faces in the catchment of the River Tay, outwith the Loch Lomond area described here. Beinn a' Chroin, An Caisteal and Cruach Ardrain in the eastern block were all well worked by the indefatigable Victorian botanists after the railway link from Glasgow and Edinburgh to Crianlarich near the head of Glen Falloch was completed in 1873. Included among the many arctic-alpines

that fell to their grasp were reticulate willow (*Salix reticulata*) and alpine woodsia (*Woodsia alpina*) (see p. 191), together with several endemic mountain
hawkweeds (*Hieracium* spp.). Beinn Chabhair – the only other eastern Munro
– never received the same attention in the past because of its distance from the
railway station at Crianlarich. Yet the hill is not without botanical interest, as
latter-day records of sheathed sedge (*Carex vaginata*) and chestnut rush show.

To the Munro-bagger, western Glen Falloch offers the most challenging
ridgewalk in the district – three (even four at a push) major peaks attainable
from the one ascent. The first Munro in line, Beinn Dubhchraig, is blessed
with a south-facing, high-level exposure of Loch Tay Limestone, most importantly rendered coarsely crystalline and crumbly through contact with the
metamorphic schists. This 'sugar' limestone is literally crammed with choice
plants, not least the rock speedwell (*Veronica fruticans*), mountain willow (*Salix
arbuscula*) and the easily overlooked hair sedge (*Carex capillaris*). Below the
exposure, the well-drained and invertebrate-rich limestone soils are inhabited
by Loch Lomondside's highest known moles. The mole's ability to thrive at
such altitudes in ground that can be frozen solid, often for weeks at a time, is
extraordinary. Common frogs, which breed in the small pools, adapt to the
usually low summer temperatures at these heights by the tadpole stage taking
two years to complete.

Rock ledges in the more calcareous schist of Beinn Dubhchraig provide further additions to the region's mountain flowers, notably the semi-parasitic
alpine bartsia (*Bartsia alpina*) and a large-flowered variety of northern rock-
cress (*Arabis petraea*), which leading botanist George Claridge Druce named
grandiflora from material he had gathered on these hills. From February
onwards a pair of ravens regularly occupy the rather barren-looking cliffs
above Loch Oss (Fig. 12.8). The advantage to the carrion-dependent ravens in

Fig. 12.8 Loch Oss; an ice-gouged corrie lochan or cirque lake at the foot of Beinn
Dubhchraig.

such an early start to their breeding cycle is the frequency of winter casualties amongst the red deer and sheep. At 850 m (2,790 ft), this is the highest raven site in the district, and the nest is lined thickly with sheep's wool to prevent the eggs chilling in the harsh conditions. Near the summit of Beinn Dubhchraig and that of neighbouring Ben Oss are found the diminutive cushions of mossy cyphel (*Minuartia sedoides*) – the region's only montane flowering species that is exclusively alpine (that is, does not also occur in the Arctic) – together with several uncommon to nationally rare liverworts indicative of the high altitude: *Scapania nimbosa*, *S. ornithopodioides* (both western in their distribution), *Anthelia juratzkana*, *Nardia breidleri* and *Moerkia blyttii*, the last one in particular associated with late snow lie. West of Ben Oss, only the grassy south face of Ben Lui falls within the Loch Lomond catchment, which is almost invariably ignored by visiting botanists in preference for the well-known floral delights occurring on the rock faces outcropping on the Orchy and Tay sides of the hill. The unexpected discovery of high-level flushes with such rarities as alpine rush (*Juncus alpinoarticulatus*) and false sedge (*Kobresia simpliciuscula*) in Ben Lui's southern corrie, previously considered too dull to repay detailed exploration, clearly illustrates that seeking out the neglected parts of even the most regularly visited areas can bring its rewards.

Finally, Meall nan Tighearn (739 m) in the remotest western corner compensates the mountain botanist for its lesser height in having an outlying outcrop of the Lawers calcareous schist, on this hill overlying the more acidic garnetiferous schist through over-folding of the Tay Nappe. In the extremely wet conditions and well out of the reach of grazing animals, some of the cliff faces are completely draped in a luxuriant curtain of vegetation. These 'hanging gardens' are principally made up of plants normally associated with lower ground, including globeflower, wood crane's-bill, meadowsweet, angelica and water avens. A good proportion of the flowering species of moderate altitude already referred to in this chapter are represented on this hill, but the addition of the strict calcicole dwarf shrub mountain avens (*Dryas octopetala*) points to the lime richness and friable nature of the Lawers schist. At least one shady cleft well up the eastern face of Meall nan Tighearn conceals the rare mountain bladder fern, one of the plants now lost to Ben Lomond.

The community of crag-nesting birds in these mountains is very similar to that already described for the scarps of the southern foothills, but with the addition of the golden eagle (see p. 193). Another upland bird, but not usually thought of as a Loch Lomondside species, is the dotterel (*Charadrius morinellus*), an attractive small wader that in summer is more or less confined to Scotland's highest mountain massifs. At the time of their spring migration, dotterel on passage are occasionally seen on Ben Lomond and the Luss Hills, but breeding almost certainly took place on one occasion. In July 1979, a male bird was observed on the stony summit ridge of Ben Oss performing its characteristic distraction display of shuffling along the ground with trailing tail feathers and outstretched, quivering wings, a performance intended to entice potential predators away from its eggs or small young. Sightings of the snow bunting (*Plectrophenax nivalis*) on Loch Lomondside during the breeding season are equally rare, although there are a few spring records of singing males being heard on the high cliffs of Ben Vorlich and A'Chrois. Following a report of a flock of over 500 snow buntings wintering at the head of Glen Luss towards the end of 1988, a pair was observed on the adjacent Doune Hill in July of the fol-

Fig. 12.9 Now very rare in Britain, the alpine woodsia has one of its strongest colonies in the Loch Lomond area.

lowing year. However, proving that the odd pair of 'snowflakes' may occasionally stay behind to nest in some remote Lomondside corrie is a challenge still waiting to be met by the energetic ornithologist prepared to cover extensive areas of suitable terrain.

Some notable upland species

The alpine woodsia (Fig. 12.9) is both one of the smallest and rarest of our native ferns. Intolerant of competition from the larger mountain plants, it favours fissured calcareous rock which it shares with little more than a few cushion mosses. Much sought after by collectors during the Victorian fern craze, alpine woodsia has been reported from three different hills within the Loch Lomond catchment area, one population quite exceptional for its large size. Numbers of plants do vary at this site, for the species is particularly vulnerable to desiccation in dry summers. The best season on record was 1990, when 340 separate tufts of the fern were counted, making it a contender for the largest individual colony in Britain of this now legally protected species.

The small mountain ringlet butterfly (Plate 16) population in Scotland is concentrated in the Grampian Highlands, with a scattering of sites throughout the Glen Falloch range. An isolated colony persists on Ben Lomond, the butterfly being most readily found in the southwestern facing corrie at around 500 m. Overwintering as a caterpillar deep within a dense tussock of mat-grass often covered by snow, the butterfly emerges towards the end of June, but can be up to a month later if the weather is poor. Mountain ringlets fly only in sunshine, their dark coloration maximising rapid absorption of heat. With the recent changes in the region's climatic pattern, the effect of the greater frequency of overcast skies on a mountain species whose breeding cycle is dependent on summer sunshine gives cause for concern.

Fig. 12.10 More than once threatened with extinction, the peregrine population has recovered in most parts of Loch Lomondside (Don MacCaskill).

On the very southern fringe of its summer range in the central Highlands, the black-throated diver (*Gavia arctica*) has only one regular breeding site on Loch Lomondside. A combination of fluctuating loch levels – which all too frequently wash out the birds' nest at the water's edge – and fishermen in boats inadvertently preventing them from incubating their eggs, together ensure that the pair is rarely successful in rearing young. Up to four pairs of red-throated divers breed at suitable sites in the region, including a man-made reservoir. It is significant that the use of boats by anglers is forbidden on this strictly controlled water, and the divers are able to nest and rear their young undisturbed.

As a breeding species, the greenshank has only a tenuous hold on the Loch Lomond area and may not nest every year. Their presence in summer amongst the peaty lochans on the Caorann Plateau was suspected for some time, but it was not until 1977 that small young were actually seen. Not only is the Caorann the greenshank's most southerly nesting site in Britain, at over 450 m it also appears to be the highest in the western Highlands.

No bird in the area has experienced changing fortunes at man's hands more than the peregrine (Fig. 12.10). Initially highly esteemed and zealously protected for the ancient art of falconry, it twice faced extinction; first by direct persecution in the interests of game preserving, followed by indirect poisoning through a build-up of the agricultural insecticides dieldrin and DDT entering the food chain. Southern Loch Lomondside would not be considered amongst the most intensively managed farmland in Scotland, yet the levels of dieldrin residues found in locally recovered peregrine corpses were higher than any others recorded in Britain. So widespread was the effect of pesticide poisoning, that throughout the region during the five year period 1966–70, only one pair was known to rear young. Following legislation restricting certain uses of these toxic chemicals, the recovery in the peregrine population since the mid-1970s has been remarkable. In one favoured part of the southern foothills, where prey is abundant in the fertile valleys below, up to five pairs have been recorded nesting within a linear distance of 9.6 km, giving a mean distance of only 2.4 km between the occupied eyries. This is one of the highest densities of breeding peregrines recorded not only in this country, but in Europe.

The golden eagle has become the symbol of the Scottish Highlands; the very first sight of one of these magnificent raptors soaring effortlessly over a precipitous crag is an unforgettable experience. Their bulky nests are reoccupied and renovated early in the year before winter has lost its icy grip, almost always at traditional sites that have a long history of occupation. Although there is only one regularly breeding pair of eagles, in good years three nesting pairs have been recorded. Like the raven, most of the eagle's food in the Loch Lomond Highlands is obtained from deer and sheep carrion, for there are few blue hares to hunt on these rain-soaked western mountains. Eagles are occasionally seen patrolling the upper slopes of Cnoc (492 m) at the head of Glen Sloy, where there is a very isolated, high-level colony of rabbits.

Whereas a distant golden eagle may sometimes by glimpsed by visitors reluctant to stray too far from their cars, on Loch Lomondside the ptarmigan will be seen only by those prepared to make the effort to reach the high ground. The most arctic of all the resident birds, the ptarmigan was undoubtedly one of the first species to recolonise Scotland at the end of the ice age 11,000 years ago. Living most of the year round in the boulder-strewn corries, they survive the winter by feeding on heather and blaeberry shoots protruding through the thinner snow on the windswept ridges. White as the snow itself in winter and mottled as the lichen-covered rocks in summer, the colour and texture of the ptarmigan's seasonal plumages blend perfectly with their background. Loch Lomondside is at the southernmost edge of the ptarmigan's breeding range in Britain, small coveys occurring on most if not all of the Munros. The species does appear to have been more widespread in the district up to the middle of the last century, from when there is a published account of ptarmigan shooting in summer on the Luss Hills. Although already in decline by then, the extent of ptarmigan habitat on the summits of these lower hills was probably still sufficient, but with further burning, sheep grazing and trampling, the heathy vegetation was eventually replaced by grassland offering little feeding and protective cover for the birds. Climatic warming leading to a reduction in winter snow on the mountains will inevitably restrict the bird's distribution still further.

Part IV

Conservation: Past, Present and Future

13

The Long Struggle for Nature's Place

> 'In calling attention to special areas, we would begin by emphasising
> particularly the entire Loch Lomond area. It is not alone because of
> its unique scenic beauty that Loch Lomond is of importance to the
> people of the West of Scotland; the whole area, comprising as it does
> features of mountain, river, lake and island landscape, constitutes an
> almost unequalled field for the study of natural history.'
>
> Submission to the Clyde Valley Regional Planning Committee
> by the Glasgow & Andersonian Natural History Society (1945)

'The Bonny Bonny Banks of Loch Lomond' must be one of the best-known
songs the world over, for it would seem that just about every one of the two million or more visitors each year is familiar with at least the opening lines of the
chorus which tell of taking either the high road or low road back to this internationally renowned area. Yet there is another road – one that has proved long
and stony – that has been slowly making its way towards recognition of Loch
Lomondside as a living heritage landscape, a national asset of which Scotland
can feel justifiably proud.

   Although pristine areas of wild country have been set aside for birds and
beasts of the chase since the time of the medieval kings, measures to preserve
Scotland's rich diversity of breathtaking scenery and abundant wildlife to
refresh both body and mind of all the people and not just as a playground for
the privileged few are a relatively modern concept. Over the last hundred years
or so, moves to protect the nation's finest landscapes from exploitation have
become inextricably linked with calls for a system of National Parks, to safeguard in perpetuity the finest tracts of unspoiled countryside together with
their dependent flora and fauna. Focusing down to just one region, this chapter looks back at some of the milestones – both successes and setbacks – in the
progress of the conservation movement on Loch Lomondside.

The first stirrings

One of the earliest protests at what was seen as the despoliation of Loch
Lomond came in the early nineteenth century with the introduction of the first
steamboat service. Francis Jeffrey, a leading Scottish advocate who frequently
stayed at Stuckgowan House overlooking the loch, felt compelled to complain
when the small wooden-hulled paddle-steamer *Marion* (Fig. 13.1) began regularly to ply its waters in 1818. The steamer's 'hissing and roaring' he considered,
vulgarised the scene. It was probably this early development of popular tourism
unfolding on his very doorstep, together with the sweeping changes taking
place in agriculture and the advent of conifer plantation forestry, that prompt-
ed local man John Colquhoun to publish 'A Plea for the Wastes' in his book

Fig. 13.1 Launched in the early nineteenth century, the *Marion* was the first in a long line of recreational paddle-steamers on the loch (Author's collection).

Rocks and Rivers (1849), which began with an impassioned appeal for the retention of the Highland's wilderness character. After years of playing an active role in the impoverishment of Loch Lomondside's wildlife as a sportsman-collector, in this at least Colquhoun was very much ahead of his time.

Another half century passed before the idea of setting aside a representative example of the country's relatively untouched wild land was aired again. In a landmark essay entitled 'A National Park for Scotland', first published in 1904 and updated in 1909, Charles Stewart of Appin, Argyllshire, proposed not only protected status for a large tract of the western Highlands possessing a natural beauty and grandeur in a high degree, but for the strict preservation of the natural fauna within its boundaries. With discussions then underway on the potential for state-backed afforestation of the Scottish Highlands, Stewart saw an additional reason for the establishment of a park system in order to preserve those wild animals of the open moorland and hillside which would be threatened by huge areas of plantation forestry.

The first proposal for designating land specifically for nature conservation in the Loch Lomond area came from the Society for the Promotion of Nature Reserves, which was founded in 1912. Ben Lui, which just touches the area's northwestern fringe, was included in their list of potential reserves in Britain compiled in 1915. Although not stated, Ben Lui was almost certainly nominated by one of the society's driving forces – the botanist George Claridge Druce – who had previously made a study of this fine hill.

The Addison Report

In 1929, overtures were made to Government by several countryside organisations, including the newly formed Association for the Preservation of Rural

Scotland, requesting an inquiry into the need for a series of National Parks in Britain. The Government response was the setting up of a National Park Committee under the chairmanship of Dr Christopher Addison, then Parliamentary Secretary to the Ministry of Agriculture. Objectives included the examination of proposals for the safeguarding of areas of exceptional national interest and nature sanctuaries for the protection of flora and fauna.

With the exception of the Cairngorms, the *Report of the National Park Committee* (Cmd. 3851) published in 1931 did not consider any particular area in Scotland for either National Parks or nature sanctuaries, but did append the suggestions made by witnesses to the Committee. Those listed included sites only peripheral to Loch Lomond, such as the Trossachs, proposed as a National Park by the Ramblers Federation. As nature reserves, the British Correlating Committee for the Protection of Nature (made up of representatives from a number of scientific bodies) put forward Ben Lui for mountain plants and the Ardgoil Peninsula in Cowal for birds.

The early 1930s were a time of financial stringency in the country, with no steps taken by Government to implement any part of the Addison report. This lack of action galvanised the voluntary bodies into forming a Standing Committee on National Parks in 1934 to keep alive public interest and support. Amongst several areas in Scotland proposed for National Park status by the Standing Committee in the following year were some of the wilder parts of Argyll and central Perthshire, but nothing for Loch Lomondside.

Events on Loch Lomondside during the 1930s and 1940s

A move that could have given Loch Lomondside a flying start in landscape and wildlife conservation occurred in the summer of 1930, when the Duke of Montrose approached the Chancellor of the Exchequer with the offer of the Rowardennan Estate – which included Ben Lomond – in lieu of death duties. It was proposed that once the land transfer was complete, the Ben Lomond area was to be given National Park status. Seen now as a golden opportunity missed, this offer to hand over Rowardennan Estate to the nation was turned down. Despite fears fanned in the press that the whole area would be sold off abroad along with other national treasures, the land was eventually purchased by a Scottish industrialist who continued its use as a sporting estate.

The chance gone to create Britain's very first National Park in Scotland, the Lomondside peaks of Beinn Ime (Fig. 13.2), Beinn Narnain and A'Chrois were included in the Forestry Commission's 235 km² Argyll National Forest Park when it was formally opened in May 1937. This was the first of any type of large-scale park in Britain. Although the primary use of the plantable land remained the commercial production of timber, it was recognised that there were also opportunities for both recreation and nature conservation. An extension eastwards to the very shores of Loch Lomond took place in 1966, when the Stronafyne Estate north of Arrochar was purchased by the Commission, enabling a linkup of the Argyll Forest Park (the prefix 'National' now dropped) with Kenmore Wood near Tarbet which had been acquired earlier.

Not everyone felt at ease with the prospect of conifer plantations spreading all over the Scottish hills. During the mid-1930s, individual members of the Association for the Preservation of Rural Scotland expressed their concern that large-scale forestry operations such as those underway in the Aberfoyle area would transform entire landscapes to their detriment. However, the gen-

Fig. 13.2 At 1,011 m, the summit of Beinn Ime is the highest peak in the Argyll Forest Park.

eral consensus at the time was that mile upon mile of coniferous trees planted in regimented ranks could hardly materialise in a country with such varied topography as the Highlands. The result was that an agreement between the amenity and rural conservation bodies with the Forestry Commission over restricting blanket afforestation in selected areas, such as those already formalised in parts of the Lake District in England and Snowdonia in Wales, was considered unnecessary in the equally scenic regions of Scotland.

Late 1944 saw the first major environmental battle for Loch Lomondside, which followed the publication of the North of Scotland Hydro-Electric Board's plans for a massive development based on Loch Sloy, a remote lochan in the Arrochar Hills. Amongst the objectors to the project were representatives of the landowner on the grounds of loss of amenity and Dunbarton County Council who submitted a case for reserving the Sloy catchment for the primary water needs of the county. Opponents to the scheme also stressed the visual impact of siting an electric generating station at Inveruglas beside Loch Lomond. In rejecting the environmental evidence presented, the chairman of the ensuing public enquiry gave his opinion that the Inveruglas site selected for development was not in itself a noted beauty spot, being a steep and scrub-covered mountainside with no special features to commend it; the generating station's multi-pipeline intake when treated with camouflage paint would not be obtrusive and in time would be concealed by planted trees; the station itself was to be a very modest structure and would not in any appreciable degree affect the natural beauty of the area. Posterity, however, has not judged these conclusions in quite such a favourable light. By no stretch of the imagination can it be claimed that the power station and its huge intake pipes have successfully blended into the landscape, even after half a century (Fig. 13.3). Nor could the associated double row of electric pylons heading towards Glasgow be

Fig. 13.3 The Loch Sloy hydro-electric generation station at Inveruglas.

hidden from general view once they reached the more open ground of Glen Fruin. Above all, the wild solitude of Glen Sloy was lost for ever. Years after the completion of the project, complaints still rumbled on over the industrial debris abandoned at a work site in Coiregrogan Glen.

The Ramsay Reports and the Clyde Valley Regional Plan

Despite the dark shadow cast by the Second World War, the Association for the Preservation of Rural Scotland was able to set up a Scottish Council for National Parks in 1942. Acting for about 30 interested bodies, the Council pressed the Scottish Secretary of State for an assessment of potential park areas in the country. Importantly, the Council's own nominations included Loch Lomondside for the first time. Resulting from these representations, a Scottish National Parks Survey Committee was appointed in January 1944 under the chairmanship of Sir Douglas Ramsay. The Committee's remit was to identify and survey the most suitable areas for designation as National Parks. When *National Parks: A Scottish Survey* (Cmd. 6631) was published in 1945, Loch Lomond and the Trossachs headed the list in order of priority.

The selection of the Loch Lomond and Trossachs area as a potential National Park was well received by the Clyde Valley Regional Planning Committee, whose remit included Loch Lomondside, although they did not agree with the park boundaries proposed, which more or less followed the loch's western and southern shores. One of their concerns was over a Loch Lomond Draft Planning Scheme prepared by Dunbarton County Council, which zoned the loch's southern banks for residential development. The Regional Planning Committee's favoured boundaries included the improved farmland to the south of the loch, all of the surrounding hills, together with a link-up to the existing Argyll Forest Park. For their own *Clyde Valley Regional*

Plan published in 1946, the Committee turned to the Glasgow and Andersonian Natural History Society for comment on the boundaries to the plan and the identification of key wildlife sites. In their response, the Society recommended for inclusion within the plan all of the loch and its islands, the entire montane area to the north plus the Kilpatrick, Campsie and Fintry Hills to the south. Ballagan Glen and the Endrick Marshes were among several high quality geological and wildlife sites individually named. The Society added to their submission that the setting-up of local or National Nature Reserves within the defined area would meet with their full approval.

The follow-up to the Scottish National Parks Survey Committee report was the appointment of a second committee, again under the chairmanship of Sir Douglas Ramsay, to advise on the administrative and financial requirements of a National Parks system in Scotland. In the second Ramsay report *National Parks and the Conservation of Nature in Scotland* (Cmd. 7235) published in 1947, the Loch Lomond–Trossachs area remained the Committee's first choice. In the meantime, however, powerful vested interests had gathered together to oppose the very idea of National Parks in Scotland. This came not only from the major landowners unwilling to relinquish absolute control over their estates, but also from the hydro-electric and forestry industries who saw the Committee's recommendations as liable to sterilise large tracts of Scotland from future development. Even some conservationists expressed their reservations, fearing that National Park status might attract a rash of tourist-led developments aiming to cash in on the growing demand for recreational and leisure activities, rather than generate genuine public concern for the natural environment. In the face of this combined opposition the outcome was inevitable. The Government accepted the case for the creation of National Parks in England and Wales, but Scotland was passed over in the *National Parks and Access to the Countryside Act 1949.* Minimum protection was afforded to Scotland's special areas by the introduction of National Park Direction Orders (one of which covered Loch Lomond and the Trossachs), whereby the Secretary of State was empowered to scrutinise any development proposal falling within each order's designated boundaries.

The Ritchie Report and the Nature Conservancy

At the very first meeting of the second Scottish National Parks Committee held in February 1946, a supporting Scottish Wildlife Conservation Committee was appointed under Professor James Ritchie. The Ritchie Report *Nature Reserves in Scotland* (Cmd.7814) published in 1949 listed a number of proposed nature reserves and conservation areas in Scotland. No part of Loch Lomondside was included amongst these sites. Unaccountably, even Ben Lui on the northwestern fringe was left out. Just to the east of Loch Lomond, however, the Ritchie Committee suggested the eastern end of Loch Ard near Aberfoyle as a National Park Reserve, the designation to be given to any nature reserve situated within a National Park in Scotland. Gartrenich Moss nearby – which was considered the least disturbed of a series of raised bogs in the Forth Valley – was put forward as a Nature Conservation Area to preserve the site from harmful developments. Neither recommendation was adopted. Gartrenich was subsequently acquired by the Forestry Commission, the moss drained and planted with conifers.

Despite National Parks for Scotland having been rejected by Government, it did accept the Scottish Wildlife Conservation Committee's recommendation of a representative series of National Nature Reserves throughout the country, together with creation of a biological service to protect, administer and manage the reserves. This wildlife service was to be a Great Britain body, not separate from England and Wales as some had advocated. The Nature Conservancy (later, the Nature Conservancy Council) was founded by Royal Charter in 1949, a programme of National Nature Reserve acquisition beginning almost immediately. The new organisation was also given the responsibility of notifying to local planning authorities all sites regarded as having special scientific interest (SSSIs) within their administrative boundaries. In general these were often very small areas, but sufficiently important to need some statutory protection against developments likely to damage their wildlife or physical interests. Loch Lomondside's Conic Hill, with its exposures of the Highland Boundary Fault zone, was notified as a geological site in 1951, one of the very first SSSIs in Scotland.

The National Nature Reserve potential of Loch Lomond's southeastern group of wooded islands quickly attracted the newly formed Nature Conservancy's attention, in particular the floristically diverse Inchcailloch (Fig. 13.4), which was used for teaching purposes by the Botany Department of Glasgow University. Clairinsh was also earmarked, the reversion of the island's oak coppice back to semi-natural high forest more advanced than in any other formerly managed woodland in the area. It was Clairinsh in fact which was the first to gain National Nature Reserve status, declared in July 1958 by agreement with the island's owners, the Buchanan Society. At this point the Nature Conservancy was confronted with applications for housing developments on Inchcailloch and its neighbouring island of Torrinch. Clearing the earmarked building site of trees actually began on Inchcailloch, but felling was brought to

Fig. 13.4 Only just offshore, Inchcailloch is the most accessible of the five islands in the Loch Lomond National Nature Reserve.

a halt by Stirling County Council imposing a Tree Preservation Order, a stand-off only resolved by the Conservancy's purchase of the island from the would-be developer. The Nature Conservancy's now committed interest in Loch Lomondside was also drawn to the Endrick Marshes on the adjacent mainland. Ornithologically, not only was the area at the confluence of several routes used by migratory birds, but regular counts of wintering wildfowl from 1948 had shown the Endrick Marshes to harbour numbers of regional importance. The Loch Lomond National Nature Reserve, made up of Inchcailloch, Clairinsh, Torrinch, Creinch and the Aber Isle, together with the grazing marshes south of the River Endrick, was declared on 4 December 1962. The waterfowl habitat of the reserve was further recognised in 1976, when it was designated under the Ramsar Convention on Wetlands of International Importance. With subsequent extensions on the mainland to encompass all of the Endrick Marshes in the lower flood plain of the river, the extent of the reserve stands at 441 ha.

A countrywide review of existing and potential conservation sites undertaken in the 1970s identified two other Loch Lomond islands – Inchlonaig and Inchmoan – as being of National Nature Reserve standard, although to date, no firm steps have been taken towards their inclusion within the existing reserve. Ben Lui National Nature Reserve (374 ha) was declared in April 1961. Although there have been several major extensions since then, only the reserve's eastern extremity on Ben Dubhchraig falls within the Loch Lomond catchment area.

Barely had the Nature Conservancy become established in the area, when it was faced with a proposal for Scotland's largest reservoir development – the Loch Lomond Water Scheme. To increase the reservoir's storage capacity, the plan was to hold the water level at 27 ft (8.2 m) OD by means of a barrage across the only outlet to the loch. This would have raised Loch Lomond's mean annual water level by about 2 ft (0.61 m), with loss of the important shore zone plant communities of the reserve and elsewhere. Following objections from the Conservancy, together with other loch users and lochside residents, the height of the crest barrage across the River Leven was agreed at a compromise 26 ft (7.9 m) OD. Despite the overall picture having been complicated by increased rainfall experienced over the same period, most riparian property owners on both the mainland and islands remain adamant that the artificially raised water level is responsible for the unprecedented rate of shore erosion witnessed since the scheme became operational in 1971 (Fig. 13.5).

The Queen Elizabeth Forest Park

By late 1949, the Rowardennan Estate (including Ben Lomond) was again facing sale to meet death duties. This time the Government did step in to purchase the estate through the National Land Fund. Set up just after the Second World War, the National Land Fund was specifically aimed at acquiring areas of high scenic value. Such land was to be dedicated to those who died in the conflict and made available in perpetuity to everyone seeking the peace and tranquillity of the countryside. Initially it seemed the estate would be entrusted to the care of the National Trust for Scotland, a body that was empowered to hold land. Founded in 1931, the Trust already had a presence on Loch Lomondside, having been gifted two small islands – Bucinch and Ceardach – in 1943. In the event, the estate passed to the Forestry Commission, and the land was incorporated into the Queen Elizabeth Forest Park, which officially

Fig. 13.5 The exposed roots of this alder illustrate how rapidly the shoreline of Loch Lomond has eroded in recent years.

opened on 19 June 1954. When it came to the preservation of the area's natural beauty, it cannot be said that during the early years of the park's existence the Commission's management on Loch Lomondside fully lived up to the ideals and expectations of the National Land Fund. Scant attention was paid to landscape design, with straight-edged blocks of foreign conifers laid out unsympathetically to the terrain. With the planted trees in each block even-aged, harvesting at commercial maturity would be by clear-felling, leaving behind a scene of ugliness impossible to disguise. The Forestry Commission's treatment of the large stands of former coppice oak woodland within the park also left something to be desired. Classified in a woodland census as little more than scrub, one forest policy statement dismissed such woodlands as not justifying their existence. Under a management plan entitled 'Rehabilitation of the Hard Wood Areas' – which was not quite what it seemed – a planting programme of conifers began in the Rowardennan oak woods by utilising existing clearings, cutting openings in the canopy and by direct underplanting. The practice continued right up to 1969, by which time some two-thirds of the native deciduous woodland in the Commission's ownership on the east side of Loch Lomond had been converted to mixed stands.

In 1973, a study of the Rowardennan oak woods was carried out jointly by the Forestry Commission and the Nature Conservancy Council (the name of the agency had changed in that same year) to examine the possibilities of reversing the coniferisation of the native hardwood areas. Time passed, and it was not until May 1989, after the adoption in 1984 of the Commission's indigenous species-friendly broad-leaved woodland policy, that the 300 ha Loch Lomond Oakwoods Forest Nature Reserve was created with SSSI status. Within the Forest Nature Reserve, a phased programme of removing the introduced

Fig. 13.6 The Queen Elizabeth Forest Park successfully blends commercial forestry with recreational activities and wildlife conservation.

conifers began at their earliest economic stage. Forest Enterprise (the operational arm of the Forestry Commission) was to receive an environmental award in recognition of this restorative step.

Since its inception, the Queen Elizabeth Forest Park (Fig. 13.6) as a multipurpose forest has developed into one of the most popular destinations in west central Scotland for outdoor recreational pursuits, attracting up to a million visitors per year.

A National Scenic Area

Aware that the face of the Scottish Highlands was undergoing change at a rapid pace with the boom in post-war forestry planting and hydro-electric schemes, the National Trust for Scotland commissioned W. H. Murray – a well-known Scottish mountaineer and writer – to undertake a survey of all the Highlands' key scenic areas. Published in 1962, *Highland Landscape* enumerated and described 21 places of outstanding beauty. That Loch Lomond had for so long remained free from the most unsightly tourist developments, Murray concluded to be little short of a miracle. He was not impressed, however, with the conspicuous siting of the Hydro-Electric Board's generating station at Inveruglas, further warning that a plan already approved to carry power from Loch Awe hydro-electric scheme across Glen Falloch would involve pylons up to 76 m tall, an intrusion on the skyline that the eye could not escape.

A more comprehensive survey of Scotland's landscapes was carried out by the newly created Countryside Commission for Scotland (see below). Their report *Scotland's Scenic Heritage* (1978) named 40 areas covering one-eighth of the land and fresh waters in both the Highlands and Lowlands requiring special planning control. Although recognised as a 'cultural landscape' where the imprint of man's activities could be clearly seen, the compilers of the report concluded that Loch Lomondside lived up to its oft-sung fame. Two years later in 1980, the region was designated by the Scottish Secretary of State as a

National Scenic Area. In practice, however, Lomondside's new designation was not particularly effective as a protective mechanism and had little impact on curbing conifer afforestation or the bulldozing of unsightly hill tracks.

The Greave Report and the Countryside Commission for Scotland

Against a background of increasing private car ownership and greater mobility of the urban population, a conference looking at rural issues of the future and entitled 'The Countryside in 1970' (European Conservation Year) was held in 1965. In the published proceedings, attention was again drawn to the anomaly between Scotland and the rest of mainland Britain over the provision of National Parks. Study Group 9, considering countryside planning and development in Scotland under the chairmanship of Professor Robert Greave, singled out the combined Loch Lomond–Trossachs region as an obvious candidate for National Park status, not least because half of the proposed 1,108 km^2 was already in public ownership. Despite the optimism felt at the time, government once more failed to live up to the expectations of proponents of National Parks for Scotland. The Greave Report did, however, successfully argue the case for the setting up of a Countryside Commission for Scotland, the necessary legislation reaching the statute book in October 1967.

The Scottish Wildlife Trust

The Scottish Wildlife Trust, a voluntary conservation body formed in 1964, established one of its very first nature reserves at Ballagan Glen in the southern Campsie Hills two years later. An ash wood with wych elm, bird cherry and hazel, the crumbling calciferous cementstones of the type formation of the Ballagan Beds exposed in the glen ensure a rich ground flora. A second Loch Lomondside reserve, Loch Ardinning (Fig. 13.7) together with the adjoining Muirhouse Muir, was gifted to the Trust in 1988.

Fig. 13.7 Loch Ardinning is one of two nature reserves in Loch Lomondside's Lowland fringe administered by the Scottish Wildlife Trust.

The Loch Lomond Local Subject Plan

In 1977, following local government reorganisation, the District and Regional Councils covering Loch Lomondside produced a draft local plan which aimed to reconcile the increasing demands of recreation and tourism with the need to conserve and enhance the environment of the loch and its surrounds. The exceptional scenic quality of the area was emphasised, but the problems of developmental eyesores and discarded litter were also recognised. The more mountainous parts of Loch Lomondside – where particular attention was to be paid to wildlife conservation – were initially classified as 'wilderness areas', but on further consideration this was changed to 'remote upland areas', representing the most unspoilt and wild landscapes within the boundaries of the plan. Although key wildlife sites such as the Loch Lomond National Nature Reserve and SSSIs were identified, the Nature Conservancy Council expressed a view that, rather than be lumped in with other issues, wildlife conservation should be treated as a subject in its own right. A water zonation scheme was proposed for the loch, to protect wildlife areas considered sensitive to disturbance. Among other conservation bodies who submitted comments on the draft plan, the Royal Society for the Protection of Birds warned that the loch's waterfowl population would be adversely affected if powerboat sports were to be allowed to go on expanding indefinitely. Such was the stand taken by the Scottish Landowners Federation, the National Farmers Union and the Department of Agriculture for Scotland in concerted opposition to the proposal to bring the agricultural and forestry industries under the control of the planning authorities, that this clause had to be dropped in favour of a voluntary code of practice. Those sceptical of a voluntary approach were equally adamant that a code of practice would do nothing to prevent a repetition of the conspicuous track bulldozed up Loch Lomondside's eastern slopes at Cailness while discussions on controlling such potentially disfiguring activities were still taking place. The plan was finally adopted in 1986.

In a ten year review of the Loch Lomond Local Plan published in 1996, it was restated that the conservation of the characteristic ecological diversity of the whole area must be a priority objective.

The Friends of Loch Lomond and the Craigrostan Scheme

Founded in 1978, the Friends of Loch Lomond have attracted a worldwide membership dedicated to the protection of the area's natural beauty. As such, they have been steadfast in their support for National Park status for Loch Lomondside. The Friends of Loch Lomond came to the fore when objecting to the North of Scotland Hydro-Electric Board's plan to construct a pumped storage station and reservoir on the slopes of Ben Lomond. Named the Craigrostan Scheme, nothing before or since quite galvanised public opinion against what was perceived as yet further exploitation of Loch Lomondside's most unspoilt land. Although some parts of the development were to be underground, there would be no hiding the construction roads, the upper storage reservoir with its water draw-down scoured sides and yet more power lines draped over open country. In order to obtain temporary storage in the loch for water released from the upper reservoir, the level of control at the River Leven barrage needed to be increased, although any rise in loch level would have aggravated the existing problem of shore erosion still further. Despite the well-publicised environmental protest, the reasons for the scheme not being pushed through at that particular time probably had more to do with an unanticipated surplus in Scotland's electricity generating capacity following a severe decline in several of the country's major industries.

The National Trust for Scotland and Ben Lomond

An announcement in 1982 that the Forestry Commission was to sell off 2,110 ha of the unplantable upper slopes and summit of Ben Lomond, effectively out of public ownership, was greeted with dismay and another vigorous campaign by the Friends of Loch Lomond. The Commission was accused of asset stripping by one political figure, declaring his intention of raising the matter before Parliament. The situation was only defused when Ben Lomond was handed over to the National Trust for Scotland in March 1984, a move made possible by an exceptional grant of the full purchase price from the Countryside Commission for Scotland. Needless to say, it did not escape notice that this world famous mountain had achieved the distinction of having twice been paid for with money from the public purse. Later that year, the Forestry Commission indicated to the Trust that it was also prepared to dispose of unplanted land around the upper Cailness Burn just to the north of Ben Lomond, part of which took in the North of Scotland Hydro-Electric Board's proposed site for the Craigrostan Scheme reservoir. It was reported in the press that the Hydro-Electric Board had, in fact, submitted a bid for the area. With all the signs of another major row brewing, the Secretary of State for Scotland took the decision to block this additional sale.

Since its acquisition of Ben Lomond, the National Trust for Scotland has put considerable resources into restoring the heavily used and badly eroded path to the summit (Fig. 13.8), protecting the existing native woodland by enclo-

Fig. 13.8 Maintaining the path to the summit of Ben Lomond is a continuous commitment for the National Trust of Scotland (Alasdair Eckersall).

sure and initiating a restoration programme of heather moorland and other
upland habitats through controlling the level of stock grazing.

The spread of private investment conifer plantations

From the early 1980s onwards, most of the new forestry developments in the
region were carried out by commercial companies subsidised by planting
grants (channelled through the Forestry Commission) and generous tax
incentives to investors. Not unexpectedly, there was increasing public unrest
over the rapid loss of open ground – particularly in the southern foothills –
and the deleterious effect on Loch Lomondside's scenic attraction through
the seemingly unstoppable creeping tide of conifers, the hard-edged rectan-
gular blocks of tightly packed trees usually following property boundaries with
little consideration given to landscape design. It is to be regretted that several
local wildlife sites were damaged or destroyed by private afforestation, including the floristically rich grasslands and flushes of the Highland Boundary Fault
zone on Ben Bowie. Outwith local planning control, however, the pace of company afforestation only showed signs of slowing down following the withdrawal of tax concessions to forestry investors in the budget of March 1988. The
Chancellor of the Exchequer's action effectively gave a last minute reprieve to
the plantable land around the headwaters of the River Endrick, which was
faced with being drained and smothered in conifers.

The spectre of the 'forbidden land' scenario of the early 1900s was suddenly raised again following the completion of one private afforestation scheme
on Loch Lomondside. A barbed wired gate and oppressive signs barred access
to a popular hill area where, until the change in land use, the casual visitor had
been allowed to walk freely. This return-to-the-past experience may have acted
as the catalyst to a seemingly contradictory situation where members of the
public who had initially expressed their disapproval at the Forestry
Commission for blanketing with conifers large sections of the Kilpatrick Hills,
were equally unhappy when in 1993 these same publicly owned plantations
were offered for sale to the highest bidder in the private sector. Emphasising
their recreational potential through the close proximity of the Kilpatricks to
the Glasgow conurbation, the Friends of Loch Lomond were amongst those
who registered their objection to the sale with the Secretary of State for
Scotland. The Kilpatrick Hills plantations, together with a mixed wood of high
scenic value beside Ross Priory on the southern shore of Loch Lomond, were
taken off the market.

The Royal Society for the Protection of Birds

With the help of grant aid from the Countryside Commission for Scotland and
the Nature Conservancy Council, the Royal Society for the Protection of Birds
purchased 376 ha of the Inversnaid Estate in February 1986. About a third of
the RSPB reserve comprises mixed deciduous woodland (Fig. 13.9), the rest
hill grazings including some heather moor. To encourage natural regeneration
and protect plantings of broad-leaved trees, management has been aimed at
reducing the number of herbivores such as red deer and feral goats. On the
higher ground, a deer-fenced enclosure under a woodlands grant scheme has
been planted with Scots pine using local seed collected from the Glen Falloch
pine wood, to assist in perpetuating these trees' ancient line.

Fig. 13.9 Woodlands managed for nature conservation on the Royal Society for the Protection of Birds' Inversnaid reserve.

The Loch Lomond Regional Park

The question of some form of distinguishing status for Loch Lomondside came back on to the agenda again after the publication of the Countryside Commission for Scotland's report *A Park System for Scotland* (1974). National Parks for Scotland in the accepted sense were now firmly on the back-burner, the Commission proposing instead a tiered system headed by 'special parks'. This alternative top-tier designation proved to be a non-runner, but the *Countryside (Scotland) Act 1981* enabled the creation of Regional Parks.

Set up in 1988 with joint central government and local authority funding, the Loch Lomond Regional Park (Fig. 13.10) covered some 442 km². The Park Authority did not, however, incorporate the word 'Regional' in its own title, having not given up on attaining National Park status for the area. Although the Regional Park is principally aimed at promoting outdoor recreation without losing sight of the needs of those who gain their livelihood from the land, the Park Authority also has a duty to play its part in enhancing the natural beauty and conserving the wildlife of Loch Lomondside. Visitor centres with permanent exhibitions interpreting the park's special features have been opened at Luss and Balmaha.

Loch Lomondside as an Environmentally Sensitive Area

In May 1987, Loch Lomondside was one of the first two regions in Scotland to be designated an Environmentally Sensitive Area. Under the provisions of the *Agricultural Act 1986*, land occupiers who volunteer to enter into a management agreement based on a farm conservation plan would be offered incentive payments to undertake environmentally sensitive practices. Objectives within the designated area include protecting the landscape from badly

Fig. 13.10 The Loch Lomond Regional Park was the first of its kind in Scotland.

designed farm buildings and hill tracks, restoring stone walls and hedges to maintain the traditional appearance of the countryside, encourage natural regeneration of broad-leaved woodland by enclosure and protecting heather moor and species-rich grassland from overgrazing.

The Mountain Areas of Scotland Report

The Mountain Areas of Scotland Report (1990) was the response of the Countryside Commission for Scotland to an invitation from the Scottish Minister for Home Affairs and the Environment to study management arrangements for the country's popular mountain areas. Scenery and wildlife were to be included in their remit. The Commission concluded in their report that Loch Lomondside was a prime candidate for special status, the preferred area – which included both the Argyll and Queen Elizabeth Forest Parks – particularly important to the people of Scotland's central belt as their most readily accessible hill and loch country. This time the Commission was less hesitant in the choice of top-tier designation, proposing National Park status with an independent administrative board, planning control (which would include farming and forestry) and a high proportion of the total funding of the park to be met by central government. In this, the Commission reflected the aspirations of all proponents of National Parks for Scotland.

Predictably, publication of the report recommending National Parks for Scotland immediately marshalled the now familiar and well-organised land-owning opposition to the proposal. Instead of the hoped-for Government support for National Parks, what followed was the watered-down *Natural Heritage (Scotland) Act 1991*. This gave the Secretary of State for Scotland the power to designate Natural Heritage Areas founded on the voluntary principle and not perceived as requiring their own independent administrative body. With the exception of the anti-National Park lobby, who immediately seized upon the designation and called for Loch Lomondside to become a Natural Heritage Area, the open-to-abuse voluntary code of practice in countryside protection was greeted with little enthusiasm and to date no National Heritage Areas have been established in Scotland.

This was to be the last opportunity for the Countryside Commission for Scotland to express their support for Scottish National Parks with effective statutory protection and maximum financial backing from central government, for in April 1992 the Commission and the Scottish arm of the Nature Conservancy Council were merged to form a single agency, Scottish Natural Heritage.

The Hutchison Report

In 1991, as a follow-up to *The Mountain Areas of Scotland* Report, the Secretary of State for Scotland announced the setting up of a working party under the chairmanship of Sir Peter Hutchison to address more precisely the management issues connected with visitor trends and their effect on the natural heritage of Loch Lomondside and the Trossachs area. In their report *The Management of Loch Lomond and the Trossachs* published in 1993, the working party concluded that improvements to communications together with greater disposable wealth had combined to threaten the very features that drew people to Loch Lomondside in the first place; and that there was a real need for urgent action to safeguard the precious but inherently fragile qualities of the area. They accordingly recommended that care of the natural and cultural heritage of the area should be adopted as the fundamental principle in any future plan.

Despite the thoroughness of the Hutchison Report, an air of disillusionment quickly surfaced when it became clear that right from the outset, the working party had been precluded from considering any kind of independent administration board such as those of the National Parks in the Lake and Peak Districts of England, but only what might be achieved under the legislative framework already in place for Scotland. This was despite public opinion polls – including one undertaken by the Scottish Office in 1992 – which indicated that up to 90 per cent of Scots favoured the introduction of National Parks on lines somewhat similar to those elsewhere in the United Kingdom.

Advocates for National Park status for the region were by now well used to such knock-backs, although this time they sensed a coming change in the flow of the tide. One-day conferences held on Loch Lomondside, which were organised by the Member of Parliament for Dumbarton, continued to keep the issue of National Parks for Scotland to the forefront of public and media attention.

The Ben Lomond National Memorial Park

After lying dormant for the best part of half a century, the landscape conservation objective of the National Land Fund – under which the Rowardennan Estate was first purchased for the nation – was suddenly raised again in 1995, when attention focused on Forest Enterprise's design plan for restocking the Rowardennan plantations as the first generation of planted conifers approached the stage of harvesting. Although the Friends of Loch Lomond applauded Forest Enterprise's initiative in oak wood restoration, they strongly objected to that part of the plan under which the replanting of non-native

Fig. 13.11 The Ben Lomond National Memorial Park monument symbolises the hopes of all those who wish to see this scenic area remain unspoiled in perpetuity.

Sitka spruce would be little reduced elsewhere. Following a brief skirmish in the press between the Friends and Forest Enterprise, events moved swiftly, culminating on 3 June 1996 with the signing of a concordat between the Secretary of State for Scotland, the Forestry Commission and the National Trust for Scotland for the long-delayed dedication of the area in remembrance of the thousands of Scots who died in military service during the Second World War. Forest Enterprise produced an innovative long-term plan to replace the blocks of conifers with well-designed mixed stands of native trees, planted and harvested in much smaller lots and at different times under what is termed 'continuous cover forestry'. Apart from the scenic improvement, the age/species mixed deciduous stands will encourage and sustain a far greater variety of wildlife than the even-aged, closely planted conifers. The plan not only attracted a prestigious forest management award, but with the land to be held inalienably as a living monument to the war dead, in theory at least it removed the threat of a pumped storage hydro-electric scheme being constructed on the site. Fittingly, the Ben Lomond National Memorial Park was formally opened by the Secretary of State on Remembrance Day 1997 (Fig. 13.11).

The Millennium Forest for Scotland

In August 1996 a trust company representing the Royal Scottish Forestry Society acquired 1,214 ha of hill sheep ground at Cashell, formerly the southern-most part of the Rowardennan Estate originally purchased for the nation through the National Land Fund. As part of the Millennium Forest for Scotland project, the trust company's intention is to return a large part of the land to indigenous woodland, using principally oak on the lower ground, with Scots pine and birch ascending to ericaceous and other shrubs on the upper slopes. Within a year of the scheme's launch and extensive deer fencing being erected, some 100,000 native trees had been planted. Further north at Craigrostan between Cailness and Inversnaid, the Jensen Foundation of Denmark had acquired a large stand of oak in 1987. These former coppice woodlands were incorporated into the Millennium Forest for Scotland in 1997, work carried out including enclosure fencing, rhododendron removal and individual protection of naturally occurring seedlings by the use of tree tubes. In the same year, the National Trust for Scotland began extending its existing woodland enclosures on Ben Lomond under the Millennium scheme.

Together with the current woodland protection and replanting initiatives of Forest Enterprise and the Royal Society for the Protection of Birds, the total extent of woodland cover along the lochside's eastern slopes seems set to become the showpiece of forest restoration in Scotland. Modern day planting may never replace the genetic strains of native tree species that have been lost by man's activities over thousands of years, but with sympathetic management – which must allow for a percentage of the trees to mature, die naturally and rot down – Loch Lomondside's 'New Forest' should in time assume many of the characteristics of the original wildwood.

The Natura 2000 Network

Under the European Community Birds and Habitats/Species Directives, Britain accepted the responsibility to designate Special Protection Areas for birds considered rare or vulnerable and Special Areas of Conservation to support rare and endangered habitats, together with their associated species of plants and animals (other than birds). Both protection and conservation areas go under the umbrella of the Natura 2000 Network.

Sites proposed for Loch Lomondside take in the Endrick Marshes for wintering Greenland whitefronted geese and four of the largest wooded islands in the central basin of the loch for capercaillie as a combined Special Protection Area. Special Conservation Areas take in the River Endrick from its mouth to the Loup of Fintry (particularly for spawning river lampreys and Atlantic salmon) and a large proportion of the western acidic oak woodland on the islands and around the loch.

A look to the future

The ink was barely dry to this short history of the conservation movement in the Loch Lomond area when the new parliament in Edinburgh passed an enabling bill to establish National Parks in Scotland, with Loch Lomondside and the Trossachs chosen to be the very first. After a litany of missed opportunities and one study report after another consigned to the back of the cupboard to gather dust, Scotland will no longer stand alone as the only country in Europe not having this internationally recognised top-tier designation for its finest scenic areas. There are many issues that will have to be resolved before the proposals contained within the bill are translated into reality, but for those who have held firm for National Park status for Loch Lomondside their long struggle for nature's place is almost at an end.

How has the region fared in the 70 years since the Rowardennan Estate together with Ben Lomond was first unsuccessfully offered to the country as a National Park? In his excellent book *Loch Lomond*, published in 1931, Henry Lamond made the following appeal: 'My modest plea is that no cottager within his limited domain, that no landed proprietor within his estate, and that no Local Authority within its administration area, should countenance or tolerate anything that may result in the ultimate degradation of Loch Lomond'. Since those words were written, Loch Lomondside has witnessed the intensification of agriculture practices, an unprecedented spread of plantation-style conifers and loss of heather moor, further water storage provision including a massive hydro-electric scheme and harnessing as a major water supply the loch itself. To this should be added the vastly increased traffic that has necessitated road realignment and widening on a scale never before experienced, together with the ongoing upgrading of tourist and other leisure facilities. Resulting from the combined effect of all these competing claims for land and water, it cannot be denied that Loch Lomondside has become a little frayed around the edges, its scenic beauty and wild places all to often having to take second place to developmental interests. Overall, however, apart from the excessive distur-bance on the loch created by the recent free-for-all in fast powerboat sports – which as a keen fisherman he would have found totally unacceptable – it is unlikely that Henry Lammond would be too disappointed. Despite all the uses and abuses, the Bonny Banks have somehow managed to retain a semblance of balance between its heritage of nature and the people's needs. In a rapidly changing world, where the importance of conserving a representative variety of native flora and fauna in every region is increasingly recognised, Loch Lomondside is acknowledged as one of the finest Scottish pearls in the United Kingdom's biodiversity crown. That it should remain so, as the area enters the new millennium with a new future as part of Scotland's first National Park, is in our own hands.

References

Many of the selected works below, particularly those forming a collection of seminar papers, contain useful bibliographies that together make up an extensive list of scientific and historical titles for the area. A few less site-specific publications, which the author found useful in the preparation of the account, have been added.

Adams, C.E. et al. (1990). A Check-list of the Freshwater Invertebrate Fauna of the Loch Lomond Catchment. *The Glasgow Naturalist* 21:537–554.

Agnew, J. (1975). *The Story of the Vale of Leven*. Famedram, Gartocharn.

Anderson, M.L. (1967). *A History of Scottish Forestry* 2 vols. Thomas Nelson, Edinburgh.

Anon, (1967). *History of Croftamie and District*. Women's Rural Institute, Croftamie.

Backmeroff, C.E. & Peterken, G.F. (1988). Long-term Changes in the Woodlands of Clairinsh. *Transactions of the Botanical Society of Edinburgh* 45:253–297.

Bassett, D.A. (1958). *Geological Excursion Guide to the Glasgow District*. Geological Society of Glasgow.

Bennet, D. (1986). *The Southern Highlands* (2nd ed.). The Scottish Mountaineering Trust, Edinburgh.

Bignal, E. (1978). Mink Predation of Shelduck and other Wildfowl at Loch Lomond. *The Western Naturalist* 7:47–53.

Boney, A.D. (1978). Microscopic Plant Life in Loch Lomond. *The Glasgow Naturalist* 19:391–402.

Brown, H. (1992). Munro and Munro-ing. *The Scots Magazine*. September 1992, pp. 611–621.

Brown, M. & Mendum, J. (1995). *Loch Lomond to Stirling: A Landscape Fashioned by Geology*. Scottish Natural Heritage and British Geological Survey, Edinburgh.

Bryant, D.M. (1993). Bird Communities in Oak and Norway Spruce Woodlands on Loch Lomondside – a long-term study. *The Forth Naturalist and Historian* 16:59–69.

Calder, C. & Lindsay, L. (1992). *The Islands of Loch Lomond*. Famedram, Formartine.

Calladine, J. et al. (1990). Moorland Birds on the Campsie Fells, Touch Hills and West Ochil Hills, Stirling: Habitats, Distribution and Numbers. *The Forth Naturalist and Historian* 13:53–69.

Cameron, I.B. & Stephenson, D. (1995). *British Regional Geology: The Midland Valley of Scotland* 4th ed. British Geological Survey, London.

Christie, I.C. & Christie, E.R. (1982). *The Lepidoptera of East Loch Lomondside and Aberfoyle*. Unpublished Nature Conservancy Council Report, Balloch.

Clyde Birds. (1988–1999). Nos 1–12.

Colquhoun, J. (1878). *The Moor and the Loch*. 2 vols. William Blackwood, Edinburgh.

Corbett, L. et al. (1993). *Central Scotland: Land–Wildlife–People*. Forth Naturalist and Historian, Stirling.

Davies, M. (1978). *A Survey of the Breeding Birds of the Caorran Plateau, Loch Lomondside*. Unpublished Nature Conservancy Report, Balloch.

Dennison, E.P. & Coleman, R. (1999). *Historic Dumbarton*. Historic Scotland, Edinburgh.

Dickson, C.A. & Parks, W. (1994). Ten Years of Population Counts of Orchids at Dumbrock Loch Meadows, Stirlingshire and Problems of Management. *The Glasgow Naturalist* 22:349–360.

Dickson, J.H. (1977). *Western Scotland II: Excursion Guide*. International Union for Quaternary Research.

Dickson, J.H. et al. (1978). Palynology, Palaemagnetism and Radiometric dating of Flandrian Marine and

Freshwater Sediments of Loch Lomond. *Nature* 274:548–553.

Edlin, H.L. et al. (1973). *Queen Elizabeth Forest Park* 2nd ed. (Forestry Commission Guide). HMSO, Edinburgh.

Edlin, H.L. et al. (1976). *Argyll Forest Park* 5th ed. (Forestry Commission Guide). HMSO, Edinburgh.

Eggling, W.J. (1963). Nature Conservation in Scotland. *Transactions of the Royal Highland and Agricultural Society of Scotland* (6th series). 8:1–27.

Futter, K.R. (1990). *A Habitat Survey of the Leven Valley, Dumbarton District.* Scottish Wildlife Trust, Renton.

Gibson, J.A. (1984). The Mammals of Dunbartonshire. *West Dunbartonshire Naturalist Report* 6:11–34.

Gibson, J.A. & Mitchell, J. (1986). *An Atlas of Loch Lomond Vertebrates.* Scottish Wildlife Trust, Glasgow.

Gilbert, J.M. (1979). *Hunting and Hunting Reserves in Medieval Scotland.* John Donald, Edinburgh.

Gilbert, O.L. & Mitchell, J. (1981). Rossdhu Park, Dunbartonshire – a major site for Epiphytic Lichens. *The Glasgow Naturalist* 20:123–132.

Gordon, J.E. & Sutherland, D.G. (1993). *Quaternary of Scotland.* Chapman & Hall, London & Glasgow.

Graham, P. (1812). *General View of the Agriculture of Stirlingshire.* Board of Agriculture, Edinburgh.

Gray, R. (1864). 'Quadrupeds, Birds and Fishes of Loch Lomond and its vicinity' in *Tourist Guide Book to the Trossachs, Loch Lomond, etc.* pp.69–83. Maclure & Macdonald, Glasgow.

Habib, O.A. et al. (1997). Seasonal changes in phytoplankton community structure in relation to physico-chemical factors in Loch Lomond, Scotland. *Hydrobiologia* 350:63–79.

Hall, I.H.S. et al. (1998). *Geology of the Glasgow District.* British Geological Survey, London.

Hamilton, J.D. (1988). Recent Human Influences on the Ecology of Loch Lomond. *Proceedings of the International Association for Theoretical and*

Applied Limnology. 23: 403–413.

Holliday, F. et al. (1979). *Wildlife of Scotland.* Macmillan, London.

Huxley, T. et al. (1979). *Shore Erosion around Loch Lomond.* Countryside Commission for Scotland, Battleby.

Idle, E.T. (1968). *Rumex aquaticus* L. at Loch Lomondside. *Transactions of the Botanical Society of Edinburgh* 40:445–449.

Idle, E.T. & Mitchell, J. (1968 & 1982). The Fallow Deer of Loch Lomondside. *Deer* 1:263–265 & 5:368–369.

Idle, E.T. et al. (1970). *Elatine hydropiper* L. – New to Scotland. *Watsonia* 8:45–46.

Jardine, W.G. et al. (1980). *Field Guide to the Glasgow Region.* Quaternary Research Association, Glasgow.

Lamond, H. (1931). *Loch Lomond.* Jackson & Wylie, Glasgow.

Lawson, J. & Lawson, J. (1976). *Geology Explained around Glasgow and South West Scotland, including Arran.* David & Charles, Newton Abbot.

Lee, J.R. (1933). *The Flora of the Clyde Area.* John Smith, Glasgow.

Lee, J.R. (1953). Additions to the Flora of the Clyde Area. *The Glasgow Naturalist* 17:65–82.

Leiper, J. (1995). Early Textile Industry and Planned Villages in the Endrick Valley. *The Forth Naturalist and Historian* 18:117–125.

Linton, D.L. & Moisley, H.A. (1960). The Origin of Loch Lomond. *Scottish Geographical Magazine* 76:26–37.

Loch Lomond Bird Reports. (1972–1992). Nos.1–21.

Lockie, J.D. (1955). The Breeding Habits and Food of Short-eared Owls after a Vole Plague. *Bird Study* 2:53–69.

Lumsden, J. & Brown, A. (1895). *A Guide to the Natural History of Loch Lomond and Neighbourhood.* David Bryce, Glasgow.

McEwan, W. (1980). *Angling on Loch Lomond.* Albyn Press, Edinburgh.

Macfarlane, M.M.G. (1966). *Village and District History: Buchanan.* Women's Rural Institute, Buchanan.

MacPhail, I.M.M. (1972). *Dumbarton Through the Centuries.* Dumbarton Town Council.

MacPhail, I.M.M. (1979). *Dumbarton Castle.* John Donald, Edinburgh.

MacPhail, I.M.M. (1984). *A Short History of Dunbartonshire.* Spa Books, Stevenage.

MacPhail, I.M.M. (1987). *Lennox Lore.* Dumbarton District Libraries, Dumbarton.

McWilliam, J.M. (1936). *The Birds of the Firth of Clyde.* H.F.&G. Witherby, London; Supplement, with Gibson, J.A. (1959): *The Glasgow Bird Bulletin* 8:5–93.

Maitland, P.S. (1966). *Studies on Loch Lomond 2: The Fauna of the River Endrick.* Blackie, Glasgow.

Maitland, P.S. (1972). Loch Lomond: Man's Effects on the Salmonid Community. *Journal of the Fisheries Research Board of Canada* 29:849–860.

Maitland, P.S. & Campbell, R.N. (1992). *Freshwater Fishes of the British Isles* (New Naturalist). HarperCollins, London.

Maitland, P.S. et al. (1981). *The Ecology of Scotland's Largest Lochs.* Junk, The Hague.

Maitland, P.S. et al. (1994). *The Fresh Waters of Scotland.* John Wiley, Chichester.

Miller, R., Tivy, J. et al. (1958). *The Glasgow Region.* British Association handbook, Glasgow.

Mitchell, J. (1974). The Yew Trees of Inchlonaig. *Transactions of the Botanical Society of Edinburgh* 42:163–166.

Mitchell, J. (1978 & 1993). The Heronry at Gartfairn Wood, Loch Lomondside. *The Forth Naturalist and Historian* 3:56–67 & 16:58.

Mitchell, J. (1979). Inchmoan – The Everchanging Bird Island of Loch Lomond. *West Dunbartonshire Naturalist Report* 4:2–9.

Mitchell, J. (1980). Notes on the Hen Harrier in the Loch Lomond Area. *The Western Naturalist* 9:3–8.

Mitchell, J. (1981). The Adaptable Loch Lomondside Mole. *Scottish Wildlife* 17:18–21.

Mitchell, J. (1983 & 1995). Strange Beasts on the Bonny Banks. *Scottish Wildlife* 19:20–24 & *The Scottish Naturalist* 107:133–134.

Mitchell, J. (1984). The Peregrine Population in the Loch Lomond – Trossachs Area of Scotland between 1961 and 1981: A Review. *The Glasgow Naturalist* 20:389–399.

Mitchell, J. (1984 & 1994). The Birds of the Endrick Mouth, Loch Lomond. *The Scottish Naturalist* 1984:3–47 & 1994:3–30.

Mitchell, J. (1993). Shelduck at the Endrick Mouth, Loch Lomond. *The Glasgow Naturalist* 23: 58–59.

Mitchell, J. (1995 & 1998). Old Cornstone Workings in Dunbartonshire and West Stirlingshire, with notes on their associated flora. *The Glasgow Naturalist* 22:485–491 & 23(3):61–62.

Mitchell, J. (1996 & 1998). The Legacy of the Loch Lomondside Wolf. *The Glasgow Naturalist* 23(1):4–6 & 23(3): 59–60.

Mitchell, J. (1997). Wet Meadows in Lowland West Central Scotland – an almost forgotten Botanical Habitat. *Botanical Journal of Scotland* 49: 341–345.

Mitchell, J. (1998). Loch Lomondside Depicted and Described: 1. Myths, Marvels and Monsters. *The Glasgow Naturalist* 23(3):5–8.

Mitchell, J. (2000). Wetland Vegetation Management at the Loch Lomond National Nature Reserve. *BSBI Scottish Newsletter* 22:24–27.

Mitchell, J. & Stirling, A.McG. (1980). *Carex elongata* in Scotland. *The Glasgow Naturalist* 20:65–70.

Mitchell, J. et al. (1993). *Loch Lomond National Nature Reserve. The Reserve Record Pt.II: The Flora of the Reserve.* Unpublished Scottish Natural Heritage report, Clydebank.

Murphy, K.J. et al. (1994). *The Ecology of Loch Lomond.* Klewer Academic, Dordrecht.

Murray, J. & Pullar, L. (1910). *Bathymetrical Survey of the Freshwater Lochs of Scotland.* Challenger Office, Edinburgh.

Murray, W.H. (1982). *Rob Roy MacGregor: his life and times.* Richard Drew, Glasgow.

Paton, D. (1924). Vegetation of Beinn Laoigh. *Report of the Botanical Exchange Club for 1923* 7:268–319.

Pearsall, W.H. (1950). *Mountains and Moorlands* (New Naturalist). Collins, London.

Pilkington, N. et al. (1994 & 1996). The Inchlonaig Yews, their Tree Epiphytes and their Tree Partners. *The Glasgow Naturalist* 22:365–376 & 23(1):59.

Placido, C. et al. (1986). *Loch Lomond National Nature Reserve. The Reserve Record Pt.1: Preliminary.* Unpublished Nature Conservancy Report, Balloch.

Price, R.J. (1983). *Scotland's Environment during the last 30,000 Years.* Scottish Academic Press, Edinburgh.

Ramsay, S. & Dickson, J.H. (1997). Vegetational History of Central Scotland. *Botanical Journal of Scotland* 49:141–150.

Ratcliffe, D.A. (1968). An Ecological Account of Atlantic Bryophytes in the British Isles. *New Phytologist* 67:365–439.

Ritchie, J. (1920). *The Influence of Man on Animal Life in Scotland.* University Press, Cambridge.

Rose, J. (1981). Field Guide to the Quaternary Geology of the South Eastern Part of the Loch Lomond Basin. *Proceedings of the Geological Society of Glasgow* 122/123:12–28.

Shaw, G. (1975). The Breeding Birds of Crom Mhin, Loch Lomond. *Scottish Birds* 8:356–363.

Shaw, G. (1976). The Breeding Bird Communities of the Hillside Oakwoods of Loch Lomondside. *The Western Naturalist* 5:41–52.

Shaw, G. (1977). The Breeding Bird Community in a Scottish Yew Plantation. *Scottish Forestry* 31:74–82.

Sheail, J. (1976). *Nature in Trust: The*

History of Nature Conservation in Britain. Blackie, Glasgow.

Slack, H.D. et al. (1957). *Studies on Loch Lomond 1.* Blackie, Glasgow.

Smith, J.G. (1886). *The Parish of Strathblane and its Inhabitants from Early Times.* James Maclehose, Glasgow.

Smith, J.G. (1896). *Strathendrick and its Inhabitants from Early Times.* James Maclehose, Glasgow.

Stamp, L.D. (1946). *The Land of Britain,* pts. 22 & 23: *Dunbartonshire and Stirlingshire.* Geographical Publications, London.

Stephenson, D. & Gould, D. (1995). *British Regional Geology: The Grampion Highlands* (4th ed.). British Geological Survey, London.

Stewart D. A. (1979) *The Flandrian Vegetational History of the Loch Lomond Area.* Ph.D. thesis, University of Glasgow.

Stewart, D.A. (1983). The History of Alder, *Alnus glutinosa* L., in the Campsie Fells. *The Glasgow Naturalist* 20:333–345.

Stewart, D.A. et al. (1984). Pollen Diagrams from Dubh Lochan, near Loch Lomond. *New Phytologist* 98:531–549.

Stirling, A.McG. & Mitchell, J. (1978). Summer Snowflake. *The Glasgow Naturalist* 19:429–430.

Stirling, A.McG. & Mitchell, J. (1996). Pillwort at Loch Lomond. *The Glasgow Naturalist* 23(1): 58.

Stott, L. (1995). *The Ring of Words: Literary Loch Lomond.* Creag Darach, Milton of Aberfoyle.

Tait, N. (1995). Capercaillie on Loch Lomondside. *The Glasgow Naturalist* 5:535–537.

The Meteorological Office. (1989). *The Climate of Scotland: Some Facts and Figures.* HMSO, London.

The Royal Commission on the Ancient and Historical Monuments of Scotland. (1963). *Stirlingshire: An Inventory of the Ancient Monuments* 2 Vols. HMSO, Edinburgh.

The Royal Commission on the Ancient and Historical Monuments of Scotland. (1978). *The Archaeological Sites of Dumbarton District, Clydebank District, Bearsden and Milngavie District, Strathclyde Region.* Edinburgh.

The Royal Commission on the Ancient and Historical Monuments of Scotland & Historic Scotland. (2000). *The Historic Landscape of Loch Lomond and the Trossachs.* Edinburgh.

Thomson, G. (1988). *The Butterflies of Scotland.* Croom Helm, London.

Thomson, J. (1991). *The Balfron Heritage.* Balfron Heritage Group.

Thornton, T. (1804). *A Sporting Tour through the northern parts of England and a great part of the Highlands of Scotland.* Vernor & Hood, London.

Tims, D.W.G. et al. (1974). *The Stirling Region.* British Association handbook, Stirling.

Tippet, R. et al. (1974). *A Natural History of Loch Lomond.* University Press, Glasgow.

Tittensor, R.M. (1970). History of the Loch Lomond Oakwoods. *Scottish Forestry* 24:100–118.

Tittensor, R.M. & Steele, R.C. (1971). Plant Communities of the Loch Lomond Oakwoods. *Journal of Ecology* 59:561–582.

Trubridge, M. (1988). The Goats of the Loch. *The Scots Magazine* May 1988, pp.179–188.

Trubridge, M. (1996). Inversnaid RSPB Reserve – the first ten years. *The Forth Naturalist and Historian* 19:83–90.

University of Glasgow & University of Strathclyde. (1992). *Loch Lomond 1991.* Glasgow.

Waltho, C.M. (1979). *The Breeding Bird Community of the Aber Bogs, Loch Lomondside, in 1978.* Unpublished Nature Conservancy Report, Balloch.

Waltho, C.M. (1980). The establishment of Fen Carr in the Aber Bogs, Dunbartonshire. *West Dunbartonshire Naturalist Report* 5:14–23.

Waltho, C.M. (1982). *The Breeding Bird Community of Inchmoan, Loch Lomond, 1979–80.* Unpublished Nature Conservancy Report, Balloch.

Waugh, D.R. (1978). *The Breeding Bird Community of the Glen Douglas Woodlands.* Unpublished Nature Conservancy Report, Balloch.

Weir, T. (1976). A threat to Loch Lomond [Craigrostan hydro-electric scheme]. *Country Life* December 1976, pp.1746–1748.

Whyte, A. & Macfarlan, D. (1811). *General View of the Agriculture of the County of Dumbarton.* Board of Agriculture, Glasgow.

Willby, N.J. & Mitchell, J. (1996). *Limosella aquatica* at Loch Lomond National Nature Reserve. *The Glasgow Naturalist* 23: 58–59.

Williamson, K. et al. (1973). Bird Communities of the Mainland Section of Loch Lomond National Nature Reserve. *The Western Naturalist* 2: 15–28.

Williamson, K. (1974). Oak Wood Breeding Bird Communities in the Loch Lomond National Nature Reserve. *Quarterly Journal of Forestry* 68:9–28.

Wilson, A. et al. (1988). *The Parish of Killearn* 2nd ed. Killearn Trust.

Wood, I. (1954). *Loch Lomond and its Salmon.* The Glasgow Herald, Glasgow.

Wylie, D.D. & Dickson, J.H. (1998). The Holocene History of Scots Pine *Pinus sylvestris* L. at Loch Sloy, Scottish Highlands. *The Glasgow Naturalist* 23(3):16–23.

Index

Cervus elephus, 56, 67, 94, 96–97, 163, 169–170, 183–184, 190, 208
Ceterach officinarum, 142, 143
chaffinch, 136, 158, 162, 166, 168
Charadrius hiaticula, 121, 148, 150, 180
morinellus, 190
charr, Arctic, 115–116
North American brook, 116
Chelidonium majus, 144
Chelon labrosus, 115, 129
cherry, bird, 37, 152, 205
chiff-chaff, 166
Chironomidae, 109, 114
chough, 180
Chrysosplenium alternifolium, 162
oppositifolium, 154, 178
chub, 126
Cicuta virosa, 120–121
Cinclidotus fontinaloides, 111
Cinclus cinclus, 45, 127
cinqfoil, alpine, 186
spring, 178
Circus aeruginosus, 121
cyaneus, 98, 121, 168, 177
Cirsium eriophorum, 144
heterophyllum, 142
palustre, 147
Clan Macgregor, 64–65, 165
Claytonia sibirica, 124
climate & effects:
atmospheric pollution, 44–45, 176–177
floods, 12
frost & ice, 47–49
greenhouse effect, 51, 193
rainfall & cloud cover, 12, 13, 42–45
snow & hail, 45–46
sunshine, 46–47
temperature, 18, 47–49
wind, 49–50
cloudberry, 151, 177, 183
clubmoss, alpine, 186
interrupted, 187
lesser, 147
marsh, 118
club-rush, floating, 119
grey, 128
sea, 128
Clupea harengus, 129

Clyde Estuary, 12, 32, 34, 42, 53, 60–61, 84, 86, 115, 127, 129
Clyde Lava Plateau, 16, 22, 25–26, 29, 30, 34, 38, 176–181
Clytus arietis, 156
Cochlearia micacea, 188
officinalis, 128
pyrenaica, 182
cockle, pea-shell spp., 109
Coeloglossum viride, 134
Coenagrion puella, 121
Coenonympha pamphilus, 134
tullia, 151
Collema dichotomum, 129
Cololejeunea rossettiana, 154
columbine, 113
conifer plantations, 16, 72, 76, 167–170, 175, 197–198, 200, 203, 205, 208
Conium maculatum, 144
Conopodium majus, 141
coot, 149
copper, small, 134
Cordulia aenea, 157
Coregonus lavaretus, 83, 115, 116, 130–131, 138
cormorant, 116, 118
corncrake, 136
cornel, dwarf, 188
Cornus suecica, 188
corries & crags:
Corrie an Lochain, 46
Corrie Cuinne, 181
Coire na h'Eanachan, 162
Corries of Balglass, 30, 178, 180
Creag an Leinibh, 182
Creag Mhor, 147
Double Craigs, 178
Whangie, 102
Corvus corax, 80, 145, 165, 178 179, 182, 187, 189–190, 193
corone, 98, 137, 177, 179, 182
frugilegus, 138
monedula, 180
corydalis, climbing, 155
Corylus avellana, 37–39, 152, 205
cotton grass, broad-leaved, 147

common, 175, 177, 183
hare's-tail, 150
Countryside Commission for Scotland, 204, 205, 207, 208, 209, 210–211
cowbane, 120–121
cowberry, 162, 177, 183
cowslip, 142
cow-wheat, common, 155
wood, 155
Craigrostan, 65, 93, 162, 206–207, 213
crake, spotted, 120, 121
Crambus uliginosellus, 135
cranberry, 118, 150
crane-fly spp., 114
crane's-bill, wood, 178, 190
crannogs, 56–57
Crataegus monogyna, 152
Crenobia alpina, 163
Crex crex, 136
crossbill, common, 168
crow, carrion/hooded, 98, 137, 177, 179, 182
crowberry, 36, 162, 183
crowfoot, round-leaved, 149
water, 113
Cryptogramma crispa, 178
cuckoo, 162
Cuculus canorus, 162
cudweed, dwarf, 186
Culicoides impunctatus, 118
curlew, 121, 151, 181
Cygnus cygnus, 121, 131–132
olor, 110, 129
Cymbalaria muralis, 143
cyphel, mossy, 190
Cyprinus carpio, 126
Cystopteris montana, 185, 190
Cytisus scoparius, 148

dace, 116,
Dactylorhiza maculata, 141
purpurella, 142
daffodil, 142
daisy, oxeye, 142
dame's-violet, 124
damselfly, azure, 121
Daphnia spp., 110
Dark Ages, 59–60
Dama dama, 67, 95, 158, 166
darter, common, 148
Highland, 148, 157
death cap, 155
deer, fallow, 67, 95, 158, 166